My Brother, Theodore Roosevelt...

Corinne Roosevelt Robinson

MY BROTHER
THEODORE ROOSEVELT

From a photograph, copyright by C. Le Gendre.

Theodore Roosevelt with his little granddaughter,
Edith Roosevelt Derby, 1918.

...THER

...E ROOSEV...

...SEVELT E...

WITH ...ATIONS

NEW YORK
CHARLES SCRIBNER'S SONS
1921

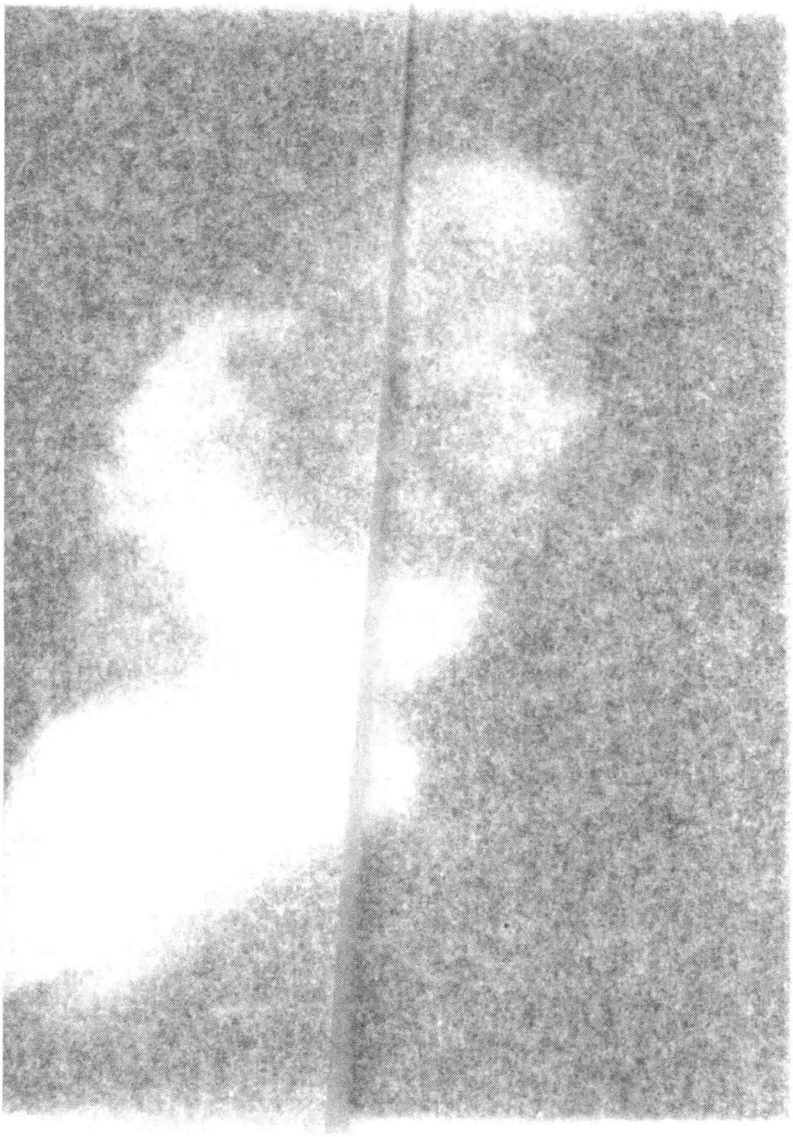

MY BROTHER THEODORE ROOSEVELT

BY
CORINNE ROOSEVELT ROBINSON

WITH ILLUSTRATIONS

NEW YORK
CHARLES SCRIBNER'S SONS
1921

Published September, 1921

THE SCRIBNER PRESS

WITH TENDER AFFECTION I DEDICATE THIS BOOK

TO MY SISTER

ANNA ROOSEVELT COWLES

WHOSE UNSELFISH DEVOTION TO HER BROTHER

THEODORE ROOSEVELT

NEVER WAVERED THROUGH HIS WHOLE LIFE, AND FOR WHOM

HE HAD FROM CHILDHOOD

A DEEP AND UNSWERVING LOVE AND ADMIRATION

PREFACE

This Preface I write to my fellow countrymen as I give into their hands these intimate reminiscences of my brother, Theodore Roosevelt.

A year and a half ago I was invited by the City History Club of New York to make an address about my brother on Washington's Birthday. Upon being asked what I would call my speech, I replied that as George Washington was the "Father of his country," as Abraham Lincoln was the "Saviour of his country," so Theodore Roosevelt was the "Brother of his country," and that, therefore, the subject of my speech would be "The Brother of His Country."

In the same way, I feel that in giving to the public these almost confidential personal recollections, I do so because of the attitude of that very public toward Theodore Roosevelt. There is no sacrilege in sharing such memories with the people who have loved him, and whom he loved so well.

This book is not a biography, it is not a political history of the times, although I have been most careful in the effort to record facts accurately, and carefully to search my memory before relating conversations or experiences; it is, I hope, a clear picture, drawn at close hand by one who, because of her relationship to him and her intercourse with him, knew his loyalty and tenderness of heart in a rare and satisfying way, and had unusual opportunity of comprehending the point of view, and therefore perhaps of clarifying the point of view, of one of the great Americans of the day.

As I have reread his letters to me, as I have dwelt upon our long and devoted friendship—for we were even more friends than brother and sister—his character stands out to me more strongly than ever before as that of "The Great Sharer." He shared all that he had—his worldly goods, his strong mentality, his wide sympathy, his joyous fun, and his tender comprehension—with all those with whom he came in contact, and especially with those closest and dearest to him—the members of his own family and his sisters.

In the spirit of confidence that my frankness will not be misunderstood, I place a sister's interpretation of a world-wide personality in the hands of my fellow Americans.

CORINNE ROOSEVELT ROBINSON.

September, 1921.

CONTENTS

ILLUSTRATIONS

MY BROTHER
THEODORE ROOSEVELT

THE STAR

Epiphany, 1919

Great soul, to all brave souls akin,
  High bearer of the torch of truth,
Have you not gone to marshal in
  Those eager hosts of youth?

Flung outward on the battle's tide,
  They met in regions dim and far;
And you, in whom youth never died,
  Shall lead them, as a star.

—Marion Couthouy Smith.

MY BROTHER THEODORE ROOSEVELT

I

THE NURSERY AND ITS DEITIES

THE first recollections of a child are dim and hazy, and so the nursery at 28 East 20th Street, in New York City, does not stand out as clearly to me as I wish it did—but the personality of my brother overshadowed the room, as his personality all through life dominated his environment.

I suppose I must have been about four, and he about seven, when my first memory takes definite form. My older sister, Anna, though only four years older than my brother Theodore, was always mysteriously classed with the "grown people," and the "nursery" consisted of my brother Theodore, my brother Elliott, a year and a half younger than Theodore, and myself, still a year and a half younger than Elliott.

In those days we were "Teedie," "Ellie," and "Conie," and we had the most lovely mother, the most manly, able, and delightful father, and the most charming aunt, Anna Bulloch, the sister of my Southern mother, with whom children were ever blessed.

Theodore Roosevelt, whose name later became the synonym of virile health and vigor, was a fragile, patient sufferer in those early days of the nursery in 20th Street. I can see him now struggling with the effort to breathe—for his enemy was that terrible trouble, asthma—but always ready to give the turbulent "little ones" the drink of water, book, or plaything which they vociferously demanded, or equally ready to weave for us long stories of animal life—stories closely resembling the jungle stories of Kipling—for Mowgli had his precursor in the brain of the little boy of seven or eight, whose knowledge of natural history even at that early age was strangely accurate, and whose imagination gave to the creatures of forest and field impersonations as vivid as those which Rudyard Kipling has made immortal for all time.

We used to sit, Elliott and I, on two little chairs, near the higher chair which was his, and drink in these tales of endless variety, and which always were "to be continued in our next"—a serial story which never flagged in interest for us, though sometimes it continued from week to week, or even from month to month.

It was in the nursery that he wrote, at the age of seven, the famous essay on "The Foregoing Ant." He had read in Wood's "Natural History" many descriptions of various species of ant, and in one instance on turning the page the author continued: "The foregoing ant has such and such characteristics." The young naturalist, thinking that this particular ant was unique, and being specially interested in its forthgoing character, decided to write a thesis on "The Foregoing Ant," to the reading of which essay he called in conclave "the grown people." One can well imagine the tender amusement over the little author, an amusement, however, which those wise "grown people" of 28 East 20th Street never let degenerate into ridicule.

No memories of my brother could be accurate without an analysis of the personalities who formed so big a part of our environment in childhood, and I feel that my father, the first Theodore Roosevelt, has never been adequately described.

He was the son of Cornelius Van Shaack and Margaret Barnhill Roosevelt, whose old home on the corner of 14th Street and Broadway was long a landmark in New York City. Cornelius Van Shaack Roosevelt was a typical merchant of his day, fine and true and loyal, but ultraconservative in many ways; and his lovely wife, to whom he addressed, later, such exquisite poems that I have always felt that they should have been given more than private circulation, was a Pennsylvanian of Quaker blood.

The first Theodore Roosevelt was the youngest of five sons, and I remember my mother used to tell me how friends of her mother-in-law once told her that Mrs. Cornelius Van Shaack Roosevelt was always spoken of as "that lovely Mrs. Roosevelt" with those "*five horrid boys*."

As far as I can see, the unpleasant adjective "horrid" was only adaptable to the five little boys from the usual standpoint of boyish mischief, untidiness, and general youthful irrepressibleness.

The youngest, my father, Theodore Roosevelt, often told us himself how he deplored the fate of being the "fifth wheel to the coach," and of how many a mortification he had to endure by wearing clothes cut down from the different shapes of his older brothers, and much depleted shoes about which, once, on overhearing his mother say, "These were Robert's, but will be a good change for Theodore," he protested vigorously, crying out that he was "tired of changes."

As the first Theodore grew older he developed into one of the most enchanting characters with whom I, personally, have ever come in contact; sunny, gay, dominant, unselfish, forceful, and versatile, he yet had the extraordinary power of being a focussed individual, although an "all-round" man. Nothing is as difficult as to achieve results in this world if one is filled full of great tolerance and the milk of human kindness. The person who achieves must generally be a one-ideaed individual, concentrated entirely on that one idea, and ruthless in his aspect toward other men and other ideas.

My father, in his brief life of forty-six years, achieved almost everything he undertook, and he undertook many things, but, although able to give the concentration which is necessary to achievement, he had the power of interesting himself in many things outside of his own special interests, and by the most delicate and comprehending sympathy made himself a factor in the lives of any number of other human beings.

My brother's great love for his humankind was a direct inheritance from the man who was one of the founders in his city of nearly every patriotic, humanitarian, and educational endeavor. I think, perhaps, the combination of the stern old Dutch blood with the Irish blood, of which my brother always boasted, made my father what he was—unswerving in duty, impeccable in honesty and uprightness, and yet responsive to the joy of life to such an extent that he would dance all night, and drive his "four-in-hand" coach so fast that the old tradition was "that his grooms frequently fell out at the corners"!

I remember that he always gave up one day of every week (and he was a very busy merchant and then banker) to the personal visiting of the poor in their homes. He was not satisfied with doing active work on many organizations, although he did the most extraordinary amount of active organization work, being one of the founders of the Children's Aid Society, of the State Aid Society, of the Sanitary Commission and Allotment Commission in the time of the Civil War, and of the Orthopædic Hospital, not to mention the Museum of Natural History and the Museum of Art—but he felt that even more than this organized effort must be the effort to get close to the hearts and homes of those who were less fortunately situated than he.

My older sister suffered from spinal trouble, and my father was determined to leave no stone unturned to make her body fit for life's joys and life's labors, and it was because of his efforts to give his little girl health—successful efforts—that in co-operation with his friends Howard Potter and James M. Brown and several others he started the great work of the New York Orthopædic Hospital, having become imbued with belief in the methods of a young doctor, Charles Fayette Taylor. Nobody at that time believed in treating such diseases in quite the way in which modern orthopædy treats them now, but my father, like his son, had the vision of things to be, and was a leader in his way, as was my brother in his.

He could not at first influence sufficient people to start the building of a hospital, and he decided that if the New York public could only *see* what the new instruments would do for the stricken children, that it could be aroused to assist the enterprise.

And so, one beautiful spring afternoon, my mother gave what was supposed to be a purely social reception at our second home, at 6 West 57th Street, and my father saw to it that the little sufferers in whom he was interested were brought from their poverty-stricken homes to ours and laid upon our dining-room table, with the steel appliances which could help them back to normal limbs on their backs and legs, thus ready to visualize to New York citizens how these stricken little people might be cured. He placed me by the table where the children lay, and explained to me how I could show the appliances, and what they were supposed to achieve; and I can still hear the voice of the first Mrs. John Jacob Astor, as she leaned over one fragile-looking child and, turning to my father, said: "Theodore, you are right; these children must be restored and made into active citizens again, and I for one will help you in your work."

That very day enough money was donated to start the first Orthopædic Hospital, in East 59th Street. Many business friends of my father used to tell me that they feared his sudden visits when, with a certain expression in his eyes, he would approach them, for then before he could say anything at all they would feel obliged to take out their pocketbooks and ask: "How much this time, Theodore?"

One of his most devoted interests was the newsboys' lodging-house in West 18th Street, and later in 35th Street, under the auspices of the Children's Aid Society. Every Sunday evening of his life he went to that lodging-house, after our early hospitable Sunday supper, to which many a forlorn relation or stranded stranger in New York was always invited, and there he would talk to the boys, giving them just such ideas of patriotism, good citizenship, and manly morality as were the themes of his son in later years.

The foundational scheme of the Children's Aid Society was, and is, to place little city waifs in country homes, and thus give them the chance of health and individual care, and a very dramatic incident occurred many years after my father's death, when my brother, as governor of New York State and candidate for the vice-presidency in 1900, had gone to the Far West to make the great campaign for the second election of William McKinley. The governors of many Western States decided to meet in the city of Portland, Ore., to give a dinner and do honor to the governor of the Empire State, and as Governor Roosevelt entered the room they each in turn presented themselves to him. The last one to come forward was Governor Brady, of Alaska, and as he shook hands with Governor Roosevelt he said: "Governor Roosevelt, the other governors have greeted you with interest, simply as a fellow governor and a great American, but I greet you with infinitely more interest, as the son of your father, the first Theodore Roosevelt."

My brother smiled and shook him warmly by the hand, and asked in what special way he had been interested in our father, and he replied: "Your father picked me up from the streets in New York, a waif and an orphan, and sent me to a Western family, paying for my transportation and early care. Years passed and I was able to repay the money which had given me my start in life, but I can never repay what he did for me, for it was through that early care and by giving me such a foster mother and father that I gradually rose in the world, until today I can greet his son as a fellow governor of a part of our great country."

I was so thrilled when my brother told me this story on his return from that campaign, that the very next Sunday evening I begged him to go with me to the old 35th Street lodging-house to tell the newsboys that were assembled there the story of another little newsboy, now the governor of Alaska, to show that there is no bar in this great, free country of ours to what personal effort may achieve.

My father was the most intimate friend of each of his children, and in some unique way seemed to have the power of responding to the need of each, and we all craved him as our most desired companion. One of his delightful rules was that on the birthday of each child he should give himself in some special way to that child, and many were the perfect excursions which he and I took together on my birthday.

The day being toward the end of September was always spent in the country, and lover as he was of fine horses, I was always given the special treat of an all day's adventure behind a pair of splendid trotters. We would take the books of poetry which we both loved and we would disappear for the whole day, driving many miles through leafy lanes until we found the ideal spot, where we unharnessed the horses and gave them their dinner, and having taken our own delicious picnic lunch, would read aloud to each other by the hour, until the early September twilight warned us that we must be on our way homeward.

In those earlier days in New York the amusements were perhaps simpler, but the hospitality was none the less generous, and our parents were indeed "given to hospitality."

My lovely Southern mother, of whom I will speak more later, had inherited from her forebears a gift for hospitality, and we young children, according to Southern customs, were allowed to mingle more with our elders than was the case with many New York children. I am a great believer in such mingling, and some of the happiest friendships of our later lives were formed with the chosen companions of our parents, but many things were done for us individually as well. When we were between thirteen and sixteen I remember the delightful little Friday-evening dances which my mother and father organized for us in 57th Street, and in which they took actual part themselves.

As I said before, my father could dance all night with the same delightful vim that he could turn to his business or his philanthropy in the daytime, and he enjoyed our pleasures as he did his own. It always seems to me sad that the relationship between father and son, or father and daughter, should not have the quality of charm, a quality which it so often lacks, and which I believe is largely lacking because of the failure of the older generation to enter into the attitude of the younger generation.

I was delicate at one period and could not dance as I had always done, and I remember when I was going to a little entertainment, just as I was leaving the house I received an exquisite bunch of violets with a card from my father, asking me to wear the flowers, and think of his wish that I should not overtire myself, but also of his sympathy that I could not do quite what I had always done.

Comparatively few little girls of fourteen have had so loverlike an attention from a father, and just such thought and tender, loving comprehension made our relationship to our father one of perfect comradeship, and yet of respectful adoration. He taught us all, when very young, to ride and to swim and to climb trees. I remember the careful way in which he would show us dead limbs and warn us about watching out for them, and then, having taught us and having warned us, he gave us full liberty to try our wings and fall by the wayside should they prove inadequate for our adventures.

After graduating from our first Shetland pony, he provided us each with a riding-horse, and always rode with us himself, and a merry cavalcade went forth from our country home, either early in the morning before he started for the train or in the soft summer evenings on his return. When at one time we were living on the Hudson River, we had hoped one autumn afternoon that he would come home early from the city, and great was our disappointment when a tremendous storm came up and we realized that he would take a later train, and that our beloved ride must be foregone. We were eagerly waiting in the hall for his return and watching the rain falling in torrents and the wind blowing it in gusts, when the depot wagon drove up to the door and my father leaped out, followed by the slight

Theodore Roosevelt, Sr., aged thirty, 1862.

Martha Bulloch Roosevelt, twenty-two years old, about 1856.

figure of a somewhat younger man. As the young man tried to put up his umbrella it blew inside out and, like a dilapidated pinwheel loosened from his hand, ran round and round in a circle. The unknown guest merrily chased the umbrella pinwheel, and my mother, who had joined us children at the window, laughingly wondered who my father's new friend was. The front door opened and the two dripping men came in, and we rushed to meet them.

I can see the laughing face of the young man become suddenly shy and a little self-conscious as my father said to my mother: "Mittie, I want to present to you a young man who in the future, I believe, will make his name well known in the United States. This is Mr. John Hay, and I wish the children to shake hands with him."

Many and many a time, long, long years after, when John Hay was secretary of state in the cabinet of the second Theodore Roosevelt, he used to refer to that stormy autumn afternoon when a delicate boy of eleven, at the instigation of his father, shook hands with him and looked gravely up into his face, wondering perhaps how John Hay was going to make his name known throughout the United States. How little did Mr. Hay think then that one day he would be the secretary of state when that same little delicate boy was President of the United States.

My father's intimacy with John Hay had come about through the fact of contact in the Civil War, when they both worked so hard in Washington together.

My father stands out as the most dominant figure in our early childhood. Not that my mother was not equally individual, but her delicate health prevented her from entering into our sports and unruly doings as our father did; but I have always thought that she, in an almost equal degree with my father, influenced my brother's nature, both by her French Huguenot and Scotch blood and her Southern ancestry.

The story of her meeting with my father has a romantic flavor to it. My grandmother, Mrs. Stephens Bulloch, lived in an old plantation above Atlanta, on the sand-hills of Georgia. There, in the old white-columned house overlooking a beautiful valley, my grandmother led a patriarchal life, the head of a large family, for she had been as a young girl the second wife of Senator John Elliott, and she not only brought up the children of that marriage but the children and stepchild of her second marriage as well. My own mother was the second daughter of Mr. and Mrs. Stephens Bulloch, but she never knew the difference between her Elliott half brother and sisters, her Bulloch half-brother and her own brother and sister.

In the roomy old home with its simple white columns there was led an ideal life, and the devotion of her children to my beautiful grandmother, as the many letters in my possession prove, was one of the inspiring factors in their lives, and became the same to our own childhood, for many were the loving stories told us by my mother and aunt of the wonderful character of their mother, who ran her Southern plantation (Mr. Bulloch died comparatively young) with all the practical ability and kindly supervision over her slaves characteristic of the Southern men and women of her time.

The aforesaid slaves were treated as friends of the family, and they became to us, her little Northern grandchildren, figures of great interest. We were never tired of hearing the stories of "Daddy Luke" and "Mom Charlotte."

The first of these two, a magnificent Nubian, with thick black lips and very curly hair, was the coachman and trusted comrade of my grandmother's children, while his wife, "Mom Charlotte," was a very fastidious mulatto, slender and handsome, who, for some illogical reason, considered her mixed blood superior to his pure dark strain. She loved him, but with a certain amount of disdain, and though on week-days she treated him more or less as an equal, on Sundays, when dressed in her very best bandanna and her most elegant prayer-book in hand, she utterly refused to have him walk beside her on the path to church, and obliged him ignominiously to bring up the rear with shamefaced inferiority. Mom Charlotte on Sundays, when in her superior mood, would look at her spouse with contempt, and say, "B' Luke, he nothin' but a black nigger; he mout' stan' out to de spring," referring to Daddy Luke's thick Nubian lips, and pointing at the well about one hundred yards distant from the porch.

There was also a certain "little black Sarah," who was the foster-sister of my uncle, Irvine Bulloch, my mother's younger brother. In the old Southern days on such plantations there was almost always a colored "pickaninny" to match each white child, and they were actually considered as foster brother or sister. Little Irvine was afraid of the darkness *inside* the house, and little Sarah was afraid of the darkness *outside* the house, and so the little white boy and the little black girl were inseparable companions, each guarding the other from the imaginary dangers of house or grounds, and each sympathetically rounding out the care-free life of the other.

My mother's brilliant half-brother, Stewart Elliott, whose love of art and literature and music took him far afield, spent much of his time abroad, and when he came back to Roswell (the name of the plantation) he was always much amused at the quaint slave customs. One perfect moonlight night he took his guitar into the grove near the house to sing to the group of girls on the porch, but shortly afterward returned much disgusted and described the conversation which he had overheard between little white Irvine and little black Sarah on the back porch. It ran as follows, both children gazing up into the sky: *Sarah:* "Sonny, do you see de Moon?" "Yes, Sarah, it do crawl like a worrum." The moon at the moment was performing the feat which Shelley poetically described as gliding, "glimmering o'er its fleecelike floor." The young musician could not stand the proximity of such masters of simile as were Irvine and Sarah, and demanded that they should be forbidden the back porch on moonlight nights from that time forth!

There was also another young slave who went by the name of "Black Bess," and was the devoted companion of her two young mistresses, Martha, my mother, and her sister, Anna Bulloch. She slept on a mat at the foot of their beds and rendered the devoted services that only the slave of the old plantation days ever gave to his or her mistress. My mother used to accompany her mother on her visits to all the outlying little huts in which the various negroes lived, and she often told us the story of a visit one day to "Mom Lucy's" little home, where a baby had just been born.

Mom Lucy had had several children, none of whom had lived but a few hours, and when my grandmother and her little daughter visited the new baby, now about a week old, the mother, still lying on her couch, looked up at my grandmother and said: "Ole Miss, I jus' done name her." "And what have you named her, Lucy?" asked my grandmother; "she is a fine baby and I am so glad you are going to have the comfort of her all your life." "Oh!" said the colored woman sadly, "I don't 'spec' her to live, dey ain't none of 'em done live, and so I jus' call her Cumsy." "Cumsy?" said my grandmother, "and what may that mean, Lucy?" "Why, ole Miss, don't you understan'? Dey all done go to deir heavenly home, and so I jus' call dis one 'Come-see-de-world-and-go,' and my ole man and me we is goin' to call her 'Cumsy' for short."

My grandmother tried to argue Lucy out of this mortuary cognomen, but with no effect, and years afterward when my mother revisited Roswell as Mrs. Theodore Roosevelt, one of the first negroes to greet her was "Come-see-the-world-and-go!"

All these stories of the old plantation were fascinating to the children of the nursery in 20th Street, and we loved to hear how the brothers and sisters in that old house played and worked, for they all did their share in the work of the household. There the beautiful half-sister of my mother, Susan Elliott, brought her Northern lover, Hilborne West, of Philadelphia, whose sister, Mary West, had shortly before married Weir Roosevelt, of New

York, the older brother of my father, Theodore Roosevelt. This same Hilborne West, a young physician of brilliant promise, adored the informal, fascinating plantation life, and loved the companionship of the two dainty, pretty girls of fourteen and sixteen, Martha and Anna Bulloch, his fiancée's young half-sisters.

Many were the private theatricals and riding-parties, and during that first gay visit Doctor West constantly spoke of his young connection by marriage, Theodore Roosevelt, who he felt would love Roswell as he did.

A year afterward, inspired by the stories of Doctor West, my father, a young man of nineteen, asked if he might pay a visit at the old plantation, and there began the love-affair with a black-haired girl of fifteen which later was to develop into so deep a devotion that when the young Roosevelt, two years later, returned from a trip abroad and found this same young girl visiting her sister in Philadelphia, he succumbed at once to the fascination from which he had never fully recovered, and later travelled once more to the old pillared house on the sand-hills of Georgia, to carry Martha Bulloch away from her Southern home forever.

I cannot help quoting from letters from Martha Bulloch written in July, 1853, shortly after her engagement, and again from Martha Roosevelt a little more than a year later, when she revisits her old home. She had been hard to win, but when her lover leaves Roswell at the end of his first visit, immediately following their engagement, she yields herself fully and writes:

Roswell, July 26, 1853.

THEE, DEAREST THEE:

I promised to tell you if I cried when you left me. I had determined not to do so if possible, but when the dreadful feeling came over me that you were, indeed, gone, I could not help my tears from springing and had to rush away and be alone with myself. Everything now seems associated with you. Even when I run up the stairs going to my own room, I feel as if you were near, and turn involuntarily to kiss my hand to you. I feel, dear Thee,—as though you were part of my existence, and that I only live in your being, for now I am confident of my own deep love. When I went in to lunch today I felt very sad, for there was no one now to whom to make the request to move "just a quarter of an inch farther away"—but how foolish I am,—you will be tired of this "rhapsody. . . ."

Tom King has just been here to persuade us to join the Brush Mountain picnic tomorrow. We had refused but we are reconsidering.

July 27th,——

We have just returned after having had a most delightful time. It was almost impossible for our horses to keep a foothold, the Mountain was so steep, but we were fully repaid by the beautiful extended view from the top, and when we descended, at the bottom, the gentlemen had had planks spread and carriage cushions arranged for us to rest, and about four o'clock we had our dinner. Such appetites! Sandwiches, chicken wings, bread and cheese disappeared miraculously.

Tom had a fire built and we had nice hot tea and about six o'clock we commenced our return. I had promised to ride back with Henry Stiles, so I did so, and you cannot imagine what a picturesque effect our riding party had,—not having any Habit, I fixed a bright red shawl as a skirt and a long red scarf on my head, turban fashion with long ends streaming. Lizzie Smith and Anna dressed in the same way, and we were all perfectly wild with spirits and created quite an excitement in Roswell by our gay cavalcade— But all the same I was joked all day by everybody, who said that they could see that my eyes were swollen and that I had been crying.

All this in a very delicate Italian hand, and leaving her lover, I imagine, a little jealous of "Henry Stiles," in spite of the "rhapsody" at the beginning of the letter!

My father's answer to that very letter is so full of deep joy at the "rhapsody," in which his beautiful and occasionally capricious Southern sweetheart indulged, that I do not think he even remembered "Henry Stiles," for he replies to her as follows:

New York, August 3rd.

How can I express to you the pleasure which I received in reading your letter! I felt as you recalled so vividly to my mind the last morning of our parting, the blood rush to my temples; and I had, as I was in the office, to lay the letter down, for a few minutes to regain command of myself. I had been hoping against hope to receive a letter from you, but *such* a letter! O, Mittie, how deeply, how devotedly I love you! Do continue to return my love as ardently as you do now, or if possible love me more. I know my love for you merits such return, and do, dear little Mittie, continue to write, (when you feel moved to!) just such "rhapsodies."

On December 3, 1853, very shortly before her wedding, Martha Bulloch writes another letter, and in spite of her original "rhapsody," and her true devotion to her lover, one can see that she has many girlish qualms, for she writes him: "I do dread the time before our wedding, darling—and I wish that it was all up and that I had died game!"

A year and a half later, May 2, 1855, Martha Roosevelt is again at the home of her childhood, this time with her little baby, my older sister, Anna, and her husband has to leave her, and she writes again:

"I long to hear you say once again that you love me. I know you do but still I would like to have a fresh avowal. You have proved that you love me dear, in a thousand ways and still I long to hear it again and again. It will be a joyful day when we meet again. I feel as though I would never wish to leave your side again. You know how much I enjoy being with mother and Anna, but all the same I am only waiting until

'Thee' comes, for you can hardly imagine what a *wanting* feeling I have when you are gone.

"Mother is out in the entry talking to one of the 'Crackers.' While I was dressing mother brought in a sweet rose and I have it in my breast pin. I have picked one of the leaves off just this moment and send it to you—for Thee—the roses are out in beautiful profusion and I wish you could see them. . . ."

A year and a half in the cold North had not dimmed the ardor of affection between the young couple.

We children of the nursery in 28 East 20th Street loved nothing better than to make my mother and aunt tell us the story of the gay wedding at the old home near Atlanta. I remember still the thrill of excitement with which I used to listen to the details of that wonderful week before the wedding when all the bridesmaids and ushers gathered at the homestead, and every imaginable festivity took place.

One of my mother's half-brothers had just returned from Europe, and fell in love at first sight with one of her beautiful bridesmaids, already, alas! engaged to another and much older man, not a member of the wedding-party. My child's heart suffered unwarranted pangs at the story of the intense attraction of these two young people for each other, and I always felt that I could see the lovely bridesmaid riding back with the man to whom she had unwittingly given her heart, under the Southern trees dripping with hanging moss. The romantic story ended tragically in an unwilling marriage, a duel, and much that was unfortunate.

But my mother and my father had no such complications in their own lives, and the Southern girl who went away with her Northern lover never regretted that step, although much that was difficult and troublous came into their early married life because of the years of war from 1861 to 1865, when Martha Bulloch's brothers fought for the South and Theodore Roosevelt did splendid and unselfish work in upholding the principles for which the North was giving its blood and brawn.

The fighting blood of James Dunwoody and Irvine Bulloch was the same blood infused through their sister into the veins of their young kinsman, the second Theodore Roosevelt, and showed in him the same glowing attributes. The gallant attitude of their mother, Mrs. Stephens Bulloch, also had its share in the making of her famous grandson.

Her son Irvine was only a lad of sixteen, while her stepson, James, was much older and was already a famous naval blockade-runner when she parted from them. Turning to her daughter Anna she prayed that she might never live to know if Irvine were killed or Richmond taken by the Northern army. I cannot but rejoice that her life passed away before such news could come to her. It must have been bitter, indeed, for her under these circumstances to face the necessity of accepting the bread of her Northern son-in-law, and it speaks volumes for the characters of both that during the whole war there was never a moment of estrangement between them or between my father and his lovely sister-in-law, Anna Bulloch, who became, because of the fact that she lived with us during those early years of our lives, one of the most potent influences of our childhood.

I, myself, remember nothing of the strain of those troubled days; but my aunt has often told me of the bedtime hour in the nursery when a certain fair-haired, delicate little boy, hardly four years old, would kneel at her side to say his evening prayer, and feeling that she would not dare interrupt his petition to the Almighty, would call down in baby tones and with bent head the wrath of the Almighty upon the rebel troops. She said that she could never forget the fury in the childish voice when he would plead with Divine Providence to "grind the Southern troops to powder."

This same lovely aunt taught us our letters at her knee, in that same nursery, having begged, in return for my father's hospitality, that she should be accepted as our first instructress, and not only did she teach us the three R's, but many and many a delightful hour was passed in listening to her wonderful renderings of the "Br'er Rabbit" stories.

Both my aunt and my mother had but little opportunity for consecutive education, but they were what it seems to me Southern women ever are—natural women of the world, and yet they combined with a perfect readiness to meet all situations an exquisite simplicity and sensitive sympathy, rarely found in the women of the North. This sensitiveness was not only evidenced in their human relationships but in all pertaining to art and literature. I have often said that they were natural connoisseurs.

I remember that my father would never buy any wine until my mother had tasted it, and experts of various kinds came to her in the same way for expressions of her opinion. She was very beautiful, with black, fine hair—not the dusky brunette's coarse black hair, but fine of texture and with a glow that sometimes seemed to have a slightly russet shade, what her French hairdresser called "noir doré," and her skin was the purest and most delicate white, more moonlight-white than cream-white, and in the cheeks there was a coral, rather than a rose, tint. She was considered to be one of the most beautiful women of the New York of her day, a reputation only shared by Mrs. Gardiner Howland, and to us, her children, and to her devoted husband she seemed like an exquisite "objet d'art," to be carefully and lovingly cherished. Her wit, as well as that of my aunt, was known by all her friends and yet it was never used unkindly, for she had the most loving heart imaginable, and in spite of this rare beauty and her wit and charm, she never seemed to know that she was unusual in any degree, and cared but little for anything but her own home and her own children. Owing to delicate health she was not able to enter into the active life of her husband and children, and therefore our earliest memories, where our activities were concerned, turn to my father and my aunt, but always my mother's gracious loveliness and deep devotion wrapped us round as with a mantle.

Theodore Roosevelt, about eighteen months old, 1860.

Theodore Roosevelt, about four years old, 1862.

And so these were the three Deities of the Nursery in which Theodore Roosevelt spent his first years, and even at that early time they realized that in that simple room in the house which the patriotic women of America are about to restore as a mecca for the American people there dwelt a unique little personality whose mentality grasped things beyond the ken of other boys of his age, and whose gallant spirit surmounted the physical difficulties engendered by his puny and fragile body.

The nursery at 28 East 20th Street in the early years of the Civil War missed its chief deity, my father. From the letters exchanged by my mother and father, preserved by each of them, I have formed a clear realization of what it meant to that nursery to lose for almost two years the gay and vigorous personality who always dominated *his* environment as did later his son.

Mr. William E. Dodge, in a very beautiful letter written for the memorial meeting of the Union League Club in February, 1878, just after my father's death, gave the following interesting account of my father's special work in the Civil War. This letter was read after an eloquent speech delivered by Mr. Joseph H. Choate. The part of the letter to which I especially refer ran as follows:

"When the shadows of the coming war began to grow into a reality he (Theodore Roosevelt) threw himself with all his heart and soul into work for the country.

"From peculiar circumstances he was unable to volunteer for military service, as was his wish, but he began at once to develop practical plans of usefulness to help those who had gone to the front.

"He became an active worker on the Advisory Board of the Woman's Central Association of Relief, that wonderful and far-reaching organization of patriotic women out of which grew the Sanitary Commission.

"He worked with the 'Loyal Publication Society,' which, as many of our members know, was a most active and useful educating power in the days when there was great ignorance as to the large issues of the conflict.

"He joined enthusiastically in the organization of the Union League Club, was for years a most valued member of its executive committees and aided in the raising and equipment of the first colored troops.

"His great practical good sense led him to see needs which escaped most other minds. He felt that the withdrawal from the homes of so many enlisted men would leave great want in many sections of the country. He saw the soldiers were more than amply clothed and fed, and their large pay wasted mostly among the sutlers, and for purposes which injured their health and efficiency. So with two others he drafted a bill for the appointment of Allotment Commissioners, who without pay should act for the War Department and arrange to send home to needy families, without risk or cost, the money not needed in the camps. For three months they worked in Washington to secure the passage of this act—delayed by the utter inability of Congressmen to understand why anyone should urge a bill from which no one could selfishly secure an advantage.

"When this was passed he was appointed by President Lincoln one of the three Commissioners from this State. For long, weary months, in the depth of a hard winter, he went from camp to camp, urging the men to take advantage of this plan.

"On the saddle often six to eight hours a day, standing in the cold and mud as long, addressing the men and entering their names.

"This resulted in sending many millions of dollars to homes where it was greatly needed, kept the memory of wives and children fresh in the minds of the soldiers, and greatly improved their morale. Other States followed, and the economical results were very great.

"Towards the close of the war, finding the crippled soldiers and the families of those who had fallen were suffering for back pay due and for pensions, and that a race of greedy and wicked men were taking advantage of their needs to plunder them, he joined in organizing the Protective War-Claim Association, which without charge collected these dues. This saved to the soldiers' families more than $1,000,000 of fees.

"He also devised and worked heartily in the Soldiers' Employment Bureau, which found fitting work for the crippled men who by loss of limb were unfitted for their previous occupations. This did wonders toward absorbing into the population of the country those who otherwise would have been dependent, and preserved the self-respect of the men. I believe it did more and vastly better work than all the 'Soldiers' homes' combined. For the work in the Allotment Commission he received the special and formal thanks of the State in a joint resolution of the Legislature."

Nothing was more characteristic of my father's attitude toward life than his letters during this period to my mother. He realized fully that in leaving his young family he was putting upon his youthful and delicate wife—whose mental suffering during the war must have been great, owing to the fact of her being a Southerner—her full share of what was difficult in the situation. He writes with the utmost frankness of his wish that she might look on the great question of which the war was a symptom from the same standpoint as his, but the beautiful love and trust which existed between them was such that in all these letters which passed so constantly during my father's labors as Allotment Commissioner, there was never the slightest evidence of hurt feelings or friction of any kind.

In the early fall of 1861 he was struggling to have passed by Congress the bill to appoint Allotment Commissioners, and spent weary days in Washington to achieve that purpose. When the bill was passed and he and Mr. William E. Dodge and Mr. Theodore Bronson were appointed as the three commissioners, he threw himself with all the ardor and unselfishness of his magnificent nature into the hard work of visiting the camps in midwinter, and persuading the reluctant soldiers to believe that it was their duty to allot a certain portion of their pay to their destitute families.

He writes on January 1, 1862:

I have stood on the damp ground talking to the troop and taking their names for six hours at a time. One of the regiments that I visited last, which is wretchedly officered and composed of the scum of our city, seemed for the first time even to recall their families. We had an order from the General of Division, and the Colonel sent his adjutant to carry out our desires. He came, dirty and so drunk that he could not speak straight, and of course got the orders wrong. All the officers seem to be *in* with the sutler while the private said he was an unmitigated thief. The delays were so great that I stood out with one of these companies after seven o'clock at night, with one soldier holding a candle while I took down the names of those who desired to send money home. The men looked as hard as I have often seen such men look in our Mission neighborhood, but after a little talking and explaining my object and reminding them of those they had left behind them, one after another put down his name, and from this company alone, they allotted, while I was there, $600.00. This would be increased afterwards by the officers, if they were decent ones, and other men absent on guard and through other reasons. I could not help thinking what a subject for a painting it would make as I stood out there in the dark night, surrounded by the men with one candle just showing glimpses of their faces,—tents all around us in the woods. One man, after putting down five dollars a month, said suddenly: "My old woman has always been good to me, and if you please, change it to ten." In a moment, half a dozen others followed his example and doubled their allotments.

I enclose a letter for Teedie [Theodore]. Do take care of yourself and the dear little children while I am away, and remember to enjoy yourself just as much as you can. [This sentence is so like my father. Duty was always paramount, but joy walked hand in hand with duty whenever it legitimately could.]

I do not want you not to miss me, but remember that I would never have felt satisfied with myself after this war is over if I had done nothing, and that I do feel now that I am only doing my duty. I know you will not regret having me do what is right, and I do not believe you will love me any the less for it.

Yours as ever,

THEODORE ROOSEVELT.

This particular letter is very characteristic of the father of President Roosevelt—a man of the qualities which his country has grown to associate with its beloved "Colonel." In my brother's case they were the direct inheritance from the man who stood out knee-deep in mud using his wonderful personality to make those hard-faced drafted men remember their own people at home, and at the same time writes to the lovely mother of his children to try and enjoy herself as much as possible in his absence.

My mother's answers to my father's letters were very loving. Alone, and delicate, she never dwells on loneliness or ill health, but tells him the dear details of the home he loved so well. On January 8, 1862, she writes: "Teedie came down stairs this morning looking rather sad, and said 'I feel badly—I have a tooth ache in my stomach.'—later he asked if 'Dod' (God) was a fox?!—this after being shown a picture of a very clever looking fox! He is the most affectionate and endearing little creature in his ways." One can well imagine how the lonely father, doing his distant and gruelling duty, treasured the dainty letters full of quaint stories of childish sayings. In another and later missive there is a description of a birthday supper-party in which "Teedie" is host to his cousins; it runs as follows: "Teedie, the host, was too busy with his chicken and potatoes to converse much, but as soon as he finished he made the sage remark that he 'loved chicken, roast beef and everything that was good better than salt water.' This speech occasioned a roar of laughter, and was evidently thought very witty. Teedie, too, seemed to be under the false impression that it was clever. He seemed to be inflated with vanity for some time afterwards!" How gladly the tired man, after long days in the saddle, and evenings of effort with sullen soldiers, must have turned to just such humorous accounts of the small boy who always said or did something quaint, which lost nothing in the picture drawn by the facile pen of his mother.

Theodore Roosevelt writes his wife again in January, 1862, a letter interesting because of his attitude toward the German regiments. He says:

"We are continually at work now, and to-day saw three regiments, but even at this rate, it will be long before I see you again. They were all Germans to-day—a motley crew, having few friends and frequently no characters. We had been told that we ran the risk of our lives by going to these regiments, and much more nonsense of the same kind, but the only risk we ran has been from starvation. We were out talking to the men until very late, and then found a German dinner which Dodge could eat nothing of but the brown bread. He wanted to be polite, however, and I was much amused with his statement that he would ride five miles to get such bread, which was literally a fact, however, I have no doubt, in his state of starvation.

"The men, as Germans always do, took time to consider, and we left them to describe the allotment idea to other persons. However, after due consideration, a fair number sent money home. These Germans were generally of the lowest characters, and with the exception of one regiment disappointed me, although I have no doubt they will fight well. There are some 12,000 of them.

"This morning I saw that our efforts are noticed in *The World* and *The Tribune*. You have seen, I suppose, that we have been mentioned several times in *The Times*. This is particularly satisfying as the papers threatened once to be down on us, which would lose for us the confidence of the soldiers."

The letters all give vivid accounts of his experiences, differing in interest. He speaks of General Wadsworth, the grandfather of our present United States senator, and says that the general "helped to make my bed when I spent one night with his division."

In an interim of work, on February 7, he writes of his invitation to Mrs. Lincoln's ball, at which he says he had a delightful time.

"Mrs. Lincoln in giving the Ball, stated that she gave it as a piece of economy in war time, and included those diplomats, senators, congressmen and others, that it had been previously the habit to invite at a number of formal dinners. No one lower in the army than the Division General,—not even a Brigadier, had an invitation to the Ball, and of course there was much grumbling and a proportionate amount of envy. Some complained of the supper, but I have rarely seen a better, and often a worse one. Terrapin, birds, ducks, and everything else in great profusion when I was in the dining room, although some complained of the delay in getting into the room, as we went in parties.

"I spent all of yesterday kicking my heels in the ante-room of the Secretary of War, and in making out an order for him which he promised to sign and afterwards refused. [How history repeats itself!] I was with him about two hours, altogether, and received any number of the highest kind of compliments, but I wanted a more important proof of his good feeling which I did not get. I still hope that I may get it through the President."

On February 12, 1862, comes this description of the delightful visit to Newport News and he says:

"All the officers received us in such a hospitable spirit and the weather assisted in making our stay agreeable. I passed two of the pleasantest days that I have enjoyed when away from home. General Mansfield suggested some practice with the parrot gun, and one of those sad accidents occurred, for a gun burst and two men were killed.

"We have been treated like princes here. The steamboat was put at our disposal and when, through a misunderstanding, it left before we were on board, another one was immediately sent with us. I enclose several things to keep for me."

Amongst the enclosures was a note which is sufficiently interesting to give in facsimile.

EXECUTIVE MANSION, WASHINGTON

MR. ROSEVALT.

Dear Sir:

I very much regretted that a severe headache confined me to my room on yesterday, this morning I find we are expected to hold a noon reception which will be over by three and a half o'clock at which time I will be very happy to have you ride with us.

Very truly yours

MRS. A. LINCOLN.

This quaint missive reminds me of the fact of my father's kindly tolerance of "Mrs. A. Lincoln's" little peculiarities. I remember how he used to tell us, when occasionally he was invited, as this letter says, to "ride" with her, that he would also be invited to stop at the shop where she bought her bonnets, and give his advice on which bonnet was especially becoming!

In an earlier letter, after referring to an interview with Secretary Stanton, he speaks of his apparent decision of character. But he was disappointed when he could not, in the beginning, make the secretary take his point of view about the Allotment Commission. Later, however, he received the full support of Secretary Stanton.

In a letter dated February 5 he speaks of "justified pleasure" as follows:

"I find that only about six men under fifty [he himself

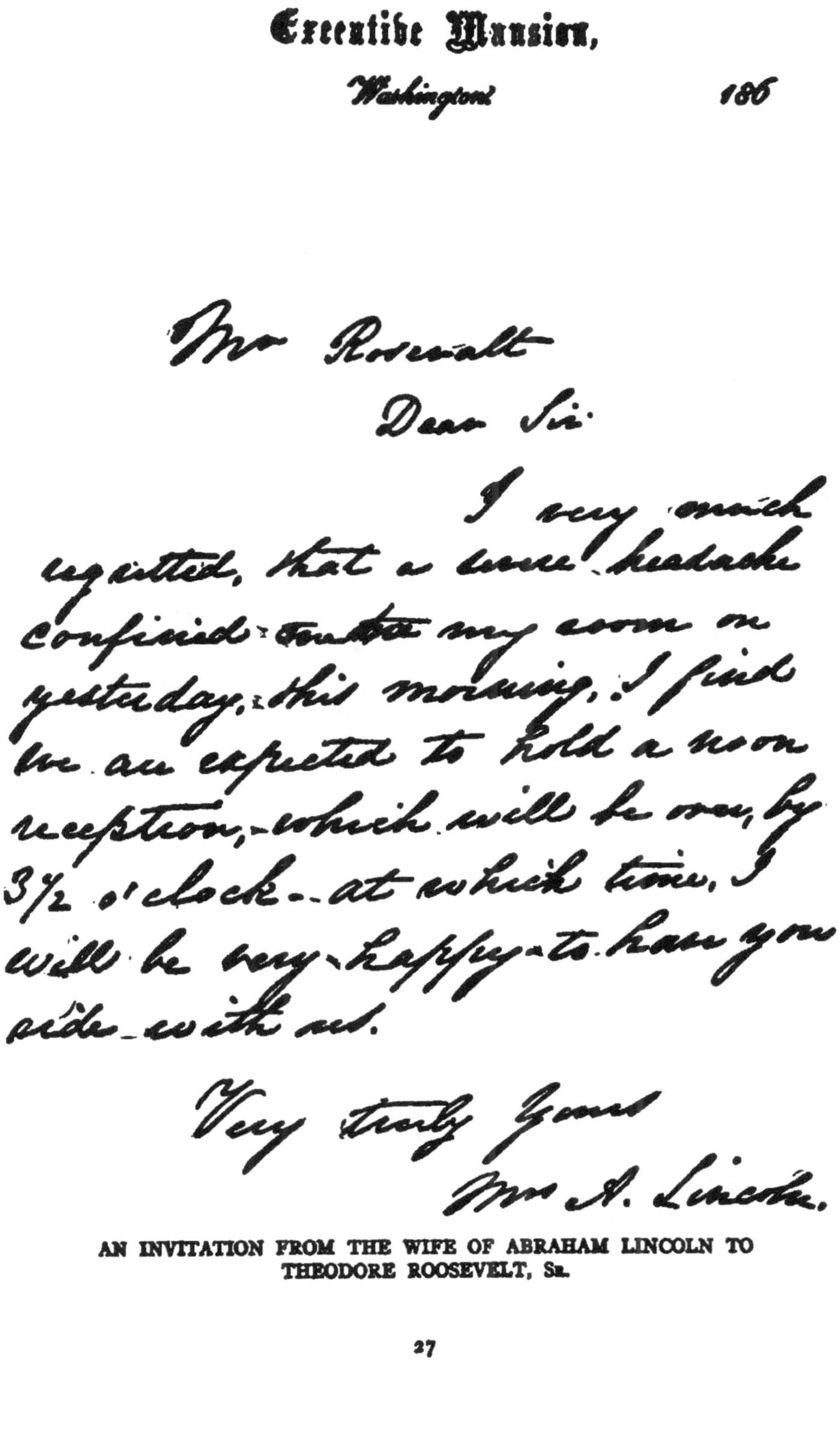

Executive Mansion,

Washington 186

Mr Roosevelt

Dear Sir:

I very much regretted, that a severe headache confined to the my room on yesterday, this morning, I find we are expected to hold a noon reception, which will be over, by 3½ o'clock – at which time, I will be very happy to have you ride – with us.

Very truly yours

Mrs A. Lincoln.

AN INVITATION FROM THE WIFE OF ABRAHAM LINCOLN TO THEODORE ROOSEVELT, Sr.

was only twenty-nine] are invited to the President's to-night, and I have determined to go for a short time, at least. There will be the largest collection of notables there ever gathered in this country, and it would probably be a sight worth remembering."

Under date of Washington, February 14, he writes again:

"I have so many acquaintances here now that I could easily find a temporary companion. Hay [John Hay] is going with me to Seward's to-night, and I am hoping to procure the pass for your mother. [My grandmother was most anxious to get back to her own people in the South]. In Baltimore I saw, or fancied I saw, on the faces of our class of the inhabitants, their feelings in consequence of the news just received of the taking of Roanoke Island. They looked very blue. The sutlers here are serious obstacles in getting allotments. As soon as *we* see a Regiment and persuade the men to make allotments, *they* send around an agent to dissuade them from signing their names, convincing them that it is a swindle because *they* want the money to be spent in Camp and go into their pockets instead of being sent home to the poor families of the men, who are in such want.

"I enclose you a flower from the bouquet on the table of the Executive Mansion. Also a piece of silk from an old-fashioned piano cover in Arlington House."

As I opened the letter, the flower fell to dust in my hands, but the little piece of green silk, faded and worn, had evidently been treasured by my mother as being a relic of Arlington House.

On February 27, 1862, his stay in Washington was drawing to a close, and my father regretted, as so many have done, that he had not kept a diary of his interesting experiences. He writes on September 27:

"All those whom I have seen here in Washington in social intercourse day by day will be characters in history, and it would be pleasant to look over a diary hereafter of my own impressions of them, and recall their utterly different views upon the policy which should be pursued by the Government. I have rarely been able to leave my room in the evening, for it has been so filled with visitors, but I have not felt the loss of liberty from the fact that those who were my guests I would have taken a great deal of trouble to see, and never could have seen so informally and pleasantly anywhere except in my own room.

"It has, of course, been more my duty to entertain those whose hospitality I was daily receiving, in the camps, by invitations to drop in during the evening; all of these are striving to make their marks as statesmen, and some, I am sure, we will hear from hereafter."

On March 1, 1862, he says:

We have all been in a state of excitement for some days past, caused by movements in the Army foreshadowing a general battle. The snow which is now falling fast, has cast a damper over all our spirits. . . . Several of the Generals have stated to me their belief that the war, as far as there was any necessity for so large an army, would be closed by some time in May,—probably the first of May. If so, my work will be all over when I return to New York, and I can once more feel that I have a wife and children, and enjoy them.

It is Sunday afternoon, and I have a peculiar longing to see you all again, the quiet snow falling outside, my own feelings being very sad and that of those around being in the same condition makes me turn to my own quiet fireside for comfort. I wish we sympathized together on this question of so vital moment to our country, but I know you cannot understand my feelings, and of course I do not expect it.

YOUR LOVING HUSBAND WHO WANTS
VERY MUCH TO SEE YOU.

One can well imagine the note of sadness in the strong young man who had relinquished his urgent desire to bear arms because of the peculiar situation in which he found himself, but who gave all his time and thought and physical endurance to the work vitally needed, and which he felt he could have handled better with the sympathy of his young wife, whose anxiety about her mother and brothers was so poignant and distressing. Never, however, in the many letters exchanged between the parents of my brother, Theodore Roosevelt, was there one word which was calculated to make less possible the close family love and the great respect for each other's feelings.

In the last letter quoted above, one feels again that history does indeed repeat itself, when one thinks that it was written in March, 1862, and that those "generals" of whom my father speaks were expecting that no large army would be needed after May 1 of that year, when in reality the long agony of civil war was to rack our beloved country for nearly three years more. This was proven shortly after to my father, and in the following October he is writing again from Baltimore, and this time in a less wistful mood:

Since I last wrote you I have enjoyed my pleasantest experiences as Allotment Commissioner. The weather was lovely our horses good and Major Dix accompanied us from the Fortress to Yorktown. It was about twenty-five miles of historic ground passing over the same country that General McClellan had taken his army along last spring.

First comes the ruins of the little town of Hampton, then through Big Bethel where Schanck was whipped, to the approaches to Yorktown. There ravines have been cut through miles of roads made, and immense breastworks thrown up by our army.

Suydam was away but the rest of General Keyes' staff received us most hospitably, and after dinner furnished us with fresh horses to visit the regiments, one of their number accompanying us.

I had practise for both my French and German in the Enfans Perdus, Colonel Comfort's regiment and it was quite late before our return. As I had broken my eyeglasses I had to trust entirely to my horse who jumped over the ditches in a most independent manner. We all sat up together until about twelve except Bronson who had seemed used up all day, and had not accompanied me to the regiments. He seemed to feel the shock of the fall when the car ran off the track, and not to recover from it so easily as myself.

Next morning we rode another twenty-five miles to Newport News to see the Irish Brigade. General Corcoran was there, and accompanied us to the regiments first suggesting Irish whiskey to strengthen us. At dinner ale was the beverage and after dinner each Colonel seemed to have his own particular tope. On our return they made an Irish drink called "scal thun" and about one o'clock gave us "devilled bones." The servant was invited in to sing for us and furnished with drinks at odd times by the General, who never indulged, however, himself to excess. We then went the grand rounds with the General at two in the morning, arrested two officers for not being at their posts and returned at half past three, well prepared to rest quietly after a very fatiguing day, and one of the most thoroughly Irish nights that I ever passed.

Next morning (yesterday) we had a delightful ride over to Fortress Monroe, and had lunch at General Dix's before leaving in the boat.

A dozen of the officers were down at the boat, and we felt as we bid goodbye to some of them, like leaving old friends. . . .

Dearest: a few words more and I must close. Bronson has a very bad cold and decides that he will leave me to-morrow. If well enough he will undoubtedly call on you. Of course this makes me doubly homesick but I must see it through.

Goodbye. Yours as ever,

Theodore Roosevelt.

Again on October 18, having apparently been able to return for a brief visit to his family, he writes from Niagara:

"I was able to get a top berth and retired for the 31st time in two months to spend the night on the railroad. My three nights at home have made it hard, rather than easier, to continue my journeys.

"All our party started from Albany to Fonda, and I had a hard day's work for the men had been deceived by the bounty and were suspicious about everything regarding the Allotment Commission. The officers' dinner was a good deal like pigs eating at a trough. When at night three companies had not yet been visited, I determined to do it wholesale. I had two tents pitched and occupied one already prepared, placing a table, candles and allotment roll in each. I then had the three companies formed into three sides of a square and used all my eloquence. When I had finished they cheered me vociferously. I told them I would be better able to judge who meant the cheers by seeing which company made most allotments. [This sentence of my father's makes me think so much of my brother's familiar "shoot; don't shout!" when he would receive vociferous cheers for any advice given.] I thus raised the spirit of competition and those really were the best that I had taken during the day. By eight o'clock we found our work done, dark as pitch, and rain descending in torrents, but still the work was done."

These letters give, I think, a vivid picture of my father's persistence and determined character, and the quality of "getting there," which was so manifestly the quality of his son as well, and at the same time the power of enjoyment, the natural affiliation with his humankind, and always the thoughtfulness and consideration for his young wife left with her little charges at home.

In that same home the spirit of the war permeated through the barriers of love raised around the little children of the nursery, and my aunt writes of the attitude of the small, yellow-haired boy into whose childish years came also the distant din of battle, arousing in him the military spirit which even at four

Elliott Roosevelt, aged five and a half years, about 1865.

Corinne Roosevelt, about four years old, 1865.

Theodore Roosevelt, aged seven, 1865.

years of age had to take some expression. She says: "Yesterday Teedie was really excited when I said to him that I must fit his zouave suit. His little face flushed up and he said, 'Are me a soldier laddie too?' and when I took his suggestion and said, 'Yes and I am the Captain,' he was willing to stand for a moment or two to be fitted." Even then Theodore Roosevelt responded to his country's call, and equally to the discipline of the superior officer!

II

GREEN FIELDS AND FOREIGN FARING

FROM the nursery in 20th Street my early memories turn with even greater happiness to the country place which my parents rented at Madison, N. J., called Loantaka, where we spent several summers. There the joy of a sorrel Shetland pony became ours—(Pony Grant was his name)—a patriotic effort to commemorate the name of the great general, still on the lips of every one, whose indomitable will and military acumen had at that very moment been the chief factor in bringing the Civil War to a close. I, however, labored under the delusion that he, the general, was named after the pony, which seemed to me at the time much the more important of the two personalities. The four-legged Grant was quite as determined and aggressive as his two-legged namesake, and he never allowed any of us to be his master. When my father first had him brought to the front door of the country home at Madison, I shall never forget the thrill of excitement in the breasts of the three little children of the nursery. "Who will jump on his back?" called out my father gaily.

It has always been the pride of my life that, although I was only about four years old, I begged for the privilege before the "boys" were quite ready to decide whether to dare the ferocious glance in his dark eyes. Owing to my temerity he was presented to me, and from that time on was only a loan to my brothers. Each in turn, however, we would climb on his back, and each in turn would be repeatedly thrown over his head, but having shown his ability to eject, he would then, satisfied by thus proving his superiority, become gentle as a really gentle lamb. I qualify my reference to lambs, remembering well the singularly *ungentle* lamb which later became a pet also in the family.

In those country days before the advent of the motor, the woods and lanes of New Jersey were safe haunts for happy childhood, and we were given much liberty, and, accompanied by our two little cousins from Savannah, John and Maud Elliott, who spent those two summers with us, having suffered greatly from the devastating war, we roamed at will, leading or riding our pony, playing endless games, or making believe we were Indians—always responsive to some story of Theodore's which seemed to cast a glamour around our environment.

I can still feel the somewhat uncanny thrill with which I received the suggestion that a large reddish stain on a rock in the woods near by was the blood of a white girl, lately killed by the chief of the Indian tribe, to which through many mysterious rites we were supposed to belong. I remember enticing there in the twilight our very Hibernian kitchen-maid, and taking delight in her shrieks of terror at the sight of the so-called blood.

My brother always felt in later years, and carried the feeling into practice with his own children, that liberty in the summer-time, for a certain period at least, stimulated greatly the imagination of a child. To rove unhampered, to people the surroundings with one's own creations, to watch the habits of the feathered or furry creatures, and insensibly to react to the beauty of wood and wind and water—all this leaves an indelible impression on the malleable nature of a young child, and we five happy cousins, in spite of Theodore's constant delicacy, were allowed this wonderful freedom to assimilate what nature had to give.

I never once remember that we came to the "grown people" with that often-heard question "What shall we do next?" The days never seemed long enough, the hours flew on golden wings. Often there would be days of suffering for my brother, even in the soft summer weather, but not as acute as in the winter-time, and though my father or my aunt frequently had to take Theodore for change of air to one place or another, and rarely, even at his best, could he sleep without being propped up in bed or in a big chair, still his spirit was so strong and so recuperative that when I think of my earliest country memories, he seems always there, leading, suggesting, explaining, as all through my life when the nursery was a thing of the past and the New Jersey woodlands a faint though fair green memory, he was always beside me, leading, suggesting, explaining still.

It was in those very woodlands that his more accurate interest in natural history began. We others—normal and not particularly intelligent little children—joyed in the delights of the country, in our games and our liberty, but he was not only a leader for us in everything, but he also led a life apart from us, seriously studying the birds, their habits and their notes, so that years afterward the result of those long hours of childish concentration took form in his expert knowledge of bird life and lore—so expert a knowledge that even Mr. John Burroughs, the great nature specialist, conceded him equality of information with himself along those lines.

It was at Lowantaka, at the breakfast-table one day, after my father had taken the train to New York—this was the second year of our domicile there, and the sad war was over—that my mother received a peculiar-looking letter. I remember her face of puzzled interest as she opened it and the flush that came to her cheek as she turned to my aunt and said: "Oh, Anna, this must be from Irvine!" and read aloud what would now seem like a "personal" on a page of the New York *Herald*. It was as follows:

"If Mrs. Theodore Roosevelt and Miss Anna Bulloch will walk in Central Park up the Mall, at 3 o'clock on Thursday afternoon of this week [it was then Tuesday] and notice a young man standing under the third tree on the left with a red handkerchief tied around his throat, it will be of interest to them."

As my mother finished reading the letter she burst into tears, for it was long since the younger brother had been heard from, as the amnesty granted to all those taking part in the Rebellion had not been extended to those who had gone to England, as had my two uncles, to assist in the building and the sailing of the *Alabama*, and letters from them were considered too dangerous to be received.

This "Irvine" had been saved when the *Alabama* sank, after her brief career, and the two brothers had settled in Liverpool, and my mother knowing the great sorrow that his mother's death had meant to this younger brother, had always longed during the intervening months to see him and tell him of that mother's undying devotion, though she herself had passed away the year before.

It seemed now to the active imaginations of the Southern sisters that somehow or other Irvine had braved the authorities, and would be able to see them and hear from their lips the story of the past five years.

One can well imagine the excitement of the children around the breakfast-table at the romantic meeting suggested by the anonymous letter. And so, on the following Thursday, the two sisters went in to New York and walked up the Mall in Central Park, and there, standing under the third tree to the left, was the young man—a thin, haggard-looking young man compared to the round-faced boy with whom they had parted so long ago, but eagerly waiting to get from them the last news of the mother who had hoped she would die before any harm could befall him. He had worked his way over in the steerage of a sailing-vessel under an assumed name, for he was afraid of bringing some trouble on my father, and had taken the method of the anonymous letter to bring to him the sisters he had loved and missed so sorely.

What a meeting it must have been under that "third tree to the left" of the old Mall of Central Park, and what reminiscences of happier childhood days those three must have indulged in in the brief hour which the brother could give his sisters before sailing back across the broad ocean, for he did not dare meet them again for fear of some unpleasant results for the Northern brother-in-law, for whom he had great admiration.

Later, of course, my uncles were given the right to return to their own country, but although they often visited us, they never settled in America again, having rooted their business interests on English soil, though their hearts always turned loyally to the country of their birth.

In taking into consideration the immediate forebears of my brother, Theodore Roosevelt, I would once more repeat that to arrive at a true comprehension of his many-sided character one must realize the combination of personalities and the different strains of blood in those personalities from whom he was descended in summing up the man he was.

The stability and wisdom of the old Dutch blood, the gaiety and abandon of the Irish strain that came through the female side of his father's people, and on his mother's side the great loyalty of the Scotch and the fiery self-devotion of the French Huguenot martyrs, mixed as it was with the light touch which shows in French blood of whatever strain—all this combined to make of the boy born of so varied an ancestry one who was akin to all human nature.

In April, 1868, the little boy of nine and a half shows himself, indeed, as father to the man in several characteristic letters which I insert here. They were written to his mother and father and the little sister Conie when the above members of the family were paying a visit to Savannah, and are as follows:

New York April 28th, 1868.

MY DEAR MAMMA

I have just received your letter! What an excitement! How nice to read it. What long letters you do write. I don't see how you can write them. My mouth opened wide with astonishment when I heard how many flowers were sent in to you. I could revel in the buggie ones. I jumped with delight when ~~I found you had heard a mocking-bird. Get some~~ of its feathers if you can. Thank Johnny for the feathers of the soldier's cap, ~~give him~~ my love also. We cried when you wrote about Grand-Mamma. Give My love to the good natured (to use your own expresion) handsome lion, Conie, Johnny, Maud, and Aunt Lucy. I am sorry the trees have been cut down. Aunt Annie, Edith and Ellie send their love to you and all, I send mine to. I send this picture to Conie. In the letters you write to me tell me how many curiosities and living things you have got for me. I miss Conie very much. I wish I were with you and Johnny for I could hunt for myself. There is Conie's letter.

MY DEAR CONIE:

As I wrote so much in Mamma's letter I cannot write so much in yours. I have got four mice, two white skined, red eyed velvety creatures, very tame for I let them run all over me, they trie to get down the back of my neck and under my vest, and two brown skined, black eyed, soft as the others but wilder. Lordy and Rosa are the names of the white mice, which are male and female. I keep them in different cages

White mouse cage. brown mouse cage.

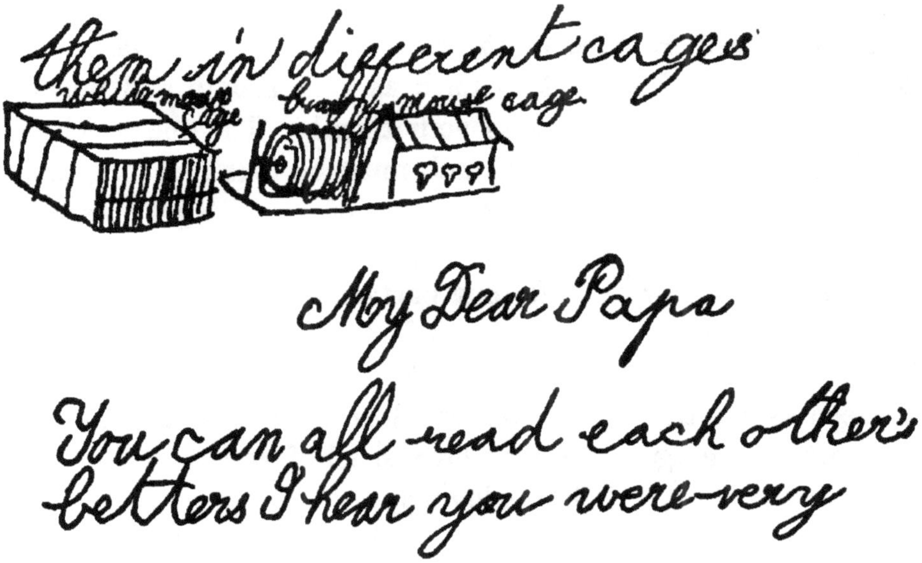
them in different cages
White mouse cage
brown mouse cage

My Dear Papa

You can all read each other's letters I hear you were very

My Dear Papa

You can all read each other's letters. I hear you were very seasick on your voyage and that Dora and Conie were seasick before you passed Sandy-hook. Give my greatest love to Johnny. You must write too. Wont you drive Mamma to some battle field for she is going to get me some trophies? I would like to have them so very much. I will have to stop now because Aunty wants me to learn my lessons.

The chaffinch is for you. The wren for Mamma. The cat for Conie.

Yours lovingly,

Theodore Roosevelt.

P. S. I liked your peas so much that I ate half of them.

New York, April 30th, 1868.

My Dear Father

I received your letter yesterday. Your letter was more exciting than Mother's. I have a request to ask of you, will you do it? I hope you will, if you will it will figure greatly in my museum. You know what supple jacks are, do you not? Please get one for Ellie and two for me. Ask your friend to let you cut off the tiger-cat's tail, and get some long moos and have it mated together. One of the supple jacks (I am talking of mine now) must be about as thick as your thumb and finger. The other must be as thick as your thumb. The one which is as thick as your finger and thumb must be four feet long and the other must be three feet long. One of my mice got crushed. It was the mouse I liked best though it was a common mouse. Its name was Brownie. Nothing particular has happened since you went away for I cannot go out in the country like you can. The trees and the vine on our piazza are buding and the grass is green as can be, and no one would dream that it was winter so short a time ago. All send love to all of you.

Yours lovingly,

Theodore Roosevelt.

The "excitement" referred to in the first letter was the wonderful reception accorded to my mother on her return to the city of her girlhood days. Her rooms in the hotel in Savannah were filled by her friends with flowers—and how she loved flowers—but not the "buggie ones" in which her young naturalist son says he would "revel!"

One can see the ardent little bird-lover as he wrote "I jumped with delight when I found you had heard a mocking-bird," and again when he says "Tell me how many curiosities and living things you have got for me." Insatiable lover of knowledge as he was, it was difficult indeed for his parents to keep pace with his thirst for "outward and visible signs of the things that be."

More than fifty years have passed since the painstaking penning of the childish letters, but the heart of his sister in reading them thrills hotly at the thought that the little "Conie" of those days was "very much" missed by her idolized brother, and how she treasured the letter written all for her, with the pictures of the cages in which he kept his beloved mice! It was sad that the pictures of the chaffinch, wren, and cat, evidently enclosed for each of the travellers, should have been lost. In the two letters to his father he enlists that comrade-father's services for his adored "museum" by the plea for "trophies from some battle field," and the urgent request for the "supple jack," the nature of which exciting article I confess I do not understand. I do understand, however, his characteristic distress that "one of my mice got crushed. It was the mouse I liked best though it was a common mouse." That last sentence brought the tears to my eyes. How true to type it was! the "common mouse" was the one he liked best of all—never the rare, exotic thing, but the every-day, the plain, the simple, and he probably liked it so much just because that little "common mouse" had shown courage and vitality and affection! All through Theodore Roosevelt's life it was to the plain simple things and to the plain simple people that he gave his most loyal devotion.

In May, 1869, because of a great desire on the part of my mother to visit her brothers in England, as well as to see the Old World of which she had read and studied so much, she persuaded my father to take the whole family abroad.

After those early summers at Madison, which still stand out so clearly in my memory, there comes a less vivid recollection of months passed at the beautiful old place at Barrytown, on the Hudson River, which my parents rented from Mr. John Aspinwall, and where a wonderful rushing brook played a big part in the joys of our holiday months.

We "younger ones" longed for another summer at this charming spot and regretted, with a certain amount of suspicion, the decision of the "Olympians" to drag us from our leafy haunts to improve our rebellious young minds, but my parents were firm in their decision, and we started on the old paddle-wheel steamship *Scotia*, as I have said, in May, 1869.

In a letter from my mother to my aunt, who had married Mr. James King Gracie, and was therefore regretfully left behind, she described with an easy pen some incidents of the voyage across the ocean, as follows:

"Elliott is the leader of children's sports and plays with the little Winthrop children all day. A short while ago Thee made up his mind suddenly that Teedie must play too, so hunted up the little fellow who was deeply enjoying a conversation with the only acquaintance he has made, a little man, whom we call the 'one too many man,' for he seems to go about with no acquaintances. His name is Mr. St. John and he is a quaint little well of knowledge,—very fond of natural history and fills Teedie's heart with delight. Teedie brought him up and introduced him to me, his eyes dancing with delight and he constantly asks me, 'Mamma, have you really conversed with Mr. St. John?' I feel so tenderly to Teedie, that I actually stopped reading the 'Heir of Redcliffe,' and talked to the poor little man who has heart complaint so badly that his voice is even affected by it.

"The two little boys were pretty seasick on Sunday and I do not know what I should have done without Robert, the bedroom steward, and an amiable deck steward, who waits on those who remain on deck at meals. He seems a wonderfully constructed creature, having amiable knobs all over his body, upon which he supports more bowls of soup and plates of eatables than you can imagine, all of which he serves out, panting over you while you take your plate, with such wide extended nostrils that they take in the Irish coast, and the draught from them cools the soup!

"Anna,—the carpet in my stateroom is filled with organic matter which, if distilled, would make a kind of anchovy paste, only fit to be the appetizer before the famous 'witches' broth,' the receipt for which Shakespeare gives in "Macbeth,"—but on the whole the *Scotia* is well ordered and cleaner than I had expected.

"On Sunday morning Thee was sick and while in bed, little Conie came into the room. He looked down from his upper berth, looking like a straw-colored Cockatoo, but Conie stopped in the middle of what she was saying and said, 'Oh Papa! you have such a lovely little curl on your forehead' with a note of great admiration in her voice and meaning it all, *really*, but her position looking up, and his looking down reminded me forcibly of the picture of the flattered crow who dropped his cheese when the fox complimented him!"

This letter, perhaps, more than almost any other, gives the quaint humor and also the tenderness of my mother's attitude toward her children and husband.

On our arrival in Liverpool we were greeted by the Bulloch uncles, and from that time on the whole European trip was one of interest and delight to the "grown people." My older sister, though not quite fifteen, was so unusually mature and intelligent that she shared their enjoyment, but the journey was of rather mitigated pleasure to the three "little ones," who much preferred the nursery at 28th East 20th Street, or their free summer activities in wood and field, to the picture-galleries and museums, or even to the wonderful Swiss mountains where they had to be so carefully guarded.

In the letters written faithfully to our beloved aunt, the note of homesickness is always apparent.

Our principal delight was in what we used to call "exploring" when we first arrived at a hotel, and in the occasional intercourse with children of our own age, or, as in Teedie's case, with some expert along the line of his own interests, but the writing and receiving of home letters stand out more strongly than almost any other memory of this time, and amongst those most treasured by Teedie and myself were the little missives written by our most intimate friend, Edith Kermit Carow, a little girl who was to have, in later days, the most potent influence of all over the life of Theodore Roosevelt. How little she thought when she wrote to her friend "Conie" from Redbank, November 19, 1869, "I was much pleased at receiving your kind letter telling me all about Teedie's birthday," that one day that very Teedie would be President Theodore Roosevelt and Edith Kermit Carow the mistress of the White House.

The old friendship of our parents for Mr. and Mrs. Carow, who lived with Mr. Carow's older sister, Mrs. Robert Kermit, in a large house backing up against the 14th Street mansion of Mr. and Mrs. Cornelius Van Schaack Roosevelt, was the natural factor in the relationship of the younger generation, and little Edith Carow and little Corinne Roosevelt were pledged friends from the time of their birth.

The "Teedie" of those days expressed always a homesick feeling when "Edie's" letters came. They seemed to fill him with a strong longing for his native land!

In the little note written on yellow, very minute writing-paper, headed by a satisfied-looking cat, "Edie" expresses the wish that "Teedie" could have been with her on a late picnic, and "Teedie," I am equally sure, wished for her presence at his eleventh-birthday festivities, which were described by my sister

Anna in a letter to our aunt, Mrs. James King Gracie. I quote a few lines from that letter, for again its contents show the beautiful devotion of my father and mother and sister to the delicate little boy—the devotion which always put their own wishes or arrangements aside when the terrible attacks of asthma came, for those attacks seemed to make them feel that no plan was too definite or important to change at once should "Teedie's" health require it. My sister writes, the letter being dated from Brussels, October 30, 1869:

"Last Thursday was dear little Teedie's birthday; he was eleven years old. We all determined to lay ourselves out on that occasion, for we all feared that he would be homesick,—for he is a great little home-boy. It passed off very nicely indeed. We had to leave Berlin suddenly the night before, for 'Teedie' was not very well; so we left Berlin on Wednesday night at eight o'clock and arrived at Cologne on Thursday morning about nine. You can imagine it was a very long trip for the three little children, although they really bore it better than we three older ones. [She one of the older ones at fourteen and a half!] It was a bitterly cold night and snowed almost all the time. Think of a snow storm on the night of the 27th of October! Teedie was delighted at having had a snow storm on his birthday morning, for he had never had *that* before. When we reached Cologne we went to the same hotel, and had the same nice rooms which we had had on our former stay there, and that of course made us feel very much more at home. Teedie ordered the breakfast, and they all had 'real tea' as a very great treat, and then Teedie ordered the dinner, at which we were all requested to appear in full dress; so Mamma came in her beautiful white silk dinner dress, and Papa in dress coat and light kid gloves. I was very cold, so only wore silk. After Teedie's dinner Papa brought in all his presents. They, Mamma and Papa, gave each of the three, writing desks marked with their names and filled with all the conveniences. Then Teedie received a number of smaller presents as well."

What parents, indeed, so fully to understand the romantic feeling of the little boy about his birthday dinner, that they were more than willing to don their most beautiful habiliments, and appear as they had so lately appeared when received at the Vienna Court! Such yielding to what by many people might have been considered as too childish a whim to be countenanced shows with special clearness the quality in my father and mother which inspired in us all such undying adoration. Another letter—not written by my older sister, but in the painstaking handwriting of a little girl of seven—describes my own party the month before. We were evidently staying in Vienna at the time, for I say: "We went to Schönbrunn, a 'shatto.'" (More frequently known as a château, but quite as thrilling to my childish mind spelled in my own unique manner!) And there in the lovely grounds my mother had arranged a charming al fresco supper for the little homesick American girl, and just as the "grown people" were in "full dress" for "Teedie's" birthday, so they gave themselves up in the grounds of the great "shatto" to making merry for the little seven-year-old girl.

After the great excitements of the birthdays came our interesting sojourn in Rome. In spite of my mother's efforts to arouse a somewhat abortive interest in art in the hearts of the three little children, my principal recollections of the Rome of 1869 are from the standpoint of the splendid romps on the Pincian Hill. In those contests of running and racing and leaping my brother Elliott was always the leader, although "Teedie" did his part whenever his health permitted. One scene stands out clearly in my mind. It was a beautiful day, one of those sunny Italian days when ilex and olive shone with a special glistening quality, and when the "Eternal City" as viewed from the high hill awoke even in the hearts of the little Philistine foreigners a subconscious thrill which they themselves did not quite understand. We were playing with the Lawrence children, playing leap-frog (how inappropriate to the Pincian Hill!) over the many posts, when suddenly there came a stir—an unexpected excite-

Corinne Roosevelt, 1869, at seven and a half years.

Theodore Roosevelt at ten years of age.

Anna Roosevelt at the age of fifteen when she spoke of herself as one of the "three older ones."

ment seemed everywhere. Word was passed that the Pope was coming. "Teedie" whispered to the little group of American children that he didn't believe in popes—that no real American would; and we all felt it was due to the stars and stripes that we should share his attitude of distant disapproval. But then, as is often the case, the miracle happened, for the crowd parted, and to our excited, childish eyes something very much like a scene in a story-book took place. The Pope, who was in his sedan-chair carried by bearers in beautiful costumes, his benign face framed in white hair and the close cap which he wore, caught sight of the group of eager little children craning their necks to see him pass; and he smiled and put out one fragile, delicate hand toward us, and, lo! the late scoffer who, in spite of the ardent Americanism that burned in his eleven-year-old soul, had as much reverence as militant patriotism in his nature, fell upon his knees and kissed the delicate hand, which for a brief moment was laid upon his fair curling hair. Whenever I think of Rome this memory comes back to me, and in a way it was so true to the character of my brother. The Pope to him had always meant what later he would have called "unwarranted superstition," but that Pope, Pio Nono, the kindly, benign old man, the moment he appeared in the flesh brought about in my brother's heart the reaction which always came when the pure, the good, or the true crossed his path.

Amongst my mother's efforts to interest us in art there was one morning when she decided positively that her little girl, at least, should do something more in keeping with the "Eternal City" than playing leap-frog on the Pincian Hill, and so, a reluctant captive, I was borne away to the Vatican Galleries, and was there initiated into the beauties of some of the frescos and sculpture. My mother, who I have already said was a natural connoisseur in all art, had especial admiration for that wonderful piece of sculpture from the hand of Michael Angelo known as "The Torso of the Vatican." This work of art stood alone in a small room, so that nothing else should take away from its effect. As those who know it well need hardly be told, it lacks both arms and both legs, and to the little girl who was summarily placed by her mother in the only chair in the small room, it seemed a very strange creation. But, with the hope of arousing artistic instinct, my lovely mother said: "Now, darling, this is one of the greatest works of art in the world, and I am going to leave you here alone for five minutes, because I want you to sit very quietly and look at it, and perhaps when I come back in the five minutes you will be able to realize how beautiful it is." And then I saw my mother's slender figure vanish into another room. Having been always accustomed to obey my parents, I virtuously and steadily kept my eyes upon the legless, armless Torso, wondering how any one *could* think it a beautiful work of art; and when my mother, true to her words, returning in five minutes with an expectant look on her face, said, "Now, darling, what do you think of the great 'Torso'?" I replied sadly, "Well, mamma, it seems to me a little 'chumpy'!" How often later in life I have heard my mother laugh immoderately as she described her effort to instil her own love of those wonderful shoulders and that massive back into her recalcitrant small daughter; and when, years after, I myself, imbued as she was with a passion for Italy and Italian art, used to wander through those same galleries, I could never go into that little room without the memory of the small girl of long ago, and her effort to think Michael Angelo's "Torso" anything but "chumpy."

Christmas in Rome was made for us as much like our wonderful Christmases at home as was possible in a foreign hotel. It had always been our custom to go to our parents' room at the pleasant hour of 6 A. M., and generally my mother had induced my long-suffering father to be dressed in some special and marvellous manner at that early hour when we "undid" the bulging, mysterious-looking stockings, and none of these exciting rites were omitted because of our distance from our native land. I think, for that reason, at the end of the beautiful Christmas Day, 1869, the special joy in the hearts of the three little American children was that they had actually forgotten that they were in Rome at all! On January 2, "Teedie" himself writes to his beloved Aunt Annie (Mrs. Gracie) on a piece of note-paper which characteristically has at the top a bird on a bough—that paper being his choice for the writing-desks which had been given to the three children on his birthday: "Will you send the enclosed to Eidith Carow. In it I described our ascent of Vesuvius, and so I will describe Pompeii to you." In a rather cramped hand he enters then into an accurate description of everything connected with Pompeii, gloating with scientific delight over the seventeen skeletons found in the Street of the Tombs, but falling for one moment into a lighter vein, he tells of two little Italian boys whom my father had engaged to come and sing for us the same evening at Sorrento, and whose faces were so dirty that my father and his friend Mr. Stevens washed them with "Kissengin Water." That extravagance seems to have been specially entertaining to the mind of the young letter-writer.

During the year abroad there were lovely times when we were not obliged to think of sculpture or painting—weeks in the great Swiss mountains when, in spite of frequent attacks of his old enemy, my father writes that "Teedie" walked many miles and showed the pluck and perseverance which were so strikingly part of his character. In another letter he is described, while suffering from a peculiarly severe attack of asthma, as being propped up all night in a big chair in the sitting-room, while his devoted mother told him stories of "when she was a little girl" at the old plantation at Roswell; and yet within two days of that very time he is following my father and brother on one of the longest walks they took in the mountains. All through the letters of that period one realizes the developing character of the suffering little boy. My mother writes in a letter to her sister: "Teedie and Ellie have walked to-day thirteen miles, and are very proud of their performance. Indeed Teedie has been further several times."

And so the year of exile had its joyous memories, but in spite of them never were there happier children than those who arrived home in America in the spring of 1870.

Earlier in our lives my father, always thinking of the problem of the fragile health of his two older children, conceived the idea of turning the third room of the second story at 28 East 20th Street into an out-of-doors piazza, a kind of open-air gymnasium, with every imaginable swing and bar and seesaw, and my mother has often told me how he called the boy to him one day—Theodore was now about eleven years of age—and said: "Theodore, you have the mind but you have not the body, and without the help of the body the mind cannot go as far as it should. You must *make* your body. It is hard drudgery to make one's body, but I know you will do it." The little boy looked up, throwing back his head in a characteristic fashion; then with a flash of those white teeth which later in life became so well known that when he was police commissioner the story ran that any recreant policeman would faint if he suddenly came face to face with a set of *false* teeth in a shop-window—he said, "*I'll make my body.*"

That was his first important promise to himself and the delicate little boy began his work; and for many years one of my most vivid recollections is seeing him between horizontal bars, widening his chest by regular, monotonous motion—drudgery indeed—but a drudgery which eventuated in his being not only the apostle but the exponent of the strenuous life.

What fun we had on that piazza! The first Theodore Roosevelt, like his son, was far ahead of his times, and fresh air was his hobby, and he knew that the children who will cry if they are made to take dull walks on dreary city streets, will romp with dangerous delight ungovernessed and unmaided in an outdoor gymnasium. I use the word "dangerous" advisedly, for one day my lovely and delicate mother had an unforgetable shock on that same piazza. She happened to look out of the window opening on to the piazza and saw two boys—one of whom, needless to say, was Theodore—carefully balancing the seesaw from the high rail which protected the children from the possibility of falling into the back yard, two stories below. Having wearied of the usual play, the aforesaid two boys thought they would add a tinge of excitement to the merriment by balancing the seesaw in such a manner as to have one boy always in the thrilling position of hanging on the farther side of the top rail, with the possibility (unless the equilibrium were kept to perfection) of seesaw, boys, and all descending unexpectedly into the back yard.

One may well imagine the horror of the mother as she saw her adventurous offspring crawling out beyond the projection of the railing, and only great self-control enabled her to reach the wooden board held lightly by the fingers of an equally criminal cousin, and by an agonized clutch make it impossible for the seesaw to slide down with its two foolhardy riders.

Needless to say, no such feat was ever performed again, but the piazza became the happy meeting-ground of all the boys and girls of the neighborhood, and there not only Theodore Roosevelt but many of his friends and family put in a stock of sturdy health which was to do them good service in later years. At the same time the children of that house were leading the normal lives of other little children, except for the individual industry of the more delicate one, who put his hours of necessary quiet into voracious reading of history, and study of natural history.

Again the summers were the special delight of our lives, and the following several summers we spent on the Hudson River, at or near Riverdale, where warm friendships were formed with the children of our parents' friends, Mr. and Mrs. William E. Dodge, Mr. and Mrs. Percy R. Pyne, Mr. and Mrs. Oliver Harriman, and Mr. Robert Colgate.

Groups of joyous children invented and carried into effect every imaginable game, and, as ever, our father was the delightful collaborator in every scheme of pleasure. There began Theodore's more active collection of birds and animals. There he advertised for families of field-mice, and the influx of the all-too-prolific little animals was terrifying to the heart of so perfect a housekeeper as my mother. The horror produced by the discovery of several of the above-named families in the refrigerator was more than trying to the nerves of one less devoted to science. My sister Anna, the most unselfish of older sisters, was the chief sufferer always, as, in spite of her extreme youth—for she was only four years older than my brother—her unusual ability and maturity made her seem more like a second mother than a sister. On one special occasion Theodore, having advertised and offered the large sum of ten cents for every field-mouse and thirty-five cents for a family, left for a trip to the Berkshire hills, and my poor sister was inundated by hundreds of active and unattractive families of field-mice, while clamoring country people demanded their ten-cent pieces or the larger sum irrelevantly offered by the absentee young naturalist. In the same unselfish manner my sister was the unwilling recipient of families of young squirrels, guinea-pigs, etc., and I can see her still bringing up one especially delicate family of squirrels on the bottle, and also begging a laundress not to forsake the household because turtles were tied to her tubs!

Those summers on the Hudson River stand out as peculiarly happy days. As I have said before, we were allowed great freedom, although never license, in the summer-time, and situated as we then were, with a group of little friends about us, the long sweet days passed like a joyous dream.

Doctor Hilborne West, the husband of my mother's half-sister, stands prominently out as a figure in those childhood times. My mother writes of him as follows: "Dr. West has made himself greatly beloved by each child. He has made boats and sailed them with Ellie; has read poetry and acted plays with Conie; and has talked science and medicine and natural history with Teedie, who always craves knowledge." In spite of his craving for knowledge the boy, now nearly fourteen years old, had evidently, however, the normal love of noise and racket, as evinced by the following "spread-eagle" letter to his aunt, who, in her turn, had gone abroad that summer.

Dobb's Ferry, July 9th, 72.

DEAR AUNTIE

We had the most splendid fun on the fourth of July. At eight o'clock we commenced with a discharge of three packs of firecrackers, which awoke most of the people. But we had only begun now, and during the remainder of the day six boxes of torpedoes and thirty-six packs of firecrackers kept the house in an exceedingly lively condition. That evening it rained which made us postpone the fireworks until next evening, when they were had with great success, excepting the balloons, which were an awful swindle. We boys assisted by firing roman candles, flowerpots and bengolas. We each got his fair share of burns.

Conie had a slight attack of asthma last night but I took her riding this morning and we hope she is well now.

We are permitted now to stay in the water as long as we please. The other day I came near being drowned, for I got caught under water and was almost strangled before I could get out. I study English, French, German and Latin now. Bamie spent the fourth at Barrytown where she had Tableaux, Dances, &c to her heart's content. Give my love to Uncles and Cousin Jimmie. Aunt Hattie &c. Tell Aunt Hattie I will never forget the beautiful jam and the splendid times we had at her cottage.

Ever your little

T. D.

Later in life, in thinking of this same uncle, whose subsequent career never squared with his natural ability, I have come to feel that sometimes people whom we call failures should not be so called,—for it is often their good fortune to leave upon the malleable minds of the next generation an inspiration of which they themselves fall sadly short. In the character of this same charming uncle there must have been some lack of fibre, for, brilliant as he was, he let his talents lie dormant. Yet, perhaps, of all those who influenced our early childhood, the effect upon us produced by his cultivation, his marvellous memory, his literary interests, and his genial good humor had more to do with the early stirring of intellectual desires in his little relatives than almost any other influence at that time. The very fact that he was not achieving a thousand worth-while things, as was my father, the very fact that he was not busied with the practical care and thought for us, as were my mother and aunt—brought about between us that delightful relationship when the older person leads rather than drives the younger into the paths of literature and learning. To have "Uncle Hill" read Shakespeare to us under the trees, and then suggest that we "dress up" and act the parts, to have "Uncle Hill" teach us parts of the famous plays of all the ages and the equally famous poems, was a delight rather than a task; and he interspersed his Shakespeare with the most remarkable, and, to our childish minds, brilliant doggerel, sometimes of his own making, that could possibly be imagined—so that Hamlet's soliloquy one day seemed quite as palatable as "Villikins and His Dinah," or "Horum, Chorum, Sumpti Vorum," the next. To show the relationship between the charming physician of Philadelphia (the home of my uncle and aunt was in that city) and the young philosopher of New York, I am tempted to insert a letter from the latter to the former written in 1873 from Paris on our second trip abroad.

"From Theodore the Philosopher to Hilborne, Elder of the Church of Philadelphia. Dated from Paris, a city of Gaul, in the 16th day of the 11th month of the 4th year of the reign of Ulysses. [I imagine that General Grant was then President.] Truly, O Hilborne! this is the first time in many weeks that I have been able to write you concerning our affairs. I have just come from the city of Bonn in the land of the Teuton, where I have been communing with our fellow labourer James of Roosevelt, surnamed The Doctor [our first cousin, young James West Roosevelt], whom I left in good health. In crossing the Sea of Atlantis I suffered much of a malady called sickness of the sea, but am now in good health, as are also all our family. I would that you should speak to the sage Leidy concerning the price of his great manuscript, which I am desirous of getting. Give my regards to Susan of West, whom I hope this letter will find in health. I have procured many birds of kinds new to me here, and have preserved them. This is all I have to say for the time being, so will close this short epistle."*

That summer of 1872 was very enchanting, although overshadowed by the thought of another "terrible trip to Europe," for after much thought my father and mother had decided that the benefits of a winter on the Nile, and a summer studying German in Dresden, would outweigh the possible disadvantage of breaking into the regular school studies of the three children of the 20th Street nursery. Therefore the whole family set sail again in the autumn of 1872.

After a delightful time with the uncles and aunts who had settled in England, and many gay excursions to Hampton Court and Bushey Park, and other places of interest, we went by way of Paris and Brindisi to Alexandria, and after some weeks in Cairo set sail on a dahabeah for three months on the Nile. In a letter from my brother Elliott to my aunt he speaks of my father's purchase of a boat. With characteristic disregard of the historic interest of the Nile he says: "Teedie and I won't mind the Nile very much, now that we have a boat to row in, perhaps it won't be so bad after all what with rowing, boxing, and Christmas and playing, in between lessons and the ruins." Reaching Egypt, the same young lover of boxing and boats writes of meeting much-beloved cousins, and again the characters of "Ellie" and "Teedie" are markedly brought out in the childish letter, for he says, "We had such a cosey tea. Frank and I poured tea and cut up chicken, while Teedie and Jimmie

*This in a boyish hand which is beginning to show the character of the young author.

[the young cousin referred to in 'Teedie's' letter to Doctor West] talked about natural history."

The experience of a winter on the Nile was a very wonderful one for the little American children, and "Ellie's" anticipations were more than carried out. Before we actually set sail I write in my journal of our wonderful trip to the pyramids and our impressions, childish ones of course, of the marvellous bazaars; and then we finally leave Cairo and start on the journey up the ancient river. I have always been so glad that our trip was before the days of the railway up to Karnak, for nothing could have been more Oriental and unlike modern life than the slow progress of our dahabeah, the *Aboo Erdan*. When there was wind we tacked and slowly sailed, for the boat was old and bulky, but when there was no wind the long line of sailors would get out on the bank of the river and, tying themselves to the rope attached to the bow, would track slowly along, bending their bronzed backs with the effort, and singing curious crooning songs.

In a letter dated December 27 I write to my aunt: "I will tell you about my presents. Amongst others I got a pair of pretty vases, and Teedie says the little birds they have on them are an entirely new species. Teedie and Father go out shooting every day, and so far have been very lucky. Teedie is always talking about it whenever he comes in the room,—in fact when he does come in the room you always hear the words 'bird' and 'skin.' *It certainly is great fun for him.*" In connection with these same shooting-trips my father writes: "Teedie took his gun and shot an ibis and one or two other specimens this morning while the crew were taking breakfast. Imagine seeing not only flocks of these birds, regarded as so rare by us in days gone by as to be selected as a subject for our game of 'twenty questions,' but also of storks, hawks, owls, pelicans, and, above all, doves innumerable. I presented Teedie with a breech-loader at Christmas, and he was perfectly delighted. It was entirely unexpected to him, although he had been shooting with it as mine. He is a most enthusiastic sportsman and has infused some of his spirit into me. Yesterday I walked through the bogs with him at the risk of sinking hopelessly and helplessly, for hours, and carried the dragoman's gun, which is a muzzle-loader, with which I only shot several birds quietly resting upon distant limbs and fallen trees; *but I felt I must keep up with Teedie.*"

The boy of fourteen, with his indomitable energy, was already leading his equally indomitable father into different fields of action. He never rested from his studies in natural history. When not walking through quivering bogs or actually shooting bird and beast, he, surrounded by the brown-faced and curious sailors, would seat himself on the deck of the dahabeah and skin and stuff the products of his sport. I well remember the excitement, and, be it confessed, anxiety and fear inspired in the hearts of the four young college men who, on another dahabeah, accompanied us on the Nile, when the ardent young sportsman, mounted on an uncontrollable donkey, would ride unexpectedly into their midst, his gun slung across his shoulders in such a way as to render its proximity distinctly dangerous as he bumped absent-mindedly against them. When not actually hunting he was willing to take part in exploration of the marvellous old ruins.

In a letter to "Edie" I say: "The other day we arrived at Edfoo, and we all went to see the temple together. While we were there Teedie, Ellie, Iesi (one of our sailors), and I started to explore. We went into a little dark room and climbed in a hole which was in the middle of the wall. The boys had candles. It was dark, crawling along the passage doubled up. At last we came to a deep hole, into which Teedie dropped, and we found out it was a mummy pit. It didn't go very far in, but it all seemed very exciting to us to be exploring mummy pits. Sometimes we sail head foremost and sometimes the current turns us all the way around—and I wish you could hear the cries of the sailors when anything happens."

They were busy days, for our wise parents insisted upon

regularity of a certain kind, and my older sister, only just eighteen, gave us lessons in both French and English in the early morning before we went on the wonderful excursions to the great temples, or before "Teedie" was allowed to escape for his shooting expeditions. I do not think the three months' absence from school was any detriment, and I am very grateful for the stimulating interest which that trip on the Nile gave to my brothers and me. I can still see in retrospect, as if it were yesterday, the great temple of Karnak as we visited it by moon-light; the majestic colossi at Medinet Haboo; and the more beautiful and delicate ruins of Philæ. Often my father would read Egyptian history to us or explain the kind of architecture which we were seeing; but always interspersed with more serious instruction were merry walks and games and wonderful picnic excursions, so that the winter on the Nile comes back to me as one of romantic interest mixed with the usual fun and cheerful intercourse of our ordinary family life. The four young men who had chartered the dahabeah *Rachel* were Messrs. Nathaniel Thayer and Frank Merriam of Boston, Augustus Jay of New York, and Harry Godey of Philadelphia, and these four friends, with the addition of other acquaintances whom we frequently met, made for my sister and my parents a delightful circle, into which we little ones were welcomed in a most gracious way.

In spite of the fact of the charms of the Nile and the fun we frequently had, I write on February 1, from Thebes, to my little playmate "Edie," with rather melancholy reminiscence of a more congenial past: "My own darling Edie," I say, "don't you remember what fun we *used* to have out in the country, and don't you remember the day we got Pony Grant up in the Chauncey's summer house and couldn't get him down again, and how we always were losing Teedie's india rubber shoes? I remember it so perfectly, and what fun it was!" I evidently feel that such adventures were preferable to those in which we were indulging in far-away Egypt, although I conscientiously describe the ear on one of the colossi at Medinet Haboo as being four feet high, and the temple, I state, with great accuracy, has twelve columns at the north and ten on either side! I seem, however, to be glad to come back from that expedition to Medinet Haboo, for I state that I wish she could see our dahabeah, which is a regular little home. I don't approve—in this same letter—of the dancing-girls, which my parents allowed me to see one evening. With early Victorian criticism I state that "there is not a particle of grace in their motions, for they only wriggle their bodies like a snake," and that I really felt they were "very unattractive"—thus proving that the little girl of eleven in 1873 was more or less prim in her tastes. I delight, however, in a poem which I copy for "Edie," the first phrase of which has rung in my ears for many a long day.

> "Alas! must I say it, fare-farewell to thee,
> Mysterious Egypt, great land of the flea,
> And thy Thebaic temples, Luxor and Karnac,
> Where the natives change slowly from yellow to black.
> Shall I ne'er see thy plain, so fraught with renown,
> Where the shadoofs go up and the shadoofs go down,
> Which two stalwart natives bend over and sing,
> While their loins are concealed by a simple shoe string."

This verse, in spite of the reference to the lack of clothes of the stalwart natives, evidently did not shock my sensibilities as much as the motions of the dancing-girls. Farther on in the letter I describe the New Year's Eve party, and how Mr. Merriam sang a song which I (Conie) liked very much, and which was called "She's Naughty But So Nice." "Teedie," however, did not care for that song, but preferred one called "Aunt Dinah," because one verse ran: "My love she am a giraffe, a two-humped camamile." [Music had apparently only charms to soothe him when suggestive of his beloved animal studies.] From Thebes also my brother writes to his aunt one of the most interesting letters of his boyhood:

Near Kom Obos, Jan. 26th, 1873.

DEAR AUNT ANNIE:

My right hand having recovered from the imaginary attack from which it did *not* suffer, I proceed to thank you for your kind present, which very much delighted me. We are now on the Nile and have been on that great and mysterious river for over a month. I think I have never enjoyed myself so much as in this month. There has always been something to do, for we could always fall back upon shooting when everything else failed us. And then we had those splendid and grand old ruins to see, and one of them will stock you with thoughts for a month. The temple that I enjoyed most was Karnak. We saw it by moonlight. I never was impressed by anything so much. To wander among those great columns under the same moon that had looked down on them for thousands of years was awe-inspiring; it gave rise to thoughts of the ineffable, the unutterable; thoughts which you cannot express, which cannot be uttered, which cannot be answered until after The Great Sleep.

[Here the little philosopher breaks off and continues in less serious mood on February 9.]

I have had great enjoyment from the shooting here, as I have procured between one and two hundred skins. I expect to procure some more in Syria. Inform Emlen of this. As you are probably aware, Father presented me on Christmas with a double-barrelled breech loading shot gun, which I never move on shore without, excepting on Sundays. The largest bird I have yet killed is a Crane which I shot as it rose from a lagoon near Thebes.

The sporting is injurious to my trousers. . . .

Now that I am on the subject of dress I may as well mention that the dress of the inhabitants up to ten years of age is nothing. After that they put on a shirt descended from some remote ancestor, and never take it off till the day of their death.

Mother is recovering from an attack of indigestion, but the rest are all well and send love to you and our friends, in which I join sincerely, and remain,

Your Most Affectionate Nephew,

T. ROOSEVELT, JR.

The adoration of his little sister for the erudite "Teedie" is shown in every letter, especially in the letters to their mutual little friend "Edie." On January 25 this admiration is summed up in a postscript which says: "Teedie is out shooting now. He is quite professionist [no higher praise could apparently be given than this remarkable word] in shooting, skinning and stuffing, and he is so satisfied." This expression seems to sum up the absolute sense of well-being during that wonderful winter of the delicate boy, who, in spite of his delicacy, always achieved his heart's desire.

In the efforts of his little sister to be a worthy companion, I find in my diary, written that same winter of the Nile, one abortive struggle on my own part to become a naturalist. On the page at the end of my journal I write in large letters:

NATURAL HISTORY

"QUAIL

"Ad. near Alexandria, Egypt, November 27th, 1872. Length 5—Expanse 13.0 Wings 5 Tail 1.3—Bill 5. Tarsus 1.2 Middle Toe 1.1 Hind Toe .3."

Under these mystic signs is a more elaborate and painstaking description of the above bird. I can see my brother now giving me a serious lecture on the subject, and trying to inspire a mind at that time securely closed to all such interests—to open at least a crack of its reluctant door, for "Teedie" felt that to walk with blind eyes in a world of such fluttering excitement as was made for him by the birds of the air showed an innate depravity which he wished with all his soul to cure in his beloved little sister. At the end of my description of the quail I fall by the wayside, and only once again make an excursion into the natural history of the great land of Egypt; only once more do I struggle with the description of a bird called this time by the curious name of "Ziczac." (Could this be "Zigzag," or was it simply my childish mind that zigzagged in its painful efforts to follow the impossible trail of my elder brother?) In my account of this, to say the least, unusual bird I remark: "Tarsus not finished." Whether *I* have not finished the tarsus, or whether the bird itself had an arrested development of some kind, I do not explain; and on the blank page opposite this final effort in scientific adventure I finish, as I began, by the words "*Natural History*," and underneath them, to explain my own unsuccessful efforts, I write: "My Brother, Theodore Roosevelt, Esq." Whether I had decided that all natural history was summed up in that magic name, or whether from that time on I was determined to leave all natural history to my brother, Theodore Roosevelt, Esq., I do not know; but the fact remains that from that day to this far distant one I have never again dipped into the mystery of mandibles and tarsi.

And so the sunny, happy days on the great river passed away. A merry eighteenth-birthday party in January for my sister Anna took the form of a moonlight ride to the great temple of Karnak, and, although we younger ones, naturally tired frequently of the effort to understand history and hieroglyphics, and turned with joy even in the shadow of the grand columns of Abydos to the game of "Buzz," still I can say with truth that the easily moulded and receptive minds of the three little children responded to the atmosphere of the great river with its mighty past, and all through the after-years the interest aroused in those early days stimulated their craving for knowledge about the land of the Pharaohs.

On our way down the river an incident occurred which, in

a sense, was also memorable. At Rhoda on our return from the tombs of Beni Hasan we found that a dahabeah had drawn up near ours, on which were the old sage Ralph Waldo Emerson and his daughter. My father, who never lost a chance of bringing into the lives of his children some worth-while memory, took us all to see the old poet, and I often think with pleasure of the lovely smile, somewhat vacant, it is true, but very gentle, with which he received the little children of his fellow countryman.

It was at this time that the story was told in connection with Mr. Emerson that some sentimental person said: "How wonderful to think of Emerson looking at the Sphinx! What a message the Sphinx must have had for Emerson." Whereupon an irreverent wit replied: "The only message the Sphinx could possibly have had for Emerson must have been 'You're another.'" I can quite understand now, remembering the mystic, dreamy face of the old philosopher, how this witticism came about.

And now the Nile trip was over and we were back again in Cairo, and planning for the further interest of a trip through the Holy Land. Mr. Thayer and Mr. Jay, two of the young friends who had accompanied us on the Nile, decided to join our party, and after a short stay in Cairo we again left for Alexandria and thence sailed for Jaffa. In my diary I write at the Convent of Ramleh between Jaffa and Jerusalem, where we spent our first night: "In Jaffa we chose our horses, which was very exciting, and started on our long ride. After three hours of delightful riding through a great many green fields, we reached this convent and found they had no room for ladies, because they were not allowed to go into one part of the building as it was against the rules, but at last Father got the old monks to allow us to come into another part of the convent for just one night."

"Father," like his namesake, almost always got what he wanted.

From that time on one adventure after another followed.

I write of many nice gallops, and of my horse lying down in the middle of streams; and, incidentally with less interest, of the Mount of Olives and the Church of the Holy Sepulchre! Antonio Sapienza proved to be an admirable dragoman, and always the practical part of the tenting cavalcade started early in the morning, and therefore as the rest of us rode over the hills in the later afternoon we would see arranged cosily in some beautiful valley the white tents, with the curling smoke from the kitchen-tent already rising with the promise of a delightful dinner.

Over Jordan we went, and what a very great disappointment Jordan was to our childish minds, which had always pictured a broad river and great waves parting for the Ark of the Covenant to pass. This Jordan was a little stream hardly more impressive than the brook at our old home at Madison, and we could not quite accustom ourselves to the disappointment. But Jerusalem with its narrow streets and gates, its old churches, the high Mount of Olives, and the little town of Bethlehem not far away, and, even more interesting from the standpoint of beauty, the vision of the Convent of Mar Saba on the high hill not far from Hebron, and beyond all else the blue sparkling waters of the Dead Sea, all remain in my memory as a wonderful panorama of romance and delight.

Arab sheiks visited us frequently in the evening and brought their followers to dance for us, and wherever my father went he accumulated friends of all kinds and colors, and we, his children, shared in the marvellous atmosphere he created. I remember, in connection with the Dead Sea, that "Teedie" and Mr. Jay decided that they could sink in it, although the guides had warned them that the salt was so buoyant that it was impossible for any living thing to sink in the waters (the Dead Sea was about the most alive sea that I personally have ever seen), and so the two adventurous ones undertook to dive, and tried to remain under water. "Teedie" fortunately relinquished the effort almost immediately, but Mr. Jay, who in a spirit of bravado struggled to remain at the bottom, suffered the ill effects from crusted salt in eyes and ears for many hours after leaving the water.

For about three weeks we rode through the Holy Land, and my memory of many flowers remains as one of the charms of that trip. Later, led in the paths of botany by a beloved friend, I often longed to go back to that land of flowers; but then to my childish eyes they meant nothing but beauty and delight.

After returning to Jerusalem and Jaffa we took ship again and landed this time at Beyrout, and started on another camping-trip to Damascus, through perhaps the most beautiful scenery which we had yet enjoyed. During that trip also we had various adventures. I describe in my diary how my father, at one of our stopping-places, brought to our tents some beautiful young Arab girls, how they gave us oranges and nuts, and how cordially they begged us, when a great storm came up and our tents were blown away, to come for shelter to their quaint little houses.

Even to the minds of the children of eleven and fourteen years of age, the great Temple of Baalbek proved a lure of beauty, and the diary sagely remarks that "It is quite as beautiful as Karnak, although in an entirely different way, as Baalbek has delicate columns, and Karnak great, massive columns." The beauty, however, is not a matter of such interest as the mysterious little subterranean passages, and I tell how "Teedie" helped me to climb the walls and little tower, and to crawl through these same unexplored dark places.

The ride into Damascus itself remains still an expedition of glamour, for we reached the vicinity of the city by a high cliff, and the city burst upon us with great suddenness, its minarets stretching their delicate, arrow-like spires to the sky in so Oriental a fashion that even the practical hearts of the little American children responded with a thrill of excitement. Again, after an interesting stay in Damascus, we made our way back to Beyrout. While waiting for the steamer there my brother Elliott was taken ill, and writes in a homesick fashion to the beloved aunt to whom we confided all our joys and woes. Poor little boy! He says pathetically: "Oh, Auntie, you don't know how I long for a finishing-up of this ever-lasting traveling, when we can once more sit down to breakfast, dinner and lunch in our own house. Since I have been sick and only allowed rice and chicken, —and very little of them—I have longed for one of our rice puddings, and a pot of that strawberry jam, and one of Mary's sponge cakes, and I have thought of when I would go to your rooms for dinner and what jolly chops and potatoes and dessert I would get there, and when I would come to breakfast we would have *buckwheat cakes*. Perhaps I am a little homesick." I am not so sure but what many an intelligent traveller, could his or her heart be closely examined, would find written upon it "lovely potatoes, chops and hot buckwheat cakes."

But all the same, in spite of "Ellie's" rhapsody, off we started on another steamer, and my father writes on March 28, 1873:

Steamer off Rhodes.

Teedie is in great spirits, as the sailors have caught for him numerous specimens, which he stuffs on deck, to the edification of a large audience.

I write during the same transit, after stopping at Athens, that "It is a very lovely town, and that I should have liked to stay there longer, but that was not to be." I also decided that although the ruins were beautiful, I did not like them as much as either Karnak or Baalbek. Having dutifully made these architectural criticisms, I turn with gusto to the fact that Tom and Fannie Lawrence, "Teedie," "Ellie," and I have such splendid games of tag on the different steamers, and that I know my aunt would have enjoyed seeing us. The tag was "con amore," while the interest in the temples was, I fear, somewhat induced. Our comprehending mother and father, however, always allowed us joyous moments between educational efforts. In a letter from Constantinople written by "Ellie" on April 7, he says: "We have had Tom and Frank Lawrence here to dinner, and we had a splendid game of 'muggins' and tried to play eucre (I don't know that this is rightly spelled) with five, but did not suceede, Teedie did make such mistakes. [Not such an expert in cards, you see, as in tarsi and mandibles!] But we were in such spirits that it made no difference, and we did nothing but shout at the top of our voices the battle cry of freedom; and the playing of a game of slapjack helped us get off our steam with hard slaps, but even then there was enough (steam) left in Teedie and Tom to have a candle fight and grease their clothes, and poor Frank's and mine, who were doing nothing at all!" As one can see by this description, the learned and rather delicate "Teedie" was only a normal, merry boy after all. "Ellie" describes also the wonderful rides in Constantinople, and many other joys planned by our indulgent parents. From that same city, called because of its many steeples The City of Minarets, "Teedie" writes to his little friend Edith:

I think I have enjoyed myself more this winter than I ever did before. Much to add to my enjoyment Father gave me a gun at Christmas, which rendered me happy and the rest of the family miserable.

I killed several hundred birds with it, and then went and lost it! I think I enjoyed the time in Egypt most, and after that I had the most fun while camping out in Syria.

While camping out we were on horseback for several hours of each day, and as I like riding ever so much, and as the Syrian horses are very good, we had a splendid time. While riding I bothered the family somewhat by carrying the gun over my shoulder, and on the journey to the Jordan, when I was on the most spirited horse I ever rode, I bothered the horse too, as was evidenced by his running away several times when the gun struck him too hard. Our tent life had a good many adventures in it.

Once it rained very hard and the rain went into our open trunks. Another time our tents were almost blown away in a rough wind, and once I hunted a couple of jackals for two or three miles as fast as the horse could go.

Yours truly,
T. Roosevelt, Jr.

This little missive sums up the joy of "Teedie's" winter in Egypt and Syria, and so it seems a fitting moment to turn to other interests and occupations, leaving the mysterious land of the pyramids and that sacred land of mountains and flowers behind us in a glow of child memories, which as year followed year became brighter rather than dimmer.

III

THE DRESDEN LITERARY AMERICAN CLUB

MOTTO "W. A. N. A."

IT was a sad change to the three young American children to settle in Dresden in two German families, after the carefree and stimulating experiences of Egypt and the Holy Land. Our wise parents, however, realized that a whole year of irregularity was a serious mistake in that formative period of our lives, and they also wished to leave no stone unturned to give us every educational advantage during our twelve months' absence from home and country. It was decided, therefore, that the two boys should be placed in the family of Doctor and Mrs. Minckwitz, while I, a very lone and homesick small girl, was put with some kind but far too elderly people, Professor and Mrs. Wackernagel. This last arrangement was supposed to be advantageous, so that the brothers and sister should not speak too much English together. The kind old professor and his wife and the daughters, who seemed to the little girl of eleven years on the verge of the grave (although only about forty years of age), did all that was in their power to lighten the agonized longing in the child's heart for her mother and sister, but to no avail, for I write to my mother, who had gone to Carlsbad for a cure: "I was perfectly miserable and very much unstrung when Aunt Lucy wrote to you that no one could mention your name or I would instantly begin to cry. Oh! Mother darling, sometimes I feel that I cannot stand it any longer but I am going to try to follow a motto which Father wrote to me, 'Try to have the best time you can.' I should be very sorry to disappoint Father but sometimes I feel as if I could not stand it any longer. We will talk it over when you come. Your own little Conie."

Poor little girl! I was trying to be noble; for my father, who had been obliged to return to America for business reasons, had impressed me with the fact that to spend part of the summer in a German family and thus learn the language was an unusual opportunity, and one that must be seized upon. My spirit was willing, but my flesh was very, very weak, and the age of the kind people with whom I had been placed, the strange, dreadful, black bread, the meat that was given only as a great treat after it had been boiled for soup—everything, in fact, conduced to a feeling of great distance from the lovely land of buckwheat cakes and rare steak, not to mention the separation from the beloved brothers whom I was allowed to see only at rare intervals during the week. The consequence was that very soon my mother came back to Dresden in answer to the pathos of my letters, for I found it impossible to follow that motto, so characteristic of my father, "Try to have the best time you can." I began to sicken very much as the Swiss mountaineers are said to lose their spirits and appetites when separated from their beloved mountains; so my mother persuaded the kind Minckwitz family to take me under their roof, as well as my brothers, and from that time forth there was no more melancholy, no bursting into poetic dirges constantly celebrating the misery of a young American in a German family.

From the time that I was allowed to be part of the Minckwitz family everything seemed to be fraught with interest and many pleasures as well as with systematic good hard work. In these days, when the word "German" has almost a sinister sound in the ears of an American, I should like to speak with affectionate respect of *that* German family in which the three little American children passed several happy months. The members of the family were typically Teutonic in many ways: the Herr Hofsrath was the kindliest of creatures, and his rubicund, smiling wife paid him the most loving court; the three daughters

—gay, well-educated, and very temperamental young women—threw themselves into the work of teaching us with a hearty good will, which met with real response from us, as that kind of effort invariably does. Our two cousins, the same little cousins who had shared the happy summer memories of Madison, New Jersey, when we were much younger, were also in Dresden with their mother, Mrs. Stuart Elliott, the "Aunt Lucy" referred to frequently in our letters. Aunt Lucy was bravely facing the results of the sad Civil War, and her only chance of giving her children a proper education was to take them to a foreign country where the possibility of good schools, combined with inexpensive living, suited her depleted income. Her little apartment on Sunday afternoons was always open to us all, and there we five little cousins formed the celebrated "D. L. A. C." (Dresden Literary American Club!)

On June 2 I wrote to my friend "Edie": "We five children have gotten up a club and meet every Sunday at Aunt Lucy's, and read the poetry and stories that we have written during the week. When the book is all done, we will sell the book either to mother or Aunt Annie and divide the money; (although on erudition bent, still of commercial mind!) *I* am going to write poetry all the time. My first poem was called 'A Sunny Day in June.' Next time I am going to give 'The Lament of an American in a German Family.' It is an entirely different style I assure you." The "different style" is so very poor that I refrain from quoting that illustrious poem.

The work for the D. L. A. C. proved to be a very entertaining pastime, and great competition ensued. A motto was chosen by "Johnnie" and "Ellie," who were the wits of the society. The motto was spoken of with bated breath and mysteriously inscribed W. A. N. A. underneath the mystic signs of D. L. A. C. For many a long year no one but those in our strictest confidence were allowed to know that "W. A. N. A." stood for "We Are No Asses." This, perhaps somewhat untruthful statement, was objected to originally by "Teedie," who firmly maintained that the mere making of such a motto showed that "Johnnie" and "Ellie" were certainly exceptions that proved that rule. "Teedie" himself, struggling as usual with terrible attacks of asthma that perpetually undermined his health and strength, was all the same, between the attacks, the ringleader in fun and gaiety and every imaginable humorous adventure. He was a slender, overgrown boy at the time, and wore his hair long in true German student fashion, and adopted a would-be philosopher type of look, effectively enhanced by trousers that were outgrown, and coat sleeves so short that they gave him a "Smike"-like appearance. His contributions to the immortal literary club were either serious and very accurate from a natural-historical standpoint, or else they showed, as comparatively few of his later writings have shown, the delightful quality of humor which, through his whole busy life, lightened for him every load and criticism. I cannot resist giving in full the fascinating little story called "Mrs. Field Mouse's Dinner Party," in which the personified animals played social parts, in the portrayal of which my brother divulged (my readers must remember he was only fourteen) a knowledge of "society" life, its acrid jealousies and hypocrisies, of which he never again seemed to be conscious.

MRS. FIELD MOUSE'S DINNER PARTY

By Theodore Roosevelt—Aged Fourteen

"My Dear," said Mrs. M. to Mr. M. one day as they were sitting on an elegant acorn sofa, just after breakfast, "My Dear, I think that we really must give a dinner party." "A What, my love?" exclaimed Mr. M. in a surprised tone. "A Dinner Party"; returned Mrs. M. firmly, "you have no objections I suppose?"

"Of course not, of course not," said Mr. M. hastily, for there was an ominous gleam in his wife's eye. "But—but why have it yet for a while, my love?" "Why indeed! A pretty question! After that odious Mrs. Frog's great tea party the other evening! But that is just it, you never have any proper regard for your station in life, and on me involves all the duty of keeping up appearances, and

The Dresden Literary American Club—Motto, "W. A. N. A." ("We Are No Asses").

From left to right: Theodore Roosevelt, aged 14¼ years; Elliott Roosevelt, aged 13½ years; Maud Elliott, aged 12¼ years; Corinne Roosevelt, aged 11¾ years; John Elliott, aged 14½ years. July 1, 1873.

after all *this* is the gratitude I get for it!" And Mrs. M. covered her eyes and fell into hysterics of 50 flea power. Of course, Mr. M. had to promise to have it whenever she liked.

"Then the day after tomorrow would not be too early, I suppose?" "My Dear," remonstrated the unfortunate Mr. M., but Mrs. M. did not heed him and continued: "You could get the cheese and bread from Squeak, Nibble & Co. with great ease, and the firm of Brown House and Wood Rats, with whom you have business relations, you told me, could get the other necessaries."

"But in such a short time," commenced Mr. M. but was sharply cut off by the lady; "Just like you, Mr. M.! Always raising objections! and when I am doing all I can to help you!" Symptoms of hysterics and Mr. M. entirely convinced, the lady continues: "Well, then we will have it the day after tomorrow. By the way, I hear that Mr. Chipmunck has got in a new supply of nuts, and you might as well go over after breakfast and get them, before they are bought by someone else."

"I have a business engagement with Sir Butterfly in an hour," began Mr. M. but stopped, meekly got his hat and went off at a glance from Mrs. M.'s eye.

When he was gone, the lady called down her eldest daughter, the charming Miss M. and commenced to arrange for the party.

"We will use the birch bark plates,"—commenced Mrs. M.

"And the chestnut 'tea set,'" put in her daughter.

"With the maple leaf vases, of course," continued Mrs. M.

"And the eel bone spoons and forks," added Miss M.

"And the dog tooth knives," said the lady.

"And the slate table cloth," replied her daughter.

"Where shall we have the ball anyhow," said Mrs. M.

"Why, Mr. Blind Mole has let his large subterranean apartments and that would be the best place," said Miss M.

"Sir Lizard's place, 'Shady Nook,' which we bought the other day, is far better *I* think," said Mrs. M. "But *I* don't," returned her daughter. "Miss M. be still," said her mother sternly, and Miss M. *was* still. So it was settled that the ball was to be held at 'Shady Nook.'

"As for the invitations, Tommy Cricket will carry them around," said Mrs. M. "But who shall we have?" asked her daughter. After some discussion, the guests were determined on. Among them were all the Family of Mice and Rats, Sir Lizard, Mr. Chipmunck, Sir Shrew, Mrs. Shrew, Mrs. Bullfrog, Miss Katydid, Sir Grasshopper,

Lord Beetle, Mr. Ant, Sir Butterfly, Miss Dragonfly, Mr. Bee, Mr. Wasp, Mr. Hornet, Madame Maybug, Miss Lady Bird, and a number of others. Messrs. Gloworm and Firefly agreed to provide lamps as the party was to be had at night. Mr. M., by a great deal of exertion, got the provisions together in time, and Miss M. did the same with the furniture, while Mrs. M. superintended generally, and was a great bother.

Water Bug & Co. conveyed everything to Shady Nook, and so at the appointed time everything was ready, and the whole family, in their best ball dresses, waited for the visitors.

. . . .

The fisrt visitor to arrive was Lady Maybug. "Stupid old thing; always first," muttered Mrs. M., and then aloud, "How charming it is to see you so prompt, Mrs. Maybug; I can always rely on *your* being here in time."

"Yes Ma'am, oh law! but it is so hot—oh law! and the carriage, oh law! almost broke down; oh law! I did really think I never should get here—oh law!" and Mrs. Maybug threw herself on the sofa; but the sofa unfortunately had one weak leg, and as Mrs. Maybug was no light weight, over she went. While Mrs. M. (inwardly swearing if ever a mouse swore) hastened to her assistance, and in the midst of the confusion caused by this accident, Tommy Cricket (who had been hired for waiter and dressed in red trousers accordingly) threw open the door and announced in a shrill pipe, "Nibble Squeak & Co., Mum," then hastily correcting himself, as he received a dagger like glance from Mrs. M., "Mr. Nibble and Mr. Squeak, Ma'am," and precipitately retreated through the door. Meanwhile the unfortunate Messrs. Nibble and Squeak, who while trying to look easy in their new clothes, had luckily not heard the introduction, were doing their best to bow gracefully to Miss Maybug and Miss Mouse, the respective mamas of these young ladies having pushed them rapidly forward as each of the ladies was trying to get up a match between the rich Mr. Squeak and her daughter, although Miss M. preferred Mr. Woodmouse and Miss Maybug, Mr. Hornet. In the next few minutes the company came pouring in (among them Mr. Woodmouse, accompanying Miss Katydid, at which sight Miss M. turned green with envy), and after a very short period the party was called in to dinner, for the cook had boiled the hickory nuts too long and they had to be sent up immediately or they would be spoiled. Mrs. M. displayed great generalship in the arrangement of the people, Mr. Squeak taking in Miss M., Mr. Hornet, Miss Maybug, and Mr. Woodmouse, Miss

Katydid. But now Mr. M. had invited one person too many for the plates, and so Mr. M. had to do without one. At first this was not noticed, as each person was seeing who could get the most to eat, with the exception of those who were love-making, but after a while, Sir Lizard, (a great swell and a very high liver) turned round and remarked, "Ee-aw, I say, Mr. M., why don't you take something more to eat?" "Mr. M. is not at all hungry tonight, are you my dear?" put in Mrs. M. smiling at Sir Lizard, and frowning at Mr. M. "Not at all, not at all," replied the latter hastily. Sir Lizard seemed disposed to continue the subject, but Mr. Moth, (a very scientific gentleman) made a diversion by saying, "Have you seen my work on 'Various Antenae'? In it I demonstrated clearly the superiority of feathered to knobbed Antenae and"—"Excuse me, Sir," interrupted Sir Butterfly, "but you surely don't mean to say—"

"Excuse *me*, if you please," replied Mr. Moth sharply, "but I *do* mean it, and if you read my work, you will perceive that the rays of feather-like particles on the trunk of the Antenae deriving from the center in straight or curved lines generally"—at this moment Mr. Moth luckily choked himself and seizing the lucky instant, Mrs. M. rang for the desert.

There was a sort of struggling noise in the pantry, but that was the only answer. A second ring, no answer. A third ring; and Mrs. M. rose in majestic wrath, and in dashed the unlucky Tommy Cricket with the cheese, but alas, while half way in the room, the beautiful new red trousers came down, and Tommy and cheese rolled straight into Miss Dragon Fly who fainted without any unnecessary delay, while the noise of Tommy's howls made the room ring. There was great confusion immediately, and while Tommy was being kicked out of the room, and while Lord Beetle was emptying a bottle of rare rosap over Miss Dragon Fly, in mistake for water, Mrs. M. gave a glance at Mr. M., which made him quake in his shoes, and said in a low voice, "Provoking thing! *now* you see the good of no suspenders" —"But my dear, you told me not to"—began Mr. M., but was interrupted by Mrs. M. "Don't speak to me, you—" but here Miss Katydid's little sister struck in on a sharp squeak. "Katy kissed Mr. Woodmouse!" "Katy didn't," returned her brother. "Katy did," "Katy didn't," "Katy did," "Katy didn't." All eyes were now turned on the crimsoning Miss Katydid, but she was unexpectedly saved by the lamps suddenly commencing to burn blue!

"There, Mr. M.! Now you see what you have done!" said the lady of the house, sternly.

"My dear, I told you they could not get enough oil if you had the party so early. It was your own fault," said Mr. M. worked up to desperation.

Mrs. M. gave him a glance that would have annihilated three millstones of moderate size, from its sharpness, and would have followed the example of Miss Dragon Fly, but was anticipated by Madame Maybug, who, as three of the lamps above her went out, fell into blue convulsions on the sofa. As the whole room was now subsiding into darkness, the company broke up and went off with some abruptness and confusion, and when they were gone, Mrs. M. turned (by the light of one bad lamp) an eagle eye on Mr. M. and said—, but we will now draw a curtain over the harrowing scene that ensued and say,

"Good Bye."

"Teedie" not only indulged in the free play of fancy such as the above, but wrote with extraordinary system and regularity for a boy of fourteen to his mother and father, and perhaps these letters, written in the far-away Dresden atmosphere, show more conclusively than almost any others the character, the awakening mind, the forceful mentality of the young and delicate boy. On May 29, in a letter to his mother, a very parental letter about his homesick little sister who had not yet been taken from the elderly family in which she was so unhappy, he drops into a lighter vein and says: "I have overheard a good deal of Minckwitz conversation which they did not think I understood; Father was considered 'very pretty' (*sehr hübsch*) and his German 'exceedingly beautiful,' neither of which statements I quite agree with." And a week or two later, writing to his father, he describes, after referring casually to a bad attack of asthma, an afternoon of tag and climbing trees, supper out in the open air, and long walks through the green fields dotted with the blue cornflowers and brilliant red poppies. True to his individual tastes, he says: "When I am not studying my lessons or out walking I spend all my time in translating natural history, wrestling with Richard, a young cousin of the Minckwitz' whom I can throw as often as he throws me, and I also sometimes cook, although my efforts in the culinary art are really confined to grinding coffee, beating eggs or making hash, and such light labors." Later he writes again: "The boxing gloves are a source of great amusement; you ought to have seen us after our 'rounds' yesterday." The foregoing "rounds" were described even more graphically by "Ellie" in a letter to our uncle, Mr. Gracie, as follows: "Father, you know, sent us a pair of boxing gloves apiece and Teedie, Johnnie, and I have had jolly fun with them. Last night in a round of one minute and a half with Teedie, he got a bloody nose and I got a bloody mouth, and in a round with Johnnie, I got a bloody mouth again and he a pair of purple eyes. Then Johnnie gave Teedie another bloody nose. [The boys by this time seemed to have multiplied their features indefinitely with more purple eyes!] We do enjoy them so! Boxing is one of Teedie's and my favorite amusements; it is such a novelty to be made to see stars when it is not night." No wonder that later "Ellie" contributed what I called in one of my later letters a "tragical" article called "Bloody Hand" for the D. L. A. C., perhaps engendered by the memory of all those bloody mouths and noses!

"Teedie" himself, in writing to his Aunt Annie, describes himself as a "bully boy with a black eye," and in the same letter, which seems to be in answer to one in which this devoted aunt had described an unusual specimen to interest him, he says:

"Dear darling little Nancy: I have received your letter concerning the wonderful animal and although the fact of your having described it as having horns and being carnivorous has occasioned me grave doubts as to your veracity, yet I think in course of time a meeting may be called by the Roosevelt Museum and the matter taken into consideration, although this will not happen until after we have reached America. The Minckwitz family are all splendid but very superstitious. My scientific pursuits cause the family a good deal of consternation.

"My arsenic was confiscated and my mice thrown (with the tongs) out of the window. In cases like this I would approach a refractory female, mouse in hand, corner her, and bang the mouse very near her face until she was thoroughly convinced of the wickedness of her actions. Here is a view of such a scene.

I am getting along very well with German and studying really hard. Your loving T. R., Secretary and Librarian of Roosevelt Museum. (Shall I soon hail you as a brother, I mean sister member of the Museum?)"

Evidently the carnivorous animal with horns was a stepping-stone to membership in the exclusive Roosevelt Museum!

The Dresden memories include many happy excursions, happy in spite of the fact that they were sometimes taken because of poor "Teedie's" severe attacks of asthma. On June 29th he writes his father: "I have a conglomerate of good news and bad news to report to you; the former far outweighs the latter, however. I am at present suffering from a slight attack of asthma. However, it is only a small attack and except for the fact that I cannot speak without blowing like an abridged hippopotamus, it does not inconvenience me very much. We are now studying hard and everything is systematized. Excuse my writing, the asthma has made my hand tremble awfully." The asthma of which he makes so light became unbearable, and the next letter, on June 30 from the Bastei in Saxon Switzerland, says: "You will doubtless be surprised at the heading of this letter, but as the asthma did not get any better, I concluded to come out here. Elliott and Corinne and Fräulein Anna and Fräulein Emma came with me for the excursion. We started in the train and then got out at a place some distance below these rocks where we children took horses and came up here, the two ladies following on foot. The scenery on the way and all about here was exceedingly bold and beautiful. All the mountains, if they deserve the name of mountains, have scarcely any gradual decline. They descend abruptly and precipitously to the plain. In fact, the sides of the mountains in most parts are bare while the tops are covered with pine forests with here and there jagged conical peaks rising from the foliage. There are no long ranges, simply a number of sharp high hills rising from a green fertile plain through which the river Elbe wanders. You can judge from this that the scenery is really magnificent. I have been walking in the forests collecting butterflies. I could not but be struck with the difference between the animal life of these forests and the palm groves of Egypt, (auld lang syne now). Although this is in one of the wildest parts of Saxony and South Germany, yet I do not think the proportion is as much as one here for twenty there or around Jericho, and the difference in proportion of species is even greater,—still the woods are by no means totally devoid of inhabitants. Most of these I had become acquainted with in Syria, and a few in Egypt. The only birds I had not seen before were a jay and a bullfinch."

The above letter shows how true the boy was to his marked tastes and his close observation of nature and natural history!

After his return from the Bastei my brother's asthma was somewhat less troublesome, and, to show the vital quality which could never be downed, I quote a letter from "Ellie" to his aunt: "Suddenly an idea has got hold of Teedie that we did not know enough German for the time that we have been here, so he has asked Miss Anna to give him larger lessons and of course I could not be left behind so we are working harder than ever in our lives." How unusual the evidence of leadership is in this young boy of not yet fifteen, who already inspires his pleasure-loving little brother to work "harder than ever before in our lives." Many memories crowd back upon me as I think of those days in the kind German family. The two sons, Herr Oswald and Herr Ulrich, would occasionally return from Leipsig where they were students, and always brought with them an aroma of duels and thrilling excitement. Ulrich, in college, went by the nickname of "Der Rothe Herzog," The Red Duke, the appellation being applied to him on account of his scarlet hair, his equally rubicund face, and a red gash down the left side of his face from the sword of an antagonist. Oswald had a very extraordinary expression due to the fact that the tip end of his nose had been nearly severed from his face in one of these same, apparently, every-day affairs, and the physician who had restored the injured feature to its proper environment had made the mistake of sewing it a little on the bias, which gave this kind and gentle young man a very sinister expression. In spite of their practice in the art of duelling and a general ferocity of appearance, they were sentimental to the last extent, and many a time when I have been asked by Herr Oswald and Herr Ulrich to read aloud to them from the dear old books "Gold Elsie" or "Old Mam'selle's Secret," they would fall upon the sofa beside me and dissolve in tears over any melancholy or romantic situation. Their sensibilities and sentimentalities were perfectly incomprehensible to the somewhat matter-of-fact and distinctly courageous trio of young Americans, and while we could not understand the spirit which made them willing, quite casually, to cut off each other's noses, we could even less understand their lachrymose response to sentimental tales and their genuine terror should a thunder-storm occur. "Ellie" describes in another letter how all the family, in the middle of the night, because of a sudden thunder-storm, crawled in between their mattresses and woke the irrelevant and uninterested small Americans from their slumbers to incite them to the same attitude of mind and body. His description of "Teedie" under these circumstances is very amusing, for he says: "Teedie woke up only for one minute, turned over and said, 'Oh—it's raining and my hedgehog will be all spoiled.'" He was speaking of a hedgehog that he had skinned the day before and hung out of his window, but even his hedgehog did not keep him awake and, much to the surprise of the frightened Minckwitz family, he fell back into a heavy sleep.

In spite of the sentimentalities, in spite of the racial differences of attitude about many things, the American children owe much to the literary atmosphere that surrounded the family life of their kind German friends. In those days in Dresden the most beautiful representations of Shakespeare were given in German, and, as the hour for the theatre to begin was six o'clock in the evening, and the plays were finished by nine o'clock, many were the evenings when we enjoyed "Midsummer Night's Dream," "Twelfth Night," "The Taming of the Shrew," and many more of Shakespeare's wonderful fanciful creations, given as they were with unusual sympathy and ability by the actors of the German Theatre.

Perhaps because of our literary studies and our ever-growing interest in our own efforts in the famous Dresden Literary American Club, we decided that the volume which became so precious to us should, after all, have no commercial value, and in July I write to my aunt the news which I evidently feel will be a serious blow to her—that we have decided that we cannot sell the poems and stories gathered into that immortal volume!

About the middle of the summer there was an epidemic of smallpox in Dresden and my mother hurriedly took us to the Engadine, and there, at Samaden, we lived somewhat the life of our beloved Madison and Hudson River days. Our cousin John Elliott accompanied us, and the three boys and their ardent little follower, myself, spent endless happy hours in climbing

FACSIMILE OF THEODORE ROOSEVELT'S LETTER

the surrounding mountains, only occasionally recalled by the lenient "Fräulein Anna" to what were already almost forgotten Teutonic studies. Later we returned to Dresden, and in spite of the longing in our patriotic young hearts to be once more in the land of the Stars and Stripes, I remember that we all parted with keen regret from the kind family who had made their little American visitors so much at home.

A couple of letters from Theodore, dated September 21 and

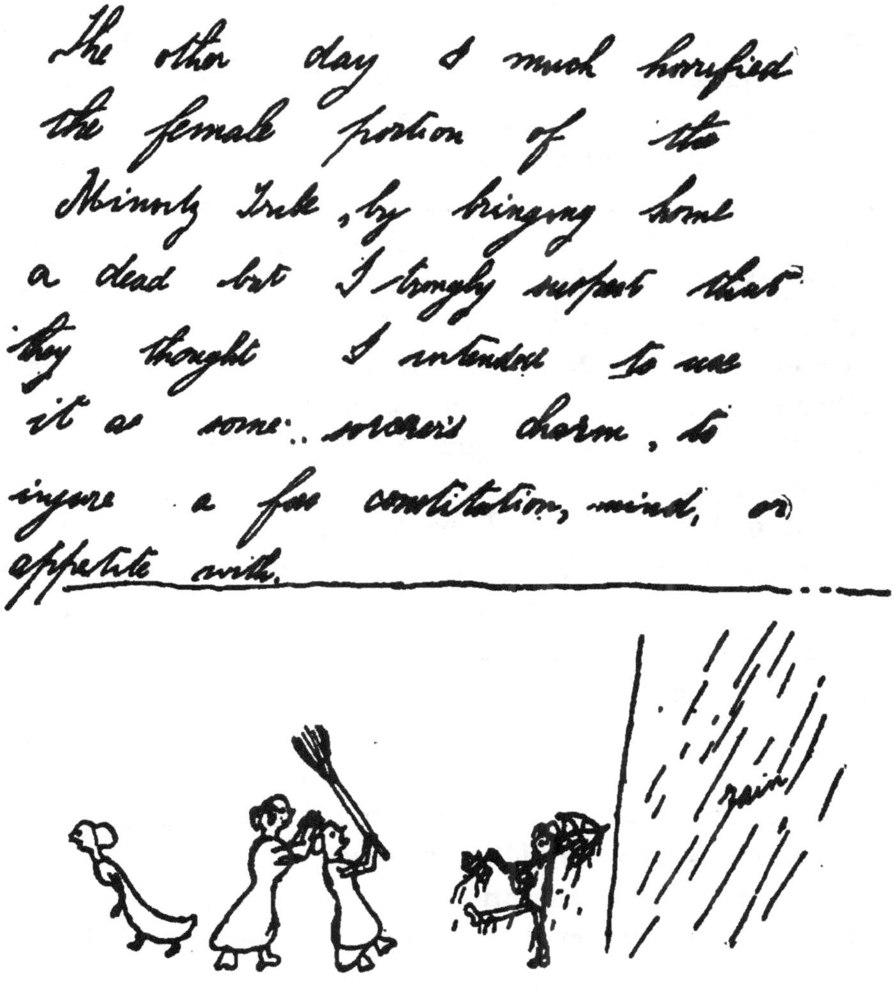
The other day I much horrified the female portion of the Minkwitz tribe, by bringing home a dead bat I strongly suspect that they thought I intended to use it as some witch's charm, to injure a fine constitution, mind, or appetite with.

OF SEPTEMBER 21, 1878, TO HIS OLDER SISTER]

October 5, bring to a close the experiences in Dresden, and show in a special way the boy's humor and the original inclination to the quaint drawings which have become familiar to the American people through the book, lately published, called "Theodore Roosevelt's Letters to His Children." On September 21,

1873, he writes to his older sister: "My dear darling Bamie,—I wrote a letter on the receipt of yours, but Corinne lost it and so I write this. Health; good. Lessons; good. Play hours; bad. Appetite; good. Accounts; good. Clothes; greasy. Shoes; holey. Hair; more 'a-la-Mop' than ever. Nails; dirty, in consequence of having an ink bottle upset over them. Library; beautiful. Museum; so so. Club; splendid. Our journey home from Samaden was beautiful, except for the fact that we lost our keys but even this incident was not without its pleasing side. I reasoned philosophically on the subject; I said: 'Well, everything is for the best. For example, if I cannot use my tooth brush tonight, at least, I cannot forget it tomorrow morning. Ditto with comb and night shirt.' In these efforts of high art, I have taken particular care to imitate truthfully the Chignons, bustles, grease-spots, bristles, and especially my own mop of hair. The other day I much horrified the female portion of the Minckwitz Tribe by bringing home a dead bat. I strongly suspect that they thought I intended to use it as some sorcerer's charm to injure a foe's constitution, mind and appetite. As I have no more news to write, I will close with some illustrations on the Darwinian theory. Your brother—Teedie."

The last letter, on October 5, was to his mother, and reads in part as follows: "Corinne has been sick but is now well, at least, she does not have the same striking resemblance to a half-starved raccoon as she did in the severe stages of the disease." After a humorous description of a German conversation between several members of his aunt's family, he proceeds to "further illustrations of the Darwinian theory" and closes his letter by signing himself "Your affectionate son, Cranibus Giraffinus."

Shortly before leaving Dresden I had my twelfth birthday and the Minckwitz clan made every effort to make it a gay festival, but perhaps the gift which I loved best was a letter received that very morning from my beloved father; and in closing this brief account of those days spent in Germany, because of his wise decision to broaden our young horizons by new

FACSIMILE OF "SOME ILLUSTRATIONS ON THE DARWINIAN THEORY," CONTAINED IN THE LETTER OF SEPTEMBER 21, 1873

FACSIMILE, ON THIS AND OPPOSITE PAGE, OF "FURTHER ILLUSTRATIONS OF THE DARWINIAN THEORY," IN HIS LETTER OF OCTOBER 5

Your aff son
Caribu Giraffine.

thoughts and new studies, I wish once more, as I have done several times in these pages, to quote from his words to the little girl in whom he was trying to instil his own beautiful attitude toward life: "Remember that almost every one will be kind to you and will love you if you are only willing to receive their love and are unselfish yourself. Unselfishness, you know, is the virtue that I put above all others, and while it increases so much the enjoyment of those about you, it adds infinitely more to your own pleasure. Your future, in fact, depends very much upon the cultivation of unselfishness, and I know that my darling little girl wishes to practise this quality, but I do wish to impress upon you its importance. As each year passes by, we ought to look back to see what we have accomplished, and also look forward to the future to make up for any deficiencies showing thus a determination to do better, not wasting time in vain regrets." In many ways these words of my father, written when we were so young and so malleable, and impressed upon us by his ever-encouraging example, became one of the great factors in making my brother into the type of man who will always be remembered for that unselfishness instilled into him by his father, and for the determination to do better each day of his life without vain regret for what was already beyond recall.

Oyster Bay—The Happy Land of Woods and Waters

After our return to America the winter of 1874 was passed at our new home at 6 West 57th Street. My brother was still considered too delicate to send to a boarding-school, and various tutors were engaged for his education, in which my brother Elliott and I shared. Friendships of various kinds were begun and augmented, especially the friendship with the little girl Edith Carow, our babyhood friend, and another little girl, Frances Theodora Smith, now Mrs. James Russell Parsons, to whose friendship and comprehension my brother always turned with affectionate appreciation. Inspired by the Dresden Literary American Club, the female members of our little coterie formed a circle known by the name of P. O. R. E., to which the "boys" were admitted on rare occasions. The P. O. R. E. had also literary ambitions, and they proved a fit sequel to the eruditionary D. L. A. C., which originated in the German family! Mr. J. Coleman Drayton, Mr. Charles B. Alexander, and my father were the only honorary members of the P. O. R. E.

The summer of 1874 proved to be the forerunner of the happiest summers of our lives, as my father decided to join the colony which had been started by his family at Oyster Bay, Long Island, and we rented a country place which, much to the amusement of our friends, we named "Tranquillity." Anything less tranquil than that happy home at Oyster Bay could hardly be imagined. Endless young cousins and friends of both sexes and of every kind of varied interest always filled the simple rooms and shared the delightful and unconventional life which we led in that enchanted spot. Again I cannot say too much of the way in which our parents allowed us liberty without license. During those years—when Theodore was fifteen, sixteen, and seventeen—every special delight seems connected with Oyster Bay. We took long rides on horseback through the lanes then so seemingly remote, so far from the thought of the broad highways which now are traversed by thousands of motors, but were then the scenes of picnics and every imaginable spree. Our parents encouraged all mental and physical activity and having, as I say, a large circle of young cousins settled around us, we were never at a loss for companionship. One of our greatest delights was to take the small rowboats with which we were provided and row away for long days of happy leisure to what then seemed a somewhat distant spot on the other side of the bay, called Yellow Banks, where we would have our picnic lunch and climb Cooper's Bluff, and read aloud or indulge in poetry contests and games which afforded us infinite amusement. One of our favorite games was called Crambo. We each wrote a question and each wrote a word, then all the words were put into one hat and all the questions into another, and after each child had drawn a question and a word, he or she was obliged to answer the question and bring in the word in a verse. Amongst my papers I find some of the old poetic efforts of those happy summer days. One is dated Plum Point, Oyster Bay, 1875. I remember the day as if it were yesterday; Theodore, who loved to row in the hottest sun, over the roughest water, in the smallest boat, had chosen his friend Edith as a companion; my cousin West Roosevelt, the "Jimmie" of earlier childhood, whose love of science and natural history was one of the joys that Theodore found in his companionship, took as his companion my friend Fannie Smith, now Mrs. Parsons, and my brother Elliott and I made up the happy six. Lying on the soft sand of the Point after a jolly luncheon, we played our favorite game, and Theodore drew the question: "Why does West enjoy such a dirty picnic?" The word which he drew was "golosh," and written on the other side of the paper in his own boyish handwriting is his attempt to assimilate the query and the word!

"Because it is his nature to,
He finds *his* idyl in the dirt,
And if you do not sympathize
But find *yours* in some saucy flirt,
Why that is your affair you know,
It's like the choosing a (?) golosh,
You doat upon a pretty face,
He takes to carrots and hogwash."

Perhaps this sample of early verse may have led him later into *other* paths than poetry!

We did not always indulge in anything as light and humorous as the above example of poetic fervor. I have in my possession all kinds of competitive essays—on William Wordsworth, Washington Irving, and Plutarch's "Lives," written by various members of the happy group of young people at Oyster Bay; but when not indulging in these literary efforts "Teedie" was always studying his beloved natural history. At that time in his life he became more and more determined to take up this study as an actual career. My father had many serious talks with

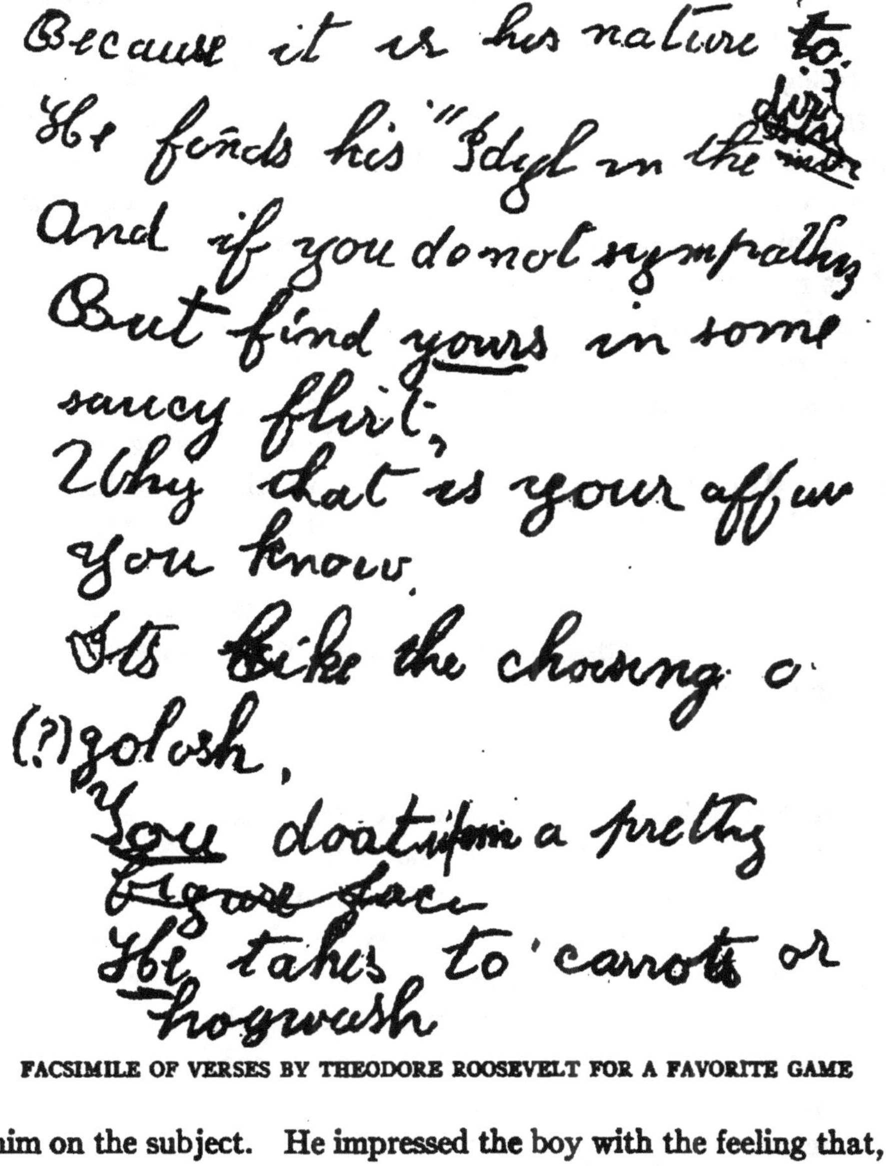

Because it is his nature to.
He finds his "Idyl in the dirt
And if you do not sympathy
But find yours in some saucy flirt,
Why that is your affair you know.
Its like the chosing o
(?) golosh,
You doat upon a pretty
~~figure~~ face
He takes to carrots or hogwash

FACSIMILE OF VERSES BY THEODORE ROOSEVELT FOR A FAVORITE GAME

him on the subject. He impressed the boy with the feeling that, if he should thus decide upon a career which of necessity could not be lucrative, it would mean the sacrifice of many of the pleasures of which our parents' environment had enabled us to partake. My father, however, also told the earnest young naturalist that he would provide a small income for him, enabling him to live simply, should he decide to give himself up to scientific research work as the object of his life. During all those summers at Oyster Bay and the winters in New York City, before going to college, "Teedie" worked along the line of his chief interest with a very definite determination to devote himself permanently to that type of study. Our parents realized fully the unusual quality of their son, they recognized the strength and power of his character, the focussed and reasoning superiority of his mentality, but I do not think they fully realized the extraordinary quality of leadership which, hitherto somewhat hampered by his ill health, was later to prove so great a factor, not only in the circle of his immediate family and friends but in the broader field of the whole country. He was growing stronger day by day; already he had learned from those fine lumbermen, "Will Dow" and "Bill Sewall," who were his guides on long hunting trips in the Maine woods, how to endure hardship and how to use his rifle as an adept and his paddle as an expert.

His body, answering to the insistence of his character, was growing stronger day by day, and was soon to be an instrument of iron to use in the future years.

Mr. Arthur Cutler was engaged by my parents to be at Oyster Bay during these summers to superintend the studies of the two boys, and with his able assistance my brother was well prepared for Harvard College, which he entered in September, 1876. It seems almost incredible that the puny, delicate child, so suffering even three years before, could have started his college life the peer, from a physical standpoint, of any of his classmates. A light-weight boxer, a swift runner, and in every way fitted to take his place, physically as well as mentally, in the arena of college life, he entered Harvard College.

In looking back over our early childhood there stands out clearly before me, as the most important asset of the atmosphere of our home, the joy of life, combined with an earnest effort for

Theodore Roosevelt, Oyster Bay,
September 21, 1875.

Theodore Roosevelt, December, 1876,
aged eighteen.

spiritual and intellectual benefit. As I write I can hear my father's voice calling us to early "Morning Prayers" which it was his invariable custom to read just before breakfast. Even this religious service was entered into with the same joyous zest which my father had the power of putting into every act of his life, and he had imbued us with the feeling that it was a privilege rather than a duty to be present, and that also the place of honor while we listened to the reading of the Bible was the seat on the sofa between him and the end of the sofa. When we were little children in the nursery, as he called to us to come to prayers, there would be a universal shout of "I speak for you and the cubby-hole too," the "cubby-hole" being this much-desired seat; and as my brother grew to man's estate these happy and yet serious memories were so much a part of him that when the boy of eighteen left Oyster Bay that September afternoon in 1876, to take up the new life which the entrance into college always means for a young man, he took with him as the heritage of his boyhood not only keen joy in the panorama of life which now unrolled before him but the sense of duty to be performed, of opportunity to be seized, of high resolve to be squared with practical and effective action, all of which had been part of the teaching of his father, the first Theodore Roosevelt.

IV

COLLEGE CHUMS AND NEW-FOUND LEADERSHIP

DURING the winter and summer of 1876, preceding that September when Theodore Roosevelt left his home for Harvard College, he had entered more fully into the social life of the boys and girls of his immediate acquaintance. As a very young boy, there was something of the recluse about him, although in his actual family (and that family included a number of cousins) he was always the ringleader. His delicate health and his almost abnormal literary and scientific tastes had isolated him somewhat from the hurly-burly of ordinary school life, and even ordinary vacation life; but during the winter of 1876 he had enjoyed to the full a dancing-class which my mother had organized the winter before, and that dancing-class sowed the seeds of many friendships. The Livingston, Clarkson, Potter, and Rutherfurd boys, and amongst the girls my friends Edith Carow, Grace Potter, Fannie Smith, Annie Murray, and myself, formed the nucleus in this dancing-class, and the informal "Germans" (as they were called in those days) and all the merriment connected with happy skating-parties and spring picnics in Central Park cemented relationships which lasted faithfully through later days. My brother Elliott, more naturally a *social* leader, influenced the young naturalist to greater interest in his *humankind*, and when the spring merged into happy summer at Oyster Bay, Theodore was already showing a keener pleasure in intercourse with young people of his own age.

In a letter to "Edith" early in the summer, I write of an expedition which he took across the bay to visit another girl friend. He started at five o'clock in the morning and reached the other shore at eight o'clock. Thinking it too early to pay a call, he lay down on a large rock and went to sleep, waking up to find his boat had drifted far away. When he put on his spectacles he could see the boat at a distance, but, of course, did not wish to swim with his clothes on, and decided to remove them temporarily. Having secured the boat, he forgot that it might be wise to put on his clothes before sleeping again under the dock. To his perfect horror, waking suddenly about an hcur later, the boat, clothes, and all had vanished. At the same moment he heard the footsteps of his fair inamorata on the wooden planks of the dock above his head. She had walked down with a friend to greet the admirer whom she expected at about nine o'clock. His description of his feelings as he lay shivering, though not from cold, while above him they calmly discussed his probable arrival and the fact that they thought they would wait there to greet him, can probably be imagined. The girls, after a period of long waiting, walked away into the woods, and the self-conscious young man proceeded to swim down a hidden creek where he thought the tide had taken his recalcitrant boat, and where, sure enough, he found it. The sequel to this little story throws much light on masculine human nature, for he conceived an aversion to the lady who so unconsciously had put him in this foolish position, and rowed defiantly back to Oyster Bay without paying the proposed visit!

During that summer my father, who always gave his children such delightful surprises, drilled us himself in a little play called "To Oblige Benson," in which Theodore took the part of an irascible and absent-minded farmer, and our beloved cousin John Elliott the part of an impassioned lover, while my friend Fannie Smith and I were the heroines of the adventures. My father's efforts to make Theodore into a farmer and John into a lover were commendable though not eminently successful, but all that he did for us in those ways gave to his children a certain ease in writing and speaking which were to be of great value in later years. Fannie Smith, to show how Theodore still dominated the little circle from the standpoint of intellect, writes that same July: "I have no power to write sensibly to-day. If I were writing to Theodore I would have to say something of this kind, 'I have enjoyed Plutarch's last essay on the philosophy of Diogenes excessively.'" In his early college days, however, he seems temporarily to put the "philosophy of Diogenes" aside, and to become a very normal, simple, pleasure-loving youth, who, however, always retained his earnest moral purpose and his realization that education was a tool for future experience, and, therefore, not to be neglected.

He writes on November 26, 1876: "I now belong to another whist club, composed of Harry Minot, Dick Saltonstall and a few others. They are very quiet fellows but also very pleasant. Harry Minot was speaking to me the other day about our making a collecting trip in the White Mountains together next summer. I think it would be good fun." The result of that collecting trip will be shown a little later in this chapter. On December 14 he writes again: "Darling Pussie [his pet name for me]: I ought to have written you long ago but I am now having examinations all the time, and am so occupied in studying for them that I have very little time for myself, and you know how long it takes me to write a letter. My only excitement lately has been the dancing class which is very pleasant. I may as well describe a few of my chief friends." He then gives an account of his specially intimate companions, and speaks as follows of one whose name has become prominent in the annals of his country's history as able financier, secretary of state, and colonel in the American Expeditionary Force—Robert Bacon: "Bob Bacon is the handsomest man in the class and is as pleasant as he is handsome. He is only sixteen, but is very large." He continues to say that he would love to bring home a few of his friends at Christmas time, and concludes: "I should like a party very much if it is *perfectly* convenient." The party proved a delightful Christmas experience, and the New York girls and Boston boys fraternized to their hearts' content. On his return to Cambridge after these Christmas holidays he writes one of his amusing, characteristic little notes, interspersed with quaint drawings. "Darling Pussie: I delivered your two notes safely and had a very pleasant journey on in the cars. To drown my grief at parting from you all, I took refuge, not in the flowing bowl, but in the *Atlantic Monthly* and *Harper's Magazine*—not to mention squab sandwiches. A journey in the cars always renders me sufficiently degraded to enjoy even the love stories in the latter magazine. I think that if I was forced to travel across the continent, towards the end of my journey, I should read dime novels with avidity. Good-bye darling. Your loving Tedo."

The signature was followed by accurate representations of *Harper's Magazine*, *Atlantic Monthly*, and the squab sandwich, which he labels "my three consolations"!

A letter dated February 5, 1877, shows the Boston of those days in a very pleasant light. He begins: "Little Pussie: I have had a very pleasant time this week as, in fact, I have every week. It was cram week for 'Conic Sections' but, by using most of my days for study, I had two evenings, besides Saturday, free. On Wednesday evening, Harry Jackson gave a large sleighing party; this was great fun for there were forty girls and fellows and two matrons in two huge sleighs. We sang songs for a great part of the time for we soon left Boston and were dragged by our eight horses rapidly through a great many of the pretty little towns which form the suburbs of Boston. One of the girls looked quite like Edith only not nearly as pretty as her ladyship. We came home from our sleigh ride about nine and then danced until after twelve. I led the German with Harry Jackson's cousin, Miss Andrews. After the party, Bob Bacon, Arthur Hooper, myself and some others, came out in a small sleigh to Cambridge, making night hideous with our songs. On Saturday I went with Minot Weld to an Assembly (a juvenile one I mean) at Brookline. This was a very swell affair, there being about sixty couples in the room. I enjoyed myself very much indeed. . . . I came home today in time for my Sunday-school class; I am beginning to get very much interested in my scholars, especially in one who is a very orderly and bright little fellow —two qualities which I have not usually found combined. Thank Father for his dear letter. Your loving brother, Ted."

The above letter shows how normal a life the young man was leading, how simply and naturally he was responding to the friendly hospitality of his new Boston friends. Boston had welcomed him originally for the sake of his older sister, who, during two charming summer visits to Bar Harbor, Maine, had made many New England friends. The Sunday-school which he mentions, and to which he gave himself very faithfully, proved a big test of character, for it was a great temptation to go with the other fellows on Saturday afternoons to Chestnut Hill or Brookline or Milton, where open house was kept by the Lees, Saltonstalls, Whitneys, and other friends, and it was very hard either to refuse their invitation from the beginning or to leave the merry parties early Sunday morning and return to Cambridge to be at his post to teach the unruly little people of the slums of Cambridge. So deeply, however, had the first Theodore Roosevelt impressed his son with the necessity of giving himself and the attainments with which his superior advantages had endowed him to those less fortunate than he, that all through the first three years of his college life he only failed to appear at his Sunday-school class twice, and then he arranged to have his class taken by a friend. Truly, when *he* put his hand to the plough he never turned back.

On March 27 of his first year at college he writes again in his usual sweet way to his younger sister: "Little Pet Pussie: 95 per cent *will* help my average. I want to pet you again awfully! You cunning, pretty, little, foolish Puss. My easy chair would just hold myself and Pussie." Again on April 15: "Little Pussie: Having given Motherling an account of my doings up to yesterday, I have reserved the more frivolous part for little pet Pussie. Yesterday, in the afternoon, Minot Weld drove me over to his house and at six o'clock we sallied forth in festive attire to a matinée 'German' at Dorchester which broke up before eleven o'clock. This was quite a swell affair, there being about 100 couples. . . . I spent last night with the Welds and walked back over here to Forest Hill with Minot in the afternoon, collecting a dozen snakes and salamanders on the way." Still the natural historian, even although on pleasure bent; so snakes and salamanders hold their own in spite of "swell matinée Germans." From Forest Hill that same Sunday he writes a more serious letter to his father: "Darling Father: I am spending my Easter vacation with the Minots, who, with their usual kindness, asked me to do so. I did not go home for I knew I should never be able to study there. I have been working pretty steadily, having finished during the last five days, the first book of Horace, the sixth book of Homer, and the 'Apology of Socrates.' In the afternoon, some of the boys usually come out to see me and we spend that time in the open air, and on Saturday evening I went to a party, but during the rest of the time I have been working pretty faithfully. I spent today, Sunday, with the Welds and went to their church where, although it was a Unitarian Church, I heard a really remarkably good sermon about 'The Attributes of a Christian.' I have enjoyed all your letters very much and my conscience reproaches me greatly for not writing you before, but as you may imagine, I have had to study pretty hard to make up for lost time, and a letter with me is very serious work. Your loving son, T. R. Jr."

On June 3, as his class day approaches, and after a visit to Cambridge on the part of my father, who had given me and my sister and friends Edith Carow and Maud Elliott the treat of accompanying him, Theodore writes: "Sweet Pussie: I enjoyed your visit so much and so did all of my friends. I am so glad you like my room, and next year I hope to have it even prettier when you all come on again." His first class day was not specially notable, but he finished his freshman year standing high in his class and having made a number of good friends, although at that period I do not think that he was in any marked degree a leader amongst the young men of the class. He was regarded more as an all-round good sport, a fellow of high ideals from which he never swerved, and one at whom his companions, who, except Harry Minot, had not very strong literary affiliations, were always more or less surprised because of the way in which their otherwise perfectly normal comrade sank into complete oblivion when the magic pages of a book were unrolled before him.

That summer, shortly after class day, he and Harry Minot took their expedition to the Adirondacks with the following results, namely: a catalogue written in the mountains of "The Summer Birds of the Adirondacks in Franklin County, N. Y., by Theodore Roosevelt, Jr., and H. D. Minot." This catalogue was sent to me by Mr. John D. Sherman, Jr., of Mt. Vernon, N. Y. He tells me that it was originally published in 1877 and favorably mentioned soon after publication in the *Nuttall Bulletin*. Mr. Sherman thinks that the paper was "privately" published, and it was printed by Samuel E. Casino, of Salem, who, when a mere boy, started in the natural-history-book business. The catalogue shows such careful observation and such perseverance in the accumulation of data by the two young college boys that I think the first page worthy of reproduction as one of the early evidences of the careful study Theodore Roosevelt had given to the subject which always remained throughout his life one of the nearest to his heart.

His love of poetry in those days became a very living thing, and the summer following his first college year was one in which the young people of Oyster Bay turned with glad interest to the riches not only of nature but of literature as well. I find among my papers, painstakingly copied in red ink in my brother's handwriting, Swinburne's poem "The Forsaken Garden." He had sent it to me, copying it from memory when on a trip to the Maine woods. Later, on his return, we would row by moonlight to "Cooper's Bluff" (near which spot he was eventually

THE SUMMER BIRDS

OF THE ADIRONDACKS IN FRANKLIN COUNTY, N. Y.

By THEODORE ROOSEVELT, JR., AND H. D. MINOT

The following catalogue (written in the mountains) is based upon observations made in August, 1874, August, 1875, and June 22d to July 9th, 1877, especially about the Saint Regis Lakes, Mr. Minot having been with me, only during the last week of June. Each of us has used his initials in making a statement which the other has not verified.

THEODORE ROOSEVELT, Jr.

The general features of the Adirondacks, in those parts which we have examined, are the many lakes, the absence of *mountain*-brooks, the luxuriant forest-growth (the taller deciduous trees often reaching the height of a hundred feet, and the White Pines even that of a hundred and thirty), the sandy soil, the cool, invigorating air, and both a decided wildness and levelness of country as compared with the diversity of the White Mountain region.

The *avifauna* is not so rich as that of the latter country, because wanting in certain "Alleghanian" birds found there, and also in species belonging especially to the Eastern or North-eastern Canadian fauna. Nests, moreover, seem to be more commonly inaccessible, and rarely built beside roads or wood-paths, as they often are in the White Mountains. M.

1. **Robin.** *Turdus migratorius* (Linnæus). Moderately common. Sometimes found in the woods.

2. **Hermit Thrush.** *Turdus Pallasi* (Cabanis). Common. Sings until the middle of August (R.).

3. **Swainson's Thrush.** *Turdus Swainsoni* (Cabanis). The commonest thrush.

4. **Cat-bird.** *Mimus Carolinensis* (Linnæus). Observed beyond the mountains to the northward, near Malone.

5. **Blue Bird.** *Sialia sialis* (Linnæus). Common near Malone.

6. **Golden-crowned "Wren."** *Regulus satrapa* (Lichten.). Quite common; often heard singing in June.

7. **Chickadee.** *Parus atricapillus* (Linnæus). Rather scarce in June. Abundant in August (R.).

8. **Hudsonian Chickadee.** *Parus Hudsonicus* (Forster). Found in small flocks at Bay Pond in the early part of August (R.).

9. **Red-bellied Nuthatch.** *Sitta Canadensis* (Linnæus). Common. The White-bellied Nuthatch has not been observed here by us.

10. **Brown Creeper.** *Certhia familiaris* (Linnæus). Common.

11. **Winter Wren.** *Troglodytes hyemalis* (Vieillot). Moderately common.

FACSIMILE OF THE FIRST PAGE OF THE "CATALOGUE OF SUMMER BIRDS," MADE IN 1877 BY THEODORE ROOSEVELT, JR., AND H. D. MINOT to build his beloved home, Sagamore Hill), and there, having climbed the sandy bulwark, we would sit on the top of the ledge looking out on the shimmering waters of the Sound, and he would recite with a lilting swing in the tone of his voice which matched the rhythm of the words:

> "In a coign of the cliff between lowland and highland,
> By the sea down's edge, twixt windward and lee,
> Walled round by rocks like an inland island,
> The ghost of a garden fronts the sea.
> A girdle of brush-wood and thorn encloses
> The steep-scarred slope of the blossomless bed,
> Where the weeds that grew green from the graves of its roses—
> Now lie dead."

He always loved the rhythm of Swinburne, just as he loved later the wonderful ringing lines of Kipling, which he taught to his children and constantly repeated to himself.

In the summer of 1877 the two brothers, Elliott and Theodore, decided to row from Oyster Bay in their small boats to Whitestone, near Flushing, where my aunt Mrs. Gracie was living in an old farmhouse. Elliott was really the sailor of the family, an expert sailor, too, and loved to manage his 20-footer, with able hand, in the stormiest weather, but Theodore craved the actual effort of the arms and back, the actual sense of meeting the wave close to and not from the more sheltered angle of a sailboat; and so the two young brothers who were perfectly devoted to each other started on the more adventurous trip together. They were caught in one of the sudden storms of the Long Island Sound, and their frail boats were very nearly swamped, but the luck which later became with Theodore Roosevelt almost proverbial, was with them, and the two exhausted and bedraggled, wave-beaten boys arrived sorely in need of the care of the devoted aunt who, as much as in the days when she taught their A B C's to the children of the nursery of 20th Street, was still their guardian angel.

In September, 1877, Theodore returns as a sophomore to Cambridge and writes in October again: "Sweet Pussie: Thank you ever so much, darling, for the three, cunning, little books which I am going to call my 'Pussie Books.' They were just what I wanted. In answer to your question, I may say that it does not seem to make the slightest difference to Brooks and Hooper that they have been dropped, although Brooks is universally called 'Freshie.' My respect for the qualities of my classmates has much increased lately, by the way, as they now no longer seem to think it necessary to confine their conversation exclusively to athletic subjects. I was especially struck by this the other night, when, after a couple of hours spent in boxing and wrestling with Arthur Hooper and Ralph Ellis, it was proposed to finish the evening by reading aloud from Tennyson and we became so interested in 'In Memoriam' that it was past one o'clock when we separated." (Evidently the lover of books was beginning to be a leader in making his associates share his love of the poets.)

In November he writes again: "I sat up last night until twelve, reading 'Poems & Poets'; some of the boys came down to my room and we had a literary coffee party. They became finally interested in Edgar Poe—probably because they could not understand him." My brother always had a great admiration for Edgar Allan Poe, and would chant "The Raven" and "Ulalume" in a strange, rather weird, monotonous tone. He especially delighted in the reference to "the Dank Tarn of Auber" and the following lines:

"I knew not the month was October,
I knew not the day of the year,—"

Poe's rhythm and curious, suggestive, melancholy quality of perfection affected strongly his imagination, and he placed him high in rank amongst the poets of his time.

One can picture the young men, strong and vigorous, wrestling and boxing together in Theodore Roosevelt's room, and then putting aside their athletic contests, making their coffee with gay nonchalance, and settling down to a night of poetry, led in the paths of literature by the blue-eyed young "Berserker," as my mother used to call Theodore in those college days.

During the summer of 1877 my father accompanied my sister Anna to Bar Harbor on one of her annual excursions to that picturesque part of the Maine coast, where they visited Mr. George Minot and his sisters. He writes to my mother in his usual vein of delightful interest in people, books, and nature, and seems more vigorous than ever, for he describes wonderful walks over the mountains and speaks of having achieved a reputation as a mountain-climber. How little any of the family who adored him realized that from a strain engendered by that climbing the seed of serious trouble had been sown in that splendid mechanism, and that in a few short months the vigorous and still young man of forty-six was to lay down that useful life which had been given so ardently and unselfishly for the good of his city and the joy and benefit of his family.

At this time, however, when Theodore went back to college as a sophomore, there was no apprehension about my father's health, and the first term of the college year was passed in his usual happy activities.

Shortly after the New Year my father's condition became serious, due to intestinal trouble, and the following weeks were passed in anxious nursing, the distress of which was greatly accentuated by the frightful suffering of the patient, who, however, in spite of constant agony, bore the sudden shattering of his wonderful health with magnificent courage. My brother Theodore could not realize, as did my brother Elliott, who was at home, the serious condition of our father, for it was deemed best that he should not return from college, where difficult examinations required all his application and energy. Elliott gave unstintedly a devotion which was so tender that it was more like that of a woman, and his young strength was poured out to help his father's condition. The best physicians searched in vain for remedy for the hidden trouble, but in spite of all their efforts the first Theodore Roosevelt died, February 9, 1878, and the gay young college sophomore was recalled to a house of mourning. In spite of the sorrow, in spite of a sense of irreparable loss, there was something infinitely inspiring in the days preceding and following my father's death. When New York City knew that its benefactor lay in extreme illness, it seemed as if the whole city came to the door of his home to ask news of him. How well I remember the day before his death, when the papers had announced that there was but little hope of his recovery. The crowd of individuals who filled 57th Street in their effort to hear the physicians' bulletin concerning his condition was huge and varied. Newsboys from the West Side Lodging House, little Italian girls from his Sunday-school class, sat for hours on the stone steps of 6 West 57th Street, our second home, waiting with anxious intensity for news of the man who meant more to them than any other human being had ever meant before; and those more fortunate ones who had known him in another way drove unceasingly up in their carriages to the door and looked with sympathetic interest at the children of the slums who shared with them such a sense of bitter bereavement and loss in the premature death of one so closely connected with all sides of his beloved native city.

Meanwhile, the family of the first Theodore Roosevelt seemed hardly able to face the blank that life meant when he left them, but they also felt that the man who had preached always that "one must live for the living" would have wished "his own" to follow out his ideal of life, and so each one of us took up, as bravely as we could, our special duties and felt that our close family tie must be made stronger rather than weaker by the loss that we had sustained.

On March 3, 1878, my brother writes from Cambridge:

My own darling, sweet, little treasure of a Pussie: Oh! I have so longed for you at times during the last few days. Darling one, you can hardly know what an inestimable blessing to a fellow it is to have such a home as I have. Even now that our dear father has been taken away, it is such a great pleasure to look forward to a visit home; and indeed, he has only 'gone before,' and oh! what living and loving memories he has left behind him. I can *feel* his presence sometimes when I am sitting alone in the evening; I have not felt nearly as sad as I expected to feel, although, of course, there are every now and then very bitter moments. I am going to bring home some of his sweet letters to show you. I shall always keep them, if merely as talismans against evil. Kiss little mother for me, and my love to Aunt Susie and Uncle Hill. [My mother and I were staying in Philadelphia with my aunt Mrs. West.] Tell the latter, Uncle Hill, I am looking forward to spending a month of nude happiness with him next summer among the wilds of Oyster Bay.

YOUR LOVING TEDDY.

When my brother speaks of keeping my father's letters to him as "talismans against evil," he not only expressed the feeling of desire to keep near him always the actual letters written by my father, but far more the spirit with which these letters are permeated. Years afterward, when the college boy of 1878 was entering upon his duties as President of the United States, he told me frequently that he never took any serious step or made any vital decision for his country without thinking first what position his father would have taken on the question. The day that he moved into the White House happened to be September 22, the day of my father's birth, and dining with him that night in the White House for the first time, we all mentioned this fact and felt that it was a good omen for the future, and my brother said that every time he dated a letter that day he felt with a glow of tender memory the realization that it was his father's birthday, and that his father's blessing seemed specially to follow him on that first day when he made his home in the beautiful old white mansion which stands in the heart of

America for all that America means to her sons and daughters.

Several other equally loving letters in that March of 1878 proved how the constant thoughts of the young sophomore turned to the family at home, and also his own sense of loss in his father's death, but I think the many interests and normal surroundings brought their healing power to the boy of nineteen, and at the end of that year of his college life he had become a well-rounded character. His mind, intelligently focussed upon many intellectual subjects, had broadened in scope, and physically he was no longer the delicate, dreamy boy of earlier days. The period of his college life, although not one of as unusual interest as perhaps other periods in his life, was of inestimable value in the forming of his character. Had Theodore Roosevelt continued to be abnormally developed along the scientific and intellectual side of his nature, he would never have become the "All-American" which he was destined to be. It was necessary for him to fall into more commonplace grooves; it was necessary for him to meet the young men of his age on common ground, to get the "give-and-take" of a life very different from the more or less individual life which, owing to his ill health and intellectual aspirations, he had hitherto led, and already, by the end of the second year of college, he was beginning to take a place in the circle of his friends which showed in an embryonic way the leadership which later was to be so strongly evidenced.

On October 8, 1878, returning to Cambridge as a junior, he writes to his mother: "Darling, beloved, little motherling: I have just loved your dear, funny, pathetic, little letter, and I am now going to write you the longest letter I ever write, and if it is still rather short, you must recollect that it takes Teddy-boy a long time to write. I have enjoyed Charlie Dickey's being here extremely, and I think I have been of some service to him. We always go to prayers together; for his own sake, I have not been much with him in the daytime, but every evening, we spend a good part of the time together in my room or his. He is just the same, honest, fine fellow as ever, and unless I am very much mistaken, is going to make a thorough success in every way of college. My studies do not come very well this year, as I have to work nearly as hard on Saturday as on any other day—six, seven or eight hours. Some of the studies are extremely interesting, however, especially Political Economy and Metaphysics. These are both rather hard, requiring a good deal of work, but they are even more interesting than my Natural History courses; and all the more so from the fact that I radically disagree on many points with the men whose books we are reading, (Mill and Ferrier). One of my zoological courses is rather dry, but the other I like very much, though it necessitates ten or twelve hours' work a week. My German is not very interesting, but I expect that my Italian will be when I get further on. For exercise, I have had to rely on walking, but today I have regularly begun sparring. I practice a good deal with the rifle, walking to and from the range, which is nearly three miles off; my scores have been fair, although not very good. Funnily enough, I have enjoyed quite a burst of popularity since I came back, having been elected into several different clubs. My own friends have, as usual, been perfect trumps, and I have been asked to spend Sundays with at least a half-dozen of them, but I have to come back to Cambridge Sunday mornings on account of Sunday School, which makes it more difficult to pay visits. I indulged in a luxury the other day in buying 'The Library of British Poets,' and I delight in my purchase very much, but I have been so busy that I have hardly had time to read it yet. I shall really have to have a new bookcase for I have nowhere to put my books. . . . Your loving son, T. Jr."

The above letter is of distinct interest for several reasons: first of all, because of the affectionate pains taken by the young man of now nearly twenty to keep his mother informed about all his activities, intellectual, physical, and social. So many young men of that age are careless of the great interest taken by their mothers and do not share with them the joys and difficulties of college life. All through his life, from his boyhood to the very last weeks of his busy existence, my brother Theodore was a great sharer. This is all the more unusual because, as a rule, the man of intellectual pursuits is apt to deny himself to the claims of family and friends, but not so with Theodore Roosevelt, except during the period of some specially hard task, when he would give himself to it to the exclusion of every other interest. Unless during such rare periods, no member of his family ever went to him for guidance or solace or interest without the most generous and most loving response. In the above letter he shows his response to the tender inquiries of his mother, so lately widowed, and he wishes to give her all the information that she desires. One can see that the young junior, as he now was, was coming into his own in more ways than one. He is working harder intellectually; already metaphysics and political economy are catching up with "natural history" in his affections, and, in fact, outdistancing the latter. His individual point of view is shown by the fact that he "radically disagrees on many points with Mill and Ferrier," and he again shows the persevering determination, so largely a part of his character, in the way in which he walks to and fro the three miles to practise with his rifle at the range. The modest way in which he speaks of his "burst of popularity" is also very characteristic, for he received the unusual distinction of being invited to join several of the most popular clubs. Altogether, this letter in which he tells, although he makes no point of it, of his still faithful service at Sunday-school, no matter how much it interferes with the gay week-end visits which he so much enjoys, and the glimpse which he gives us of his love of poetry as an offset to his harder studies, seems to me to depict in a lovable and admirable light the young Harvard student.

Having written in this accurate way to his mother, within a month he writes to his younger sister:

Sweet Pussie: I am spending Sunday with Minot Weld. It is a beautiful day and this afternoon we are going to drive over to Dick Saltonstall's where we shall go out walking with

Miss Rose Saltonstall and Miss Alice Lee, and drive home by moonlight after tea. I have begun studying fairly hard now, and shall keep it up until Christmas. I am afraid I shall not be able to come home for Thanksgiving; I really have my hands full, especially now that my Political Economy Professor wishes me to start a Finance Club, which would be very interesting indeed, and would do us all a great deal of good, but which will also take up a great deal of time. Of course, I spend a good deal of my spare time in the Porcellian Club which is great fun. Night before last, Harry Shaw and I gave a little supper up there, the chief items on the bill of fare were partridges and Burgundy,—I, confining myself to the partridges. I am going to cut Sunday school today for the second time this year, but when the weather is so beautiful as this, I like every now and then to spend Sunday with a friend. Harry Chapin is going to take my class for me today. Good-bye sweet one,—

YOUR LOVING TEDO.

Here again we see the growth of the young man, the growth of his influence in his class, for it is to him that the Political Economy professor turns to start a finance club, and we see also the proportionate all-round development, for not only does he read poetry, start finance clubs, differ with Mill and Ferrier on abstract subjects, but also joins with Harry Shaw in a little supper of partridges and Burgundy—he confining himself, I would have my readers know, to the partridges! Theodore Roosevelt was growing in every way and especially becoming the more all-round man, and it was well that this growth should take place, for if the all-round man can still keep focussed ideals and strong determination to achieve in individual directions, it is because of the all-round qualities that he becomes the leader of men. Again the happy Christmas holidays came, but this time shadowed by the great blank made by my father's loss, and in February, 1879, he writes again—now of happy coasting-parties at the Saltonstalls', where began his intimate relationship with lovely Alice Lee, who later became his wife. One can see the merry young people flying, as he says, "like the wind," on their long toboggans, and then having a gay dance at the hospitable house of Mrs. Lee.

In March he writes: "I only came out second best in the sparring contest, but I do not care very much for I have had uncommonly good luck in everything this year from studies to society. I enjoyed my trip to Maine very much indeed; of course, I fell behind in my studies, but by working pretty hard last week, I succeeded in nearly catching up again." This trip to Maine cemented the great friendship between my brother and those splendid backwoodsmen, Bill Sewall and Will Dow, who were later to be partners in his ranching venture in the Far West. Bill Sewall was a strong influence in my brother's young manhood, and for him great admiration was conceived by the young city boy and, later, by the college student. The splendid, simple, strong man of the woods, though not having had similar educational advantages, was still so earnest a reader and so natural a philosopher that his attitude toward books and life had lasting influence over his young companion.

About this same time, March, 1879, my brother wrote me one of the sweetest and most characteristic of his little love-letters. It was dated from the Porcellian Club on March 28, and enclosed a diminutive birch-bark book of poetry, and the letter ran as follows: "Wee Pussy, I came across such a funny, wee book of poetry today, and I send it to a wee, funny Kitty Coo, with Teddy's best love." The page on which the sweet words are written is yellow, but the little birch-bark book is still intact, and the great love engendered by the tender thought of, and expression of that thought to, his sister is even deeper than when the sweet words were actually written.

On May 3 he writes in a humorous vein: "Pet Pussie: At last the deed is done and I have shaved off my whiskers! The consequence, I am bound to add, is that I look like a dissolute democrat of the Fourth Ward; I send you some tintypes I had

PORCELLIAN CLUB.

Monday Mar 25th.

Wee Pussy,

I came across such a funny, wee book of poetry to-day, and I send it to a wee, funny Kitty Coo, with Teddy's best love.

LETTER TO CORINNE ROOSEVELT ACCOMPANYING "BIRCH BARK POEMS"

taken; the front views are pretty good, although giving me an expression of glum misery that I sincerely hope is not natural. The side views do not resemble me any more than they do Michael Angelo or John A. Weeks. The next four months are going to be one 'demnition grind' but by great good luck, I shall be able to leave here June 5th, I think." The whiskers were permanently removed and never again reappeared, except on his hunting trip the following year, and I think he felt, himself, that the lack of them added a touch of elegance to his appearance, for he writes again within a day or two: "I rode over on Saturday morning (very swell with hunting crop and beaver) to Chestnut Hill where I took lunch with the Lees." He is beginning to be quite a gentleman of fashion, and so the care-free days glide by, another summer comes, with pleasant visits, and another Maine woods excursion; but even when writing in the midst of house-parties of bewildering gaiety, he adds at the end of a long letter in August, 1879, "For my birthday, among the books I most want are the complete editions of Prescott, Motley, and Carlyle," and signs himself "Your loving St. Buv.," a new pet name which he had given himself and which was a conglomerate of St. Beuve, for whose writings he had great admiration, and the brother for whom his little sister had such great admiration.

His last year at college was one of equal growth, although the development was not as apparent as in his junior year, and in June, 1880, he graduated with honors, a happy, successful Harvard alumnus. A number of his New York friends went on for class day, and all made merry together, and not long afterwards he and his brother Elliott started on a hunting trip together. Elliott, who as a young child had been the strong one, when Theodore was a delicate little boy, had, during the years of adolescence, been somewhat of an invalid and could not go to college; our father, wise as ever, decided he must have his education in another way, and he arranged for Elliott to spend several years largely in the open air. He became a splendid shot, and my brother Theodore always felt that Elliott was far the better hunter of the two. The brothers were devoted to each other, and were each the complement of the other in character. Theodore writes from Wilcox's farm, Illinois, August 22, 1880: "Darling Pussie: We have been having a lovely time so far, have shot fair quantities of game, are in good health, though our fare and accommodations are of the roughest. The shooting is great fun; you would laugh to see us start off in a wagon, in our rough, dirty, hunting-suits, not looking very different from our driver; a stub-tailed, melancholy looking pointer under the front seat, and a yellow, fool idea of a setter under the back one, which last is always getting walked on and howling dismally. We enjoy the long drives very much: the roads are smooth and lovely, and the country, a vast undulating prairie, cut up by great fields of corn and wheat with few trees. The birds are not very plentiful, but of great variety; we get prairie chickens in the stubble fields, plover in the pastures, snipe in the 'slews,' and ducks in the ponds. We hunt about an hour or two in a place, then get into our wagon and drive on, so that, though we cover a very large tract of country, we are not very tired at the end of the day, only enough to make us sleep well. The climate is simply superb, and though the scenery is not very varied, yet there is something very attractive to me in these great treeless, rolling plains, and Nellie [his pet name for Elliott] and I are great chums, and in the evening, sit and compare our adventures in 'other lands' until bedtime which is pretty early."

And again he writes a few weeks later from Chicago, in a very bantering vein:

September 12, 1880—Darling Pussie: We have come back here after a week's hunting in Iowa. Elliott revels in the change to civilization—and epicurean pleasures. As soon as we got here he took some ale to get the dust out of his throat; then a milk punch because he was thirsty; a mint julep because it was hot; a brandy mash "to keep the cold out of his stomach"; and then sherry and bitters to give him an appetite. He took a very simple dinner—soup, fish, salmi de grouse, sweetbread, mutton, venison, corn, macaroni, various vegetables and some puddings and pies, together with beer, later claret and in the evening, shandigaff. I confined mvself to roast beef and potatoes; when

Theodore Roosevelt in his twenty-second year. Elliott Roosevelt in his twenty-first year.

Portrait taken in Chicago, July, 1880, on the way to the hunting trip of that season.

I took a second help he marvelled at my appetite—and at bedtime, wondered why in thunder *he* felt "stuffy" and *I* didn't. The good living also reached his brain, and he tried to lure me into a discussion about the intellectual development of the Hindoos, coupled with some rather discursive and scarcely logical digressions about the Infinity of the Infinite, the Sunday school system, and the planet Mars, together with some irrelevant remarks about Texan "Jack Rabbits" which are apparently about as large as good-sized cows. Elliott says that these remarks are incorrect and malevolent; but I say they pay him off for his last letter about my eating manners! We have had very good fun so far, in spite of a succession of untoward accidents and delays. I broke both my guns, Elliott dented his, and the shooting was not as good as we had expected; I got bitten by a snake and chucked headforemost out of the wagon.

YOUR SEEDY BROTHER, THEO.

Nothing could better exemplify the intimate, comprehending relationship of the two brothers than the above letter, in which, with exaggerated fun, Theodore "pays Elliott off" for his criticisms of the future President's eating manners! All through their lives—alas! Elliott's life was to end prematurely at the age of thirty-three—the same relationship endured between them. Each was full of rare charm, joy of life, and unselfish interest in his fellow man, and thus they had much in common always.

The hunting trip described so vividly in these two letters was, in a sense, the climax of this period of my brother's life. College days were over, the happy summer following his graduation was also on the wane, and within a brief six weeks from the time these letters were written, Theodore Roosevelt, a married man, was to go forth on the broader avenues of his life's destiny.

V

THE YOUNG REFORMER

"Lift up thy praise to Life
That set thee in the strenuous ways,
And left thee not to drowse and rot
In some thick perfumed and luxurious plot.

"Strong, strong is Earth
With vigor for thy feet,
To make thy wayfaring
Tireless and fleet,

"And good is Earth,
But Earth not all thy good,
O thou with seeds of suns
And star-fire in thy blood."

THE early part of the year 1881 was spent by Theodore Roosevelt and his young wife with my mother at 6 West 57th Street, and was devoted largely to literary work and efforts to acquaint himself with the political interests of the district in which we lived.

During the following summer, they travelled in Europe; he climbed Swiss mountains and showed his usual capacity for surmounting obstacles. June 16, 1881, he writes from Paris in connection with artistic wanderings in the Louvre. "I have not admired any of the French painters much excepting Greuze. Rubens' 'Three Wives' are reproduced in about fifty different ways, which I think a mistake. No painter can make the same face serve for Venus, the Virgin, and a Flemish lady." And again on August 24 from Brussels: "I know nothing at all, in reality, of art, I regret to say, but I do know what pictures I like. I am not at all fond of Rubens; he is mentally a fleshly, sensuous painter, and yet his most famous pictures are those relating to the Divinity. Above all, he fails in his female figures. Rubens' women are handsome animals except his pictures of rich Flemish house-wives, but they are either ludicrous or ugly when meant to represent either the Virgin or a Saint. I think they are not much better as heathen goddesses. I do not like a chubby Minerva, a corpulent Venus, or a Diana who is so fat that I know she could never overtake a cow, let alone a deer. Rembrandt is by all odds my favorite. I am very much attracted by his strongly contrasting coloring and I could sit for hours examining his heads; they are so life-like and impressive. Van Helst I like for the sake of the realism with which he presents to one, the bold, rich, turbulent Dutchman of his time. Vandyke's heads are wonderful; they are very life-like and very powerful—but if the originals were like them, I should hardly have admired one of them. Perhaps, the pictures I really get most enjoyment out of are the landscapes, the homely little Dutch and Flemish interiors, the faithful representations of how the people of those times lived and made merry and died, which are given us by Jan Steen, Van Ostade, Teniers, and Ruysdael. They bring out the life of that period in a way no written history could do, and interest me far more than pictures of Saints and Madonnas. I suppose this sounds heretical but it is true. This time I have really *tried* to like the holy pictures but I cannot; even the Italian masters seem to me to represent good men and insipid, good women, but rarely anything saintly or divine. The only pictures I have seen with these attributes are Gustav Doree's! He alone represents the Christ so that your pity for him is lost in intense admiration and reverence. Your loving brother."

The above letter is one unusual in its type, because it was rare for Theodore Roosevelt to write as much about art. He always loved certain types of pictures, but his busy, active career had but small time for the more æsthetic interests! All these criticisms by the young man not yet twenty-three have their value because they show so distinctly the character of the young man himself. One sees the interest which he takes in his humankind as represented by certain types of Dutch pictures, and also his love for spiritual beauty, when not belittled by insipidity. Perhaps the last sentence of this letter is most characteristic of all of his own vital spirit. He does not wish to pity the Christ; he almost insists that pity must be lost in admiration and reverence. Pity always seemed to Theodore Roosevelt an undesirable quality; tenderest sympathy he gave and craved—but never pity.

After this brief artistic sojourn he plunged with great energy, on his return, into the drudgery of political life in his own district. Many were the criticisms of his friends and acquaintances at the thought of his taking up city or state politics from a serious standpoint. At that time, even more than now, "politics" was considered as something far removed from the life of any one brought up to other spheres than that of mud-slinging and corruption. All "politics" was more or less regarded as inextricably intertwined with the above. Theodore Roosevelt, however, realized from the very beginning of his life that "armchair" criticism was ineffectual, and, because ineffectual, undesirable. If one were to regard oneself in the light of a capable critic, the actual criticism immediately obligated the person indulging in it to *do* something about the matter. He often used to quote the old story of "Squeers" in "Nicholas Nickleby," that admirable old novel of Charles Dickens, in which "Do the Boys' Hall" was so amusingly described. Mr. Squeers, the master of the above school, would call up a pupil and ask him to spell window. He pronounced it "winder," and the pupil in turn would spell it "w-i-n-d-e-r." The spelling would not be corrected but the boy would receive the injunction to "go and wash it," and my brother always said that while he did not approve of "Squeers' " spelling—nor indeed of other methods practised by him—that the "go and wash it" was an admirable method to follow in political life. The very fact that, although by no means a wealthy man, he had a sufficient competence to make it unnecessary for him to earn his own living, made him feel that he must devote his life largely to public affairs. He realized that unless the men of his type and caliber interested themselves in American government, the city, state, and country in which they lived would not have the benefit of educated minds and of incorruptible characters. He therefore set himself to work to learn the methods used in ordinary political life, and, by learning the methods, to fit himself to fight intelligently whatever he found unworthy of free American citizenship.

He has described this part of his life in his own autobiography. He has told of how he met Joseph Murray, a force in the political district, who became his devoted adherent, and how he decided himself to become one of the "governing class." This effort resulted in his nomination for the New York State Assembly, and on January 1, 1882, Theodore Roosevelt became outwardly, what inwardly he had always been, a devoted public servant. That winter remains in my mind as one of intense interest in all of his activities. We were all living at my mother's home in 57th Street, and he spent part of the week in Albany, returning, as a rule, on Friday for the week-end. Many were the long talks, many the humorous accounts given us of his adventures as an assemblyman, and all the time we, his family, realized that an influence unusual in that New York State Assembly was beginning to be felt. Already, by the end of a month or so, he was known as "the Young Reformer," ardent and earnest, who pleaded for right thinking, and definite practical interpretation of right thinking. His name was on the lips of many before he had been three months an assemblyman, and already his native city was beginning to take a more than amused interest in his activities.

A certain highbrow club called "The 19th Century Club," whose president was the editor of the *Evening Post* (a paper neither then nor later *always* in accord with the ideals and methods of Theodore Roosevelt!), invited the young assemblyman to make an address before its members. He accepted the invitation, feeling, as he always did, that it was well to give the type of message that *he* wished to give to the type of citizens of which that club was composed. Following my invariable custom whenever it was possible for me to do so, I accompanied him to the meeting. The method of procedure in "The 19th Century Club" was as follows: The speaker of the evening was allowed to choose his own subject, announced, of course, several weeks in advance, and he was given a half-hour in which to develop his idea. A second speaker was invited to rebut the first speaker. The speaker of the evening was then allowed ten minutes to rebut the rebutter. It is, I think, of special interest to remember that the young assemblyman, twenty-three years of age, chose for his subject the same theme on which the man of sixty, who was about to die, wrote his last message to his countrymen.

Theodore Roosevelt announced that he would speak to "The 19th Century Club" on "Americanism." A brilliant editor of an able newspaper was asked to make the speech in answer to the address of "the Young Reformer." As I say, I went with my brother to the meeting and sat directly under him in a front seat. It was the first time I had ever heard him speak in public and I confess to having been extremely nervous. He was never an orator, although later his speeches were delivered with great charm of manner and diction, but at this early stage of his career he had not the graces of an older and more finished speaker. I can see him now as he came forward on the platform and began with eager ardor his plea for Americanism. Every fibre of my being responded to him and to his theme, but I seemed to be alone in my response, for the somewhat chilly audience, full of that same armchair criticism of which I have spoken, gave but little response to the desire of the heart of Theodore Roosevelt, and when he had finished his half-hour's presentation of his plea, there was very little applause, and he sat down looking somewhat nervous and disappointed. Then the brilliant man, twice the age of Theodore Roosevelt, who had been chosen to reply to him, rose, and with deft oratorical manipulation rang the changes on every "ism" he could think of, using as his fundamental argument the fact that all "isms" were fads. He spoke of the superstition of spiritualism, the extravagance of fanaticism, the hypocrisy of hypnotism, the plausibility of socialism—and the highbrow members of "The 19th Century Club" were with the brilliant orator from start to finish, and as he closed his subtile argument, which left Americanism high and dry on the shores of faddism, the audience felt that "the Young Reformer" had had his lesson, and gave genuine applause to his opponent.

Half-way through that opponent's address, I confess, on my own part, to having experienced a great feeling of discouragement; not because I agreed with what he said, but because of the effect produced upon the listeners; but suddenly I saw my brother smile the same smile which used to cross his face in later years when some heckler would try to embarrass him from the back of a great hall, and he took a pencil and wrote something on his cuff. The smile was transitory but it gave me fresh hope, and I knew quite well that the audience would hear something worth while, if not to their liking, in the last ten minutes of the evening, when, as I said before, the speaker of the evening was allowed to rebut the rebutter. The clever editor sat down amidst interested applause, and "the Young Reformer" stepped once more forward to the edge of the platform. He leaned far over from the platform, so earnest, so eager was he, and this is what he said: "I believe that I am allowed ten minutes in which to refute the arguments of my opponent. I do not need ten minutes—I do not need five minutes—I hardly need one minute—I shall ask you one question, and as you answer that question, you will decide who has won this argument—myself or the gentleman on the other side of this platform. My question is as follows: If it is true that all isms are fads, I would ask you, Fellow

Citizens, what about *Patriotism?*" The audience rose to its feet; even "The 19th Century Club" could not but acknowledge that patriotism was a valuable attribute for American citizens to possess. That was the first time that Theodore Roosevelt, in public, asked of his fellow countrymen, "What about Patriotism?" but all his life long, from that time on, it was the question forever on his lips, the question which his own life most adequately answered.

In April of that same year, Theodore, an assemblyman not yet twenty-four, had already made himself so conspicuous a figure that mention of him and his attitudes was constantly in the New York press. In an envelope, put away long ago, I find an excerpt from the New York *Times*, April 5, 1882. It is yellow with age and brittle, but there was something ineffaceable and prophetic in the faded words; I quote:

"He called from the table his resolution directing an investigation by the Standing Judiciary Committee of the acts of Judge Westbrook and Ex-Attorney General Ward in connection with the gigantic stock jobbing scheme of the Manhattan Railroad Co. (Elevated). Ex-Governor Alvord *tried* to prevent resolution, but it was carried 48–22. As Mr. Roosevelt rose to speak, the House, for almost the only time during the Session, grew silent and listened to every word that he uttered."

In the midst of a body of men somewhat inclined to a certain kind of careless irreverence, it is of marked interest that "as Mr. Roosevelt rose to speak, the House, for almost the only time during the Session, grew silent and listened to every word that he uttered." To how few young men of twenty-three would "the House" accord such respect! As I say, the attitude was prophetic, for the following forty years, no matter how fiercely he was criticised, no matter what fury of invective was launched against him, no matter how jealously and vindictively he was occasionally opposed, there was never a place where Theodore Roosevelt rose to speak that he was not listened to with great attention.

In the *Sun* of the same date the account of the incident runs as follows: "Mr. Roosevelt's speech was delivered with deliberation and measured emphasis, and his charges were made with a boldness that was almost startling." Those first two years of his career as an assemblyman showed, indeed, again, that the youth was father to the man. The characteristics which marked his whole public life never showed more dominantly than as a young assemblyman in Albany. Uncompromising courage was combined with common sense, and the power of practical though never unworthy compromise was as evident then as later in his life. Those years have been fully dwelt upon in his own autobiography.

The great tragedy of his young wife's death at the birth of her first child was an even greater tragedy because the death of our lovely mother occurred twenty-four hours before her son's wife passed away. Our mother's home at 57th Street had been the background of our young married life, as it had been the foreground of our youth, and the winter of 1884 had been spent by my husband and myself at 6 West 57th Street, and the consequence was that as Theodore also made his headquarters there, we had been much together, and that very fact made it even harder to break up the home which had been so long the centre of our family life.

The next two years were almost the saddest of our happy lives. My brother had, fortunately, already interested himself in a ranching enterprise in North Dakota, and although he returned to the assembly in February, 1884, and with his usual courage finished his year of duty there, he turned gladly to the new life of the West, and became, through his absolute comprehension of the pioneer type of the cowboy and the ranchman, not only one of them from a physical standpoint, but also one of them from the standpoint of understanding their mental outlook.

In June, 1884, however, before starting for Dakota, he was to meet one of the serious political decisions of his life. That spring, when it came time to elect delegates to the Republican National Convention, he was, with the hearty approval of the great mass of his party, chosen as the chief of the four delegates-at-large from New York State. Mr. Joseph Bucklin Bishop gives in his history of "Theodore Roosevelt and His Time" a short account of that convention, of which I quote part:

"He went to the National Convention an avowed advocate of the nomination of Senator John F. Edmunds of Vermont as Republican Candidate for the Presidency in preference to James G. Blaine. The New York *Times* of June 4th, 1884, refers to him as the leader of the Younger Republicans, and says, 'when he spoke, it was not the voice of a youth but the voice of a man, and a positive practical man.'"

Mr. Bishop describes Mr. Roosevelt's efforts and the efforts of Senator Henry Cabot Lodge to secure the nomination of their choice, and then continues: "By the nomination of Mr. Blaine which followed later, Roosevelt was confronted with what, in many respects, was one of the most serious crises of his career. He had to decide which of the two courses he should choose; he must separate himself completely from his party and become an absolute Independent, or stay within his party and support its regularly appointed candidate. The nomination of Mr. Blaine had been fairly won. He was unquestionably the choice of the Convention. There was no claim that the will of the majority had been subverted either through the action of a committee on contested seats or in any other way. The problem before him was thus a quite different one from that presented to him twenty-eight years later in the National Republican Convention of 1912. In opposing the nomination of Mr. Blaine, he and his Republican Associates had been acting with a considerable body of Professional Independents. These men were without allegiance to either of the great political parties. Though he had been, during his brief public career, an avowed Republican, seeking to accomplish all his reforms through Republican aid and inside party lines, his Independent associates, as soon as the Blaine nomination was made, assumed that he would leave his party and join them in seeking to accomplish Mr. Blaine's defeat by supporting the Democratic candidate. In fact, they not merely asked but demanded that he abandon the course which he had followed since his entry into political life and upon which he had built his public career. They were sincere in their belief that he should do so. It seemed incredible to them that he could do anything else. He gave them full credit for sincerity but declared that the question was one that he must insist upon deciding for himself.

"He admitted frankly that he had worked hard for the nomination of Edmunds but he declined to say at once what course he should pursue in regard to the nomination of Mr. Blaine. Various devices were used to force him to declare his intentions, some by Republican politicians and others by leading Independents, but all in vain. He insisted upon deciding the question for himself and in his own way and time. He went direct from the Convention in Chicago to his ranch in Dakota, and several weeks later put forth a formal statement in which he defined his decision as follows: 'I intend to vote the Republican Presidential ticket. While at Chicago, I told Mr. Lodge that such was my intention but before announcing it, I wished to have time to think the matter over. A man cannot act both without and within the party; he can do either, but he cannot possibly do both. Each course has its advantages and each has its disadvantages, and one cannot take the advantages or the disadvantages separately. I went in with my eyes open to do what I could within the party. I did my best and got beaten, and I propose to stand by the result. It is impossible to combine the functions of a guerilla chief with those of a colonel in the regular army; one has a greater independence of action, the other is able to make what action he does take vastly more effective. In certain contingencies, the one can do most good; in certain contingencies the other; but there is no use in accepting a commission and then trying to play the game out on a lone hand. I am by inheritance and by education a Republican. Whatever good I have been able to accomplish in public life has been accomplished through the Republican party. I have acted with it in the past and wish to act with it in the future. I went as a regular delegate to the Chicago Convention and intend to abide by the outcome of that Convention. I am going back in a day or two to my Western ranch as I do not intend to take any part in a campaign this Fall.'" [This determination not to take part in the campaign he recalled later, for reasons which were eminently characteristic.]

"'When I started out to my ranch two months ago,' he said in October, 'I had no intention of taking any part whatever in the Presidential canvass, and the decision I have now come to is the result of revolving the matter in my mind during that time. It is altogether contrary to my character to keep a neutral position in so important and exciting a struggle, and besides any natural struggle to keep a position of some kind, I made up my mind that it was clearly my duty to support the ticket.'"

He faced the storm of disapproval and abuse calmly, and in reply to an open letter of regret and remonstrance from an Independent, he wrote: "I thank you for your good opinion of my past service. My power, if I ever had any, may or may not be as utterly gone as you think, but most certainly, it would deserve to go if I yield any more to the pressure of the Independents at present, when I consider *them* to be wrong, than I yielded in the past to the pressure of the machine when I thought *it* wrong." He declined a renomination for the assembly, which he could have had without opposition, and two separate offers of nominations for Congress, on the ground that his private interests, which he had neglected during his service in the legislature, required his attention.

His courageous attitude in connection with the disapproval of the Independents was indeed characteristic. He was invariably willing to run the risk of the disapproval of any faction when he had positively made up his own mind as to the right or wrong of any question, and he set his mind and heart upon those "private interests" of which he speaks.

In a later chapter I give several of his letters of this period in connection with a trip which he arranged for the members of his family to the Elkhorn Ranch and the Yellowstone Park in 1890. All his craving for the out-of-door life, all his sympathy with pioneer enterprise, such as his heroes Daniel Boone and Davy Crockett had indulged in, were satisfied by those long days on the open prairies, and by the building of his ranch-houses with the assistance of his old friends, Bill Sewall and Will Dow, the two stanch Maine lumbermen, uncle and nephew, with whom he had made many an excursion in the Maine woods in earlier days. Theodore Roosevelt, however, was not to be allowed by his country to remain too long the rider and dreamer under cottonwood-trees, or even a potent influence for good in Western affairs, as he became. Already rumors were abroad that he would be the choice of the Republican party for the nominee for mayor of New York City, and he was recalled from the wilds of North Dakota to a stirring triangular campaign in which Henry George, representing "Single Tax" beliefs, Abraham S. Hewitt, Democratic nominee, and the young ranchman from Dakota battled lustily against each other, with the result that Mr. Hewitt was elected mayor of New York.

In the autumn of 1886 he sailed for Europe to marry his old friend Edith Carow, and for a brief period led a life of leisure and travel. Only very rarely in his busy existence had he time for just that life again, and the consequence is that some of his letters at that period have an unusual value. He humorously described some of his travels in Italy in a letter dated December, 1886, as follows: "My lack of knowledge of the language has given me some soul-harrowing moments,—a mixture of broken English with German and French proving but an indifferent substitute for Italian, so I sometimes get what I do not want, as when yesterday, an effort to state that after dinner we wished only black coffee, expressed with deprecatory waves of the hand and the idiomatic phrase, 'c'est genuch' produced in addition, cheese, pastry, and fruit, all brought by the waiter in a wild hope that some one of those might satisfy what he evidently supposed was my untranslatable demand."

A little later, from Sorrento, he writes in characteristic fashion, showing that even in so romantic and enthralling a spot as Rome he was still "on duty bent" from the standpoint of writing articles for the *Century*. He says: "I finished six articles for the *Century* on ranch life while in Rome and sent them off. I do not know whether the *Century* will want them or not. I read them all to Edith and her corrections and help were most valuable to me. Now I am wondering why my 'Life of Benton' has not come out. Here, [at Sorrento] I generally take a moderate walk with Edith every morning, and then a brisk rush by myself. I had no idea that it was in me to enjoy the 'dolce far niente' even as long as I have. Luckily, Edith would dislike an extended stay in Europe as much as I would."

In this letter, after speaking of ranch losses which necessitated selling his beloved hunter, Sagamore, he signs himself, "Your extravagant and irrelevant but affectionate brother, the White Knight," the latter being a reference to the character in "Alice in Wonderland," from which enchanting book we invariably quoted in ordinary conversation or letters.

From Venice, in February, he writes: "Venice is perfectly lovely. It is more strange than any other Italian town, and the architecture has a certain florid barbarism about it,—Byzantine,—dashed with something stronger—that appeals to some streak in my nature." They returned to London later, and were shown many attentions, for even at that early period in his life, England recognized the statesman in Theodore Roosevelt. He speaks of Mr. Bryce the historian as a "charming man"—their friendship was to last all through my brother's life, and he mentions many other well-known young Englishmen, who have now grown old in their country's service. In a letter dated March 6 he says: "I have been having great fun in London, and have seen just the very nicest people, social, political, and literary. We have just come back from a lunch at the Jeunes', which was most enjoyable. Edith sat beside Chamberlain, who impresses me very much with his keen, shrewd intellect and quiet force. I sat between Trevelyan, who was just charming, and a Lady Leamington."

Unless I am mistaken, that was the first time my brother met Sir George Trevelyan, with whom he carried on a faithful and interesting correspondence for many years. "Mrs. Jeune has asked us to dine to meet Lord Charles Beresford and Lord Hartington, and I have been put down for the Athenæum Club, and also taken into the Reform Club. Last night, I dined at a Bohemian Club, the famous Savage Club, with Healy and one or two Parnellites, (having previously lunched with several of the Conservatives, Lord Stanhope and Seton-Carr, and others). The contrast was most amusing, but I like Healy immensely. Later on I met a brother of Stanhope's who is a radical, and listened to a most savage discussion with a young fellow named Foster, a nephew of the late Secretary of Ireland, who has also been very polite to me. I have enjoyed going to the House of Commons under the guidance of Bryce, the historian, and a dear old Conservative member named Hoare, very greatly. It is amusing to see the Conservatives, fresh-looking, well-built, thoroughly well-dressed gentlemen, honest and plucky but absolutely unable to grapple with the eighty odd, erratic Parnellite Irishmen. The last named, by the way, I know well of old,—I have met them in the New York Legislature!"

These comments by the young man of twenty-eight are along the line of comments made much later when almost all of his reactions to the men named or suggested had come true. The travellers were more than glad to get back to their native land, and by the early summer were settled at Sagamore Hill, to begin there the beautiful family life which grew in richness up to the moment of my brother's death.

June 8, 1887, he writes from Sagamore, describing amusingly

his efforts to become a polo-player. He has often expressed his own feeling about sports—he loved them, enjoyed his hunting and other athletic exercises to the full, but they were always a relaxation, never a pursuit with him. "Frank Underhill and I ride industriously around the field and brandish our mallets so as to foster the delusion among simple folk that we likewise are playing polo. Two other would-be players also come now and then; but as they have not yet even learned to sit on horse-back and strike the ball simultaneously, and, after trial, having found it impracticable to do so alternately, our games are generally duels. Yesterday, I beat Frank two out of three—and in addition, stood on my head on the sward in the enthusiasm of one mêlée where we got rather mixed. Day before yesterday, I rowed Edith to Lloyd's Neck, portaged across—at low tide, the hardest work I ever did almost,—into Huntington Harbor, then rowed out into the Sound. We took our lunch and some volumes of Thackeray. It was an ideal day—but wasn't I stiff and blistered next morning! Do come soon and stay as long as possible. Yours as ever, Theodore Roosevelt."

During that same summer I took my little niece Alice, with my children, to our old home on the Mohawk Hills for a change of air, and he writes me in his usual loving way of his warm appreciation of the pleasure I was giving the child, and sends his love to the little "yellow-haired darling," and incidentally, in the letters, says his book "Morris ["Gouverneur Morris"] goes drearily on by fits and starts, and in the intervals, I chop vigorously and have lovely rowing excursions"; and so the happy summer wore to its close and was crowned in September by the birth of his first boy, the third Theodore Roosevelt. He describes with amusement little Alice's remark—"a truthful remark," he says—"*My little brother* is a howling polly parrot." All through the letter one realizes his joy and pride in his first-born son, and shortly after that, in December of the same year, he writes me to congratulate me on the birth of my second son, Monroe, and says: "How glad I am that Ted, Junior, has a future playmate. Just won't they quarrel, though!"

Owing to the fact that in my brother's own biography he describes fully his work as civil service commissioner, police commissioner, and assistant secretary of the navy, I do not purport to give a detailed account of his labors, especially as during the period that he served in the first position, I have comparatively few letters from him, and it was not until he returned to New York in the second capacity that I saw as much of him as usual. One winter, however, we had a most characteristic intercourse. I do not remember exactly the date of that winter. I had married young, my children had been born in rapid succession, and owing to the delicacy of my health just before I was grown up, I was conscious of the fact that I was not as grounded in certain studies, especially American history, as I should have been, and I found myself with a very slim knowledge of the most important facts of my nation's birth and early growth. The consequence was that when my brother returned for a brief period to New York, I decided to consult him as to how best to study American History, thinking perhaps that I might go to Columbia College or something of that kind.

I began my effort for information by saying: "Theodore, I really know very little about American history." I can see the flash in his eyes as he turned to me. "What do you mean?" he said; "it's disgraceful for any woman not to know the history of her own country." "I know it is," I replied, "and that is just why I am consulting you about it. I know you feel I ought to know all about American history, but I also know that you preach large families, and you must remember that I have done my best in that direction in these last five years, and now I am ready to study American history!" "Do you mean really to study?" he said, looking at me sternly. "Just as really to study as whooping-cough, measles, chicken-pox, and other family pleasures will allow," I said. "Well," he replied, still sternly, and not laughing at my sally, "if you really mean to study, I will teach you myself. I will come at nine o'clock every week on Tuesday and Friday for one hour, if you will be ready promptly and give me all your attention." Needless to say, I was enchanted at the thought, and, true to his word, the busy man came at nine o'clock every Tuesday and Friday for several months, and in my library at 422 Madison Avenue I was ready with note-book and blackboard, and he lectured to me for that hour twice a week as if I were a matriculating class at Harvard College. I have now many of the notes he made for me at that time, and I shall always remember the painstaking way in which he drew the battle-fields, and explained how "one commander came up in this position at just the right moment and saved the day," or how the lack of preparedness ruined many a courageous adventure. These quiet hours come back to me with a rush of recollection as I write, and I am proud to think that he felt it was worth while to give me such instruction. Once I said to him: "How can you do this, Theodore; how can you take the time to study for these lectures?" "Oh!" he said, "I do not have to study; I could not, of course, give quite as much time as that. You see, I just happen to know my American history." He certainly did "happen to know" his American history, as was proved in many a controversy later in his life. His American history and, indeed, the history of almost every other country of the world were all at his finger-tips.

During his civil service commissionership, a period of a number of years, the letters were few and far between, but I have one dated July 28, 1889, in which he writes: "Struggle as I will, my life seems to grow more and more sedentary, and as for my polo, it is one of the things that *has* been; witness the enclosed check which is for Cranford, and I am trying to sell Diamond too;—how I hate to give it up! We have had lovely days this summer, however, at Sagamore. I took all the children down on the pond once, and made them walk out on a half-sunken log, where they perched like so many sand-snipes. I am leaving for the West soon to have a whack at the bears in the Rockies; I am so out of training that I look forward with acute physical terror to going up the first mountain. [He seems for the moment to have forgotten that his life was growing very "sedentary."] I have mortally hated being so much away from home this summer, but I am very glad I took the place [civil service commissionership] and I have really enjoyed my work. I feel it incumbent on me to try to amount to something, either in politics or literature because I have deliberately given up the idea of going into a money-making business. Of course, however, my political life is but an interlude—it is quite impossible to continue long to do much between two sets of such kittle-kattle as the spoilsmen and the mugwumps."

The seed of the birth of the Progressive party of 1912 was sown by that feeling of Theodore Roosevelt of the difficulty to do much "between two sets such as the spoilsmen and the mugwumps." The honest effort to play honest politics for honest purposes and practical ideals was the stimulating idea translated into action in that great attempt for better government called the Progressive party; but this letter of the young Civil Service Commissioner was written in 1889, and it was not until twenty-three years later that the seed fructified into a movement which, had it succeeded, would, I verily believe, have changed the fate of the world.

But to return to the Civil Service Commission. He gave faithful effort and all his intelligence to the improvement of that important service, and often had the sensation, which he was doomed to have in so many of his positions, that he was more or less beating his head against the wall. He sent me at that time a copy of a letter to the Civil Service Commissioners from an applicant who had been summoned to an examination and had not appeared. To show the ignorance of some of the applicants, I cannot resist quoting from the letter.

Alabama Mobile October 6, 1890.

To the Comishers of Sivel Serves,

My dear brothers: I am very sorry that I could not Meet you on the day you said but gentlemen, i am glad of the cause that kept me away. Let me tell you Mr. Comisher, i hav bin mard five years antel the Other Da me and my wife hav bin the onley mbrs en ow Famly. Well Sir on the Da before youre examnenashun My Wife Had a Kupple ov tuins, gest think of it, Mr. Comischer—and of course i couddnt go off and Leave her and them. i just staid home and we had a sellabration—and i invited all my friends to dinner. i wish you had been thare. i Hope i can be thare next time Mr. Comischer.

Very truly yours.

I remember my brother saying humorously that, after all, that particular gentleman might just as well have stayed away with his "tuins" and "sellabration," as he really doubted whether he could have passed the "examnenashun" had he appeared!

VI

THE ELKHORN RANCH AND NEAR-ROUGHING IT IN YELLOWSTONE PARK

From the cloistered life of American college boys, sheltered from the ruder currents of the world by the ramparts of wealth and gentle nurture, he passed, still very young, to the wild and free existence of the plains and the hills. In the silence of those vast solitudes men grow to full stature, when the original stuff is good. He came back to the East, bringing with him, as Tennyson sang, "The wrestling thews that throw the world." —From a speech by John Hay.

O lover of the things God made—
Hill, valley, mountain, plain:
The lightning from the darkened cloud,
The storm-burst with its rain.
—Roosevelt, "Hymn of Molokai."

MY brother has written so much about his own ranch, and has given so vivid a description in his autobiography of the life led there, of the wonderful stretches of the Bad Lands, of the swaying cottonwood-trees, and the big fireplace in the Elkhorn Ranch sitting-room, around which he and his fellow ranchers gathered, exhausted by a long day's cattle-herding or deer-hunting, that it hardly seems possible that I can add much to the picture already painted by his own facile hand: ranch life, however, viewed from the standpoint of the outsider or from that of the insider has a different quality, and thus no reminiscences of mine would be in any way complete were I not to describe my first delightful visit paid to Medora, Dakota, and the surrounding country, in 1890. Our party consisted of my brother and sister-in-law, my sister Mrs. Cowles, then Anna Roosevelt, our friend Robert Munro Ferguson, my husband and myself, and young George Cabot Lodge. The latter was the sixteen-year-old son of our valued friend Senator Henry Cabot Lodge, and was truly the "gifted son of a gifted father," for later he was not only to earn fame as a poet, well known to his countrymen, but in his brief life—for alas! he died in the summer of 1909—his talents were recognized in other lands as well.

I had been prepared by many tales for the charm and freedom and informal ease of life in the Bad Lands, and had often dreamed of going there; but, unlike most dreams, this one came true in an even more enchanting fashion than I had dared hope. Many had been the letters that my brother had written to me from Elkhorn Ranch several years previous to our journey. In June, 1886, he wrote: "I have never once had breakfast as late as four o'clock. Have been in the saddle all day, and have worked like a beaver, and am as rugged and happy as possible. While I do not see any very great future ahead, yet, if things go on as they are now going and have gone for the past three years, I think that each year I will net enough money to pay a good interest on the capital, and yet be adding slowly to my herd all the time. I think I have more than my capital on the ground, and this year I ought to be able to sell between two and three hundred head of steer and dry stock. I wish I could see all of you, but I certainly do enjoy the life. The other day while dining at the de Mores I had some cherries, the only fruit I have had since I left New York. I have lived pretty roughly."

I quote the above simply to show, what is not always understood, that my brother's ranching venture was, from his standpoint, a perfectly just business enterprise, and, had not the extraordinarily severe winters intervened, his capital would not have been impaired. Writing that same summer, shortly after hearing of the birth of my baby girl, he says in his loving way:

"My own darling Pussie, my sweetest little sister: How can I tell you the joy I felt when I received Douglas' first telegram; but I had not the heart to write you until I received the second the good old boy sent me, and knew you were all right. Just to think of there being a second wee, new Pussie in this big world! How I shall love to pet and prize the little thing! It will be very, very dear to Uncle Teddy's heart, which is quite large enough, however, not to lose an atom of affection for Teddy Douglas, the blessed little scamp. I have thought of you all the time for the last few weeks, and you can hardly imagine how overjoyed and relieved I felt, my own darling sister. I hope the little new Pussie will grow up like her dear mother, and that she will have many many loving ones as fond of her as her irrelevant old cowboy uncle is of Pussie, Senior. Will you be very much offended if I ask whether she now looks like a little sparsely-haired, pink polyp? My own offspring, when in tender youth, closely resembled a trilobite of pulpy consistency and shadowy outline. You dearest Pussie,—you know I am just teasing you, and how proud and fond I am of the little thing even when I have never seen it. I wish I was where I could shake old Douglas by the hand and kiss you again and again.

"Today I went down to Dickerman to make the Fourth of July speech to a great crowd of cowboys and rangers, and after, stayed to see the horse races between the cowboys and Indians."

In another letter about the same time: "If I was not afraid of being put down as cold-blooded, I should say that I honestly miss greatly and all the time, and think lovingly of all you dear ones, yet I really enjoy this life. I have managed to combine an outdoor life possessing much variety and excitement, and now and then a little adventure, with a literary life also. Three out of four days I spend the morning and evening in the Ranch house writing, and working at various pieces of writing I have now on hand. They may come to nothing, however; but on the other hand they may succeed; at any rate, I am doing some honest work whatever the result is and I am really pretty philosophical about success or failure now. It often amuses me when I indirectly hear that I am supposed to be harboring secret and bitter regret for my political career, when, as a matter of fact, I have hardly ever, when alone, given two thoughts to it since it closed, and have been quite as much wrapped up in hunting, ranching, and book-making as I ever was in Politics. Give my best love to wee Teddy and dear old Douglas; do you know, I have an excessively warm feeling for your respected spouse. I have always admired Truth, Loyalty, and Courage; and though I am really having a lovely life, just the life I care for, please be sure that I am always thinking of my own, darling sister, whom I love so much and so tenderly. Ever your affectionate brother, Thee."

On August 7 of the same year he wrote again after having paid a brief visit to the East, and returned to Dakota: "Blessed little Pussie; Mother of an increasing and vocal Israel, I did enjoy my two visits to my dear sister, and that dear old piece of peripatetic bric-à-brac, her Caledonian spouse. Everything here is much as usual. The boys were, as always, genuinely glad to see me. I am greatly attached to the Ranch and the life out here, and am really fond of the men. It is in many ways ideal; we are so very rarely able to, actually and in real life, dwell in our ideal 'hero land.' The loneliness and freedom, and the half-adventurous nature of existence out here, appeals to me very powerfully. . . . Merrifield and I are now busily planning our hunt in the mountains."

Such letters as the above filled the members of his family with a strong desire to participate to some degree, at least, in the life which he loved so dearly; but the births of various small members of the family rendered such participation impossible until the late summer of 1890.

After a brief visit to St. Paul, Minn., we took train for Medora. My brother had heralded the fact that I (then a young woman of twenty-eight) was a mighty rider (I had followed the Essex County hounds in New Jersey)! And the cowboys were quite sure, I think, that I would leap from the locomotive to the back of a bucking bronco. Our train drew up, or I should say, approximately drew up, to the little station at Medora at four o'clock in the morning, in one of the most frightful storms that I ever remember. Rain fell in torrents, and we had to get out on an embankment composed of such slippery mud that before we actually plodded to the station, our feet and legs were encased in glutinous slime; but the calls of the cowboys undauntedly rang out in the darkness, and the neighing of horses and prancing of hoofs made us realize that civilization as well as convention was a thing of the past. Will Merrifield, the superintendent of Elkhorn Ranch, and Sylvane Ferris, his able lieutenant, fully expected me to mount the extremely dangerous-looking little animal which they held by a loose rope, and they were inordinately disappointed when I pleaded the fatigue of two nights on the train, and begged that I might drive with the other less-adventurous ladies to the ranch-house, forty miles away. Before starting on this long trip we were entertained by Joe Ferris, the brother of Sylvane, who having once also been one of Theodore's cowboys, had now decided upon a more sober type of life as storekeeper in the little town of Medora. Joe and his wife were most hospitable, and above his shop in their own rooms we were given a nice warm breakfast and an equally warm welcome. After breakfast, we came down to the shop, where our luggage had already been gathered, and there we began to sort what we would take to the Ranch and what we would leave. This required a certain amount of packing and unpacking, and I was on my knees "madly thrusting," as "Alice in Wonderland" puts it, "a right-hand foot into a left-hand shoe" when Joe came up to me and said: "Mrs. Douglas (they all decided to call me Mrs. Douglas, as more informal than Mrs. Robinson), it ain't worth while for you to tire yourself like that when the best packer in all Dakota is standin' in the doorway." I looked up and sure enough a huge man, who might have just walked out of one of Bret Harte's novels, *was* "standin' in the doorway." "There he is," continued Joe; "that's Hell-Roarin' Bill, the sheriff of the county; you heard tell of how he caught that lunatic; well, Bill's the best ladies' packer that ever was, and you had better leave all your bags to him to arrange." Fearing that "Bill" might be offended if I did not use him in the capacity of a French maid, and having frequently been told of the rapid results of hurt feelings on the part of "Bill," I suavely called him to my side, and telling him of the wonderful reputation which I had heard he enjoyed, I immediately put my wardrobe in his care, and to my infinite surprise the huge backwoodsman measured up to his reputation. Very soon the cavalcade was ready, the rain had ceased to fall in such torrents, the half-misty quality in the air lent a softer beauty to the arid landscape, and a sense of adventure was the finishing touch to our expectations as we started for Elkhorn Ranch. My disappointed friends, Merrifield and Sylvane, said that "they did not believe that Mrs. Douglas would like drivin' with a 'shotgun team' much better than ridin' a buckin' bronco, but, of course, if she *thought* she wanted to go that way, she could." An hour later "Mrs. Douglas" somewhat regretted her choice of progression; true enough, it *was* a shotgun team attached to that springless wagon in which we sat! The horses had never been hitched up together before, and their methods of motion were entirely at odds. The cowboy driver, however, managed eventually to get them started, and from that moment our progress, though irrelevant, was rapid beyond words.

We forded the "Little Missouri" River twenty-three times on the way to the ranch-house, and as the banks of the river were extremely steep, it was always a question as to whether we could go fast enough down one bank to get sufficient impetus to enable us to go through the river and up the very steep bank on the other side; so that either coming or going we were in imminent danger of a complete somersault. However, we did accomplish that long, exhausting, springless drive, and gradually the buttes rose higher and higher around us, the strange formation of the Bad Lands, curious in color, became more and more marked, the cottonwood-trees more plentiful as the river broadened out, and suddenly we saw buried amidst the trees on the farther side of one of our fordings the substantially built, cosey-looking house called by my brother the Elkhorn Ranch.

In a letter written to my aunt, Mrs. Gracie, from the ranch-house I say:

"We are having the most delightful time at the Ranch. The little house is most cosey and comfortable, and Mrs. Merrifield had everything so neat and sweet for us, and as she has a girl to help her, we really do not have to rough it at all. We all make our beds and do up our rooms religiously, but even that they would willingly do for us if we would let them. We have had three cloudless days, the first of which was occupied in driving the forty miles down here, and a beautiful picturesque drive it is, winding in and out through these strange, bold Buttes, crossing the 'Little Missouri' twenty-three times! We ladies drove, but the men all rode, and very picturesque they looked filing across the river. We arrived at the Ranch house at twelve o'clock and ate a splendid dinner of Mrs. Merrifield's preparing, immediately after which we climbed up a Butte and walked to Prairie Dog town and saw the little prairie dogs. We then mounted horses and took a lovely ride, so you may imagine that we slept well.

"The next day we were all on horseback soon after breakfast, Ferris and Merrifield with us, and off we rode; this time with the intention of seeing Merrifield lasso a steer. When we came to a great bunch of cattle, the practised eyes of the two men at once discovered an unbranded heifer, which they immediately decided to lasso and brand. It was very exciting. Merrifield threw the rope, cleverly catching its legs, and then threw the heifer, which was almost the size of a cow, and then Ferris tied another rope around its neck. The ends of the ropes were slipped over the pommels of two ponies who, in the most sensible way, held the heifer while the two men built a little fire and heated the cinch ring with which they branded the creature. It was all intensely picturesque. In the afternoon, we again rode out to be with the men while they drove the deer on the bottom, and Merrifield shot one; so you see, we have had very typical experiences, especially at the round-up yesterday."

Happy days, indeed, they were, full of varied excitements. Merrifield's little boy, Frank, only eleven years old, was the chief factor in finding the herd of ponies in the morning, for it was the custom to let them loose after twilight. Many and many a time I would hear him unslip the halter of the one small pony ("Little Moke" by name) which was still tied to the ranch-house steps and on which he would leap in the early dawn to go to round up the ponies for the day's work. I would jump up and look out of the ranch window, and see the independent little fellow fording the river, starting on his quest, and an hour or so later the splashing of many feet in the water heralded the approach of "Little Moke," his young rider, and the whole bunch of four-legged friends.

The relationship between my brother and his men was one of honest comradeship but of absolute respect, each for the other, and on the part of the cowboys there was, as well, toward their "Boss," a certain reverential attitude in spite of the "man to man" equality. How I loved that first night that we sat around the fire, when the men, in their effort to give my brother all the news of the vicinity during his absence, told the type of tale which has had its equivalent only in Owen Wister's "The Virginian." "There is a sky-pilot a good many miles from here, Mr. Roosevelt," said Sylvane, "who's bringin' a suit against you." Sylvane announced this unpleasant fact with careless gaiety, stretching his long legs toward the fire. No one was ever so typically the ideal cowboy of one's wildest fancy as was Sylvane Ferris. Tall and slender, with strong fair hair and blue eyes of an almost unnatural clearness, and a splendid broad brow and aquiline nose, Sylvane looked the part. His leather chaps, his broad sombrero hat, his red handkerchief knotted carelessly around his strong, young, sunburned throat, all made him such a picture that one's eye invariably followed him as he rode a vicious pony, "wrastled" a calf, roped a steer, or branded a heifer; but now sitting lazily by the fire, such activities seemed a thing of the past, and Sylvane was ready for an hour's gossip.

"A sky-pilot? Why should a sky-pilot bring suit against me?" said my brother laughingly. [In telling this story he sometimes referred to this man as a professor.]

"Well," said Sylvane, "it was this way, Mr. Roosevelt. You see, we was all outside the ranch door when up drives the sky-pilot in a buggy. He was one of them wanderin' ones that thought he could preach as he wandered, and just about as he drove up in front of our ranch his horse went dead lame on him and his old buggy just fell to pieces. He was in a bad fix, and he said he knew you never would let him be held up like that, because he had heard you was a good man too, and wouldn't we lend him a horse, or send him with the team to the next place he was going to, some forty miles away. We felt we had to be hospitable-like, with you so far away and the sky-pilot in such a fix, so we said 'Yes,' we would send him to where he wanted to go, and there he is now, lyin' in a hut with one leg broken and one arm nearly wrenched off his body, and he's bringin' suit against you, which ain't really fair, we think."

"What do you mean, Sylvane; what have I got to do with his broken leg and arm?" said my brother, beginning to feel a trifle nervous.

"Well, you see, it is this way," said Sylvane; "he says we sent him to where he is with a runaway team and he was thrown out and broken up in pieces-like; but we says how could that team we sent him with *be* a runaway team—how *could* a team be called a runaway team when one of the horses ain't never been hitched up before, and the other ain't run away not more'n two or three times; but I guess sky-pilots are always unreasonable!"

This conclusion seemed to satisfy Sylvane entirely; the unfortunate condition of the much-battered sky-pilot aroused no sympathy in his adamantine heart, nor did he feel that the sky-pilot had the slightest cause for his suit, which later was settled in a satisfactory manner, but the conversation was typical of that evening's ranch news by the big wood-fire.

Our day at the round-up was one of the most fascinating days of my life, and I was proud to see that my city-bred brother was as agile and as active in the duties of rounding up the great steers of the plains as were the men brought up from their babyhood to such activities. We lunched at midday with the round-up wagon; rough life, indeed, but wonderfully invigorating, and as we returned in the evening, galloping over the grassy plateaus of the high buttes, I realized fully that the bridle-path would never again have for me the charm it once had had. Nothing in the way of riding has ever been so enchanting, and the curious formation of the Bad Lands, picturesque, indeed, almost grotesque in line, in conjunction with the wonderful climate of that period of the year and the mingling of tints in the sunset sky, resulted in a quality of color and atmosphere the like of which I only remember in Egypt, and made as lasting an impression upon my memory as did the land of the Nile.

During our stay, my original failure to leap, on my arrival, "from the locomotive to the back of a bucking bronco" had more or less been effaced from the memory of the cowboys by subsequent adventures, and the last day that we spent under the cottonwood-trees, by the banks of the Little Missouri, was made significant by the "surprise" gotten up by Merrifield and Sylvane for the special edification of my brother and husband. The surprise took the form of the "wrastling" of a calf by no less a person than myself! Merrifield had taught me to rope an animal, Sylvane had shown me with praiseworthy regularity the method of throwing a calf, and the great occasion was heralded amongst the other members of the party by an invitation to sit on the fence of the corral at three o'clock, the last afternoon of our visit to Elkhorn, and thus witness the struggle between a young woman of the East and a bovine denizen of the Western prairies. The corral, a plot of very muddy ground (having been watered by a severe rain the night before), was walled in by a fence, and generally used when we wished to keep the ponies from straying. On this occasion, however, it was emptied of all *but* the calf, which was to be the object of my efforts and prowess. I was then introduced by Merrifield, very much as the circus rider used to be introduced in the early Barnum and Bailey days; then followed a most gruelling pantomime; the calf, which was of an unusually unpleasant size, galloped around the corral and I, knee-deep in mud, galloped after it, and finally succeeded in achieving the first necessity, which was to rope it around the neck. After that, the method of procedure was as follows: The "wrastler"—on this occasion my unfortunate self—was supposed to get close enough to the animal in question to throw himself or herself across the back of the galloping calf, with the purpose of catching the left leg of the animal, the leg, in fact, farthest away from one's right arm. If this deed could be accomplished and the leg forcibly bent under the calf, both calf and rider would go down in an inextricable heap, and the "wrastling" of the calf would be complete.

I can feel now the mud in my boots as I floundered with agonized effort after that energetic animal. I can still sense the strain in every nerve of my body as I finally flung myself across its back, and still, also, as if it were only yesterday, do I remember the jellied sensation within me, as for some torturing minutes I lay across the heifer's spine, before, by a final Herculean effort, I caught that left leg with my right arm. The cries of "stay with him!" from the fence, the loud hand-clapping of the enthusiastic cowboys, the shrieks of laughter of my brother and my husband, all still ring in my ears, and when the deed was finally accomplished, when the calf, with one terrible lurch, actually "wrastled," so to speak, fell over on its head in the mud, all sensation left me and I only remember being lifted up, bruised and encased in an armor of oozing dirt, and being carried triumphantly on the shoulders of the cowboys into the ranch-house, having redeemed, in their opinion, at least, the reputation which my brother had given me before I visited the Bad Lands.

Years later, when the young owner of Elkhorn Ranch had reached the higher estate of President of the United States, I, as the sister of the President, was receiving with my sister-in-law at the breakfast in the White House, at his Inaugural in 1905, and was attired in my best black velvet gown and "presidential sister" white plumes; I was surrounded by senators and ambassadors, when suddenly, coming toward me, I recognized the lithe figure of my brother's quondam cowboy, Will Merrifield. He, too, had climbed the rungs of the ladder of fame, and now, as marshal of Montana, he had been intrusted by the State of Montana with the greetings of that state for the newly inaugurated President. Coming toward me with a gay smile of recognition, he shook me warmly by the hand and said: "Well, now, Mrs. Douglas, it's a sight for sore eyes to see you again; why, almost the last time I laid eyes on you, you were standing on your head in that muddy corral with your legs waving in the air." Senators and ambassadors seemed somewhat surprised, but Will Merrifield and the President's sister shook hands gaily together, and reminisced over one of the latter's most thrilling life victories. But to return to our farewell to Elkhorn Ranch in 1890.

The three weeks' visit to the ranch-house had passed on fleet wings, and it was a very sad little party that turned its face toward Medora again, in preparation for the specially planned trip to Yellowstone Park. Theodore Roosevelt, as one may well imagine, was making a very real concession to family affection by arranging this trip for us and accompanying us upon it. What he loved was roughing it; near-roughing it was not his "métier," nor, frankly, was it his "métier" to arrange a *comfortable* trip of any kind. He loved wild places and wild companions, hard tramps and thrilling adventure, and to be a part of the type of trip which women who were not accustomed to actual hunting could take, was really an act of unselfishness on his part. We paid huge sums for no comforts, and although supposed to go—as we were riding—where the ordinary travellers in stage-coach could not go in Yellowstone Park, yet there *were* times when we seemed to be constantly camping in the vicinity of tomato cans!

I write again to my aunt two weeks after we start our Yellowstone experiences:

"We have had a most delightful two weeks' camping and have enjoyed every moment. The weather has been cloudless, and though the nights were cold, we were only really uncomfortable one night. We were all in the best of health and the best of spirits, and ate without a murmur the strange meals of ham, tomatoes, greasy cakes and coffee prepared by our irresistible Chinese cook. Breakfast and dinner were always the same, and lunch was generally bread and cheese carried in our pockets and eaten by the wayside. We have really had great comfort, however, and have enjoyed the pretense of roughing it and the delicious, free, open-air life hugely,—and such scenery! Nothing in my estimation can equal in unique beauty the Yellowstone canyon, the wonderful shapes of the rocks, some like peaks and turrets, others broken in strange fantastic jags, and then the marvellous colors of them all. Pale greens and yellows, vivid reds and orange, salmon pinks and every shade of brown are strewn with a lavish hand over the whole Canyon,—and the beautiful Falls are so foamy and white, and leap with such exultation from their rocky ledge 360 feet down.

"We had one really exciting ride. We had undertaken too long an expedition, namely, the ascent of Mt. Washburn, and then to Towers' Falls in one day, during which, to add to the complications, Edith had been thrown and quite badly bruised. We found ourselves at Towers' Falls at six o'clock in the evening instead of at lunch time, and realized we were still sixteen miles from Camp, and a narrow trail only to lead us back, a trail of which our guide was not perfectly sure. We galloped as long as there was light, but the sun soon set over the wonderful mountains, and although there was a little crescent moon, still, it soon grew very dark and we had to keep close behind each other, single file, and go very carefully as the trail lay along the mountainside. Often we had to traverse dark woods and trust entirely to the horses, who behaved beautifully and stepped carefully over the fallen logs. Twice, Dodge, our guide, lost the trail, and it gave one a very eerie feeling, but he found it again and on we went. Once at about 11 P. M., Theodore suggested stopping and making a great fire, and waiting until daylight to go on, for he was afraid that we would be tired out, but we all preferred to continue, and about 11:30, to our great joy, we heard the roar of the Falls and suddenly came out on the deep Canyon, looking very wonderful and mysterious in the dim starlight. We reached our Camp after twelve o'clock, having been fifteen hours away from it, thirteen and a half of which we had been in the saddle. It was really an experience."

It was a hazardous ride and I did not terrify my aunt by some of the incidents such as the severe discomfort suffered by Mrs. Theodore Roosevelt when she was thrown and narrowly escaped a broken back, and when a few hours later my own horse sank in a quicksand and barely recovered himself in time to struggle to terra firma again, not to mention the dangers of the utter darkness when the small, dim crescent moon faded from the horizon. My brother was the real leader of the cavalcade, for the guide, Ira Dodge, proved singularly incompetent. Theodore kept up our flagging spirits, exhausted as we were by the long rough day in the saddle, and although furious with Dodge because of his ignorance of the trail through which he was supposed to guide us, he still gave us the sense of confidence, which is one's only hope on such an adventure. Looking back over that camping trip in the Yellowstone, the prominent figure of the whole holiday was, of course, my brother. He was a boy in his tricks and teasing, crawling under the tent flaps at night, pretending to be the unexpected bear which we always dreaded.

He was a real inspiration in his knowledge of the fauna and birds of the vicinity and his willingness to give us the benefit of that knowledge.

I find in my diary of that excursion a catalogue of the birds and other animals which he himself had pointed out to me, making me marvel again at the rapid observation which he had made part of his physical equipment. I note: "During the first four days we have been in the Park, we have seen chipmunk, red squirrel, little black bear, elk watering with the horses, muskrat in the streams, golden eagle, Peregrine falcon and other varieties, red-tailed hawk and pigeon hawk, Clark's crow, Canada jay, raven, bittern, Canada goose, mallard and teal ducks, chicadee, nuthatch, dwarf-thrush, robin, water oozel, sunbird, longspur, grass finch, yellow-crowned warbler, Rocky Mountain white-throated sparrow, song-sparrow, and wren."

Each one of the above I saw with the eyes of Theodore Roosevelt, and can still hear the tones of his voice as he described to me their habits of life and the differences between them and others of their kind. To him this trip must, of necessity, have been somewhat dull, based as it was upon the companionship of three women who were not hunters; but never once during those weeks did he seem anything but happy, and as far as we were concerned, to see the beauties of nature through those ardent eyes, to hear the bird-notes through those ears, attuned to each song, and to listen constantly to his stories of wood and plain, his interpretation of the lives of those mighty pioneer men of the West—all of this comes back to me, as a rare experience which I have gladly stored away in what Emerson calls "the amber of memory." How we laughed over the strange rules and regulations of the park! Fierce bears were trapped, but could not be killed without the kind permission of one of the secretaries in Washington, the correspondence on the subject affording my brother infinite amusement. *His* methods under like circumstances would have been so very different!

The experiences at Elkhorn Ranch and again in the Yellowstone Park were of special benefit to me from the standpoint of the comprehension which they gave me of the absolute sympathy which my brother felt both with the nature and the human nature of the great West. No period of the life of Theodore Roosevelt seems to me quite as important, in the influence which it was to bear upon his future usefulness to his country, as was that period in which, as man to man, he shared the vigorous work and pastimes of the men of that part of our country. Had he not actually lived the life not only of the hunter and cattleman, but had he not taken actual part as sheriff in the methods of government of that part of our country, he would never have been able to interpret the spirit of the West as he did. He would never have been recognized *as* such an interpreter, and when the time came that America could no longer look from an uninterested distance at the Spanish iniquities in Cuba, the fact that Theodore Roosevelt had become so prominent a figure in the West proved the essential factor in the flocking to his standard of that mass of virile manhood which, under his leadership, and that of the then army doctor, Leonard Wood, became the picturesque, well-known "Rough Rider" Volunteer Cavalry of the Spanish-American War.

At Elkhorn Ranch, also, the long silences and stretches of solitude had much to do with the mental growth of the young man. There he read and wrote and thought deeply. His old guide Bill Sewall was asked not long since about his opinion of my brother as a religious man. His answer was as follows: "I think he read the Bible a great deal. I never saw him in formal prayer, but as prayer is the desire of the heart, I think he prayed without ceasing, for the desire of his heart was always to do right." Thus, sharing the hardships and the joys of their primitive life with his comrades of the West, the young rancher became an integral part of that country, which never failed to rouse in him the spirit of high adventure and romance.

Theodore Roosevelt, himself, in a letter to John Hay, written long after our visit to his ranch and our gay excursion to the

Yellowstone, describes the men of that part of the world. He was taking an extended trip, as President, in 1903, on the first part of which journey Mr. Hay had accompanied him, and at Oyster Bay, on his return, he writes to his secretary of state in order to give him further details of the trip:

"From Washington, I turned southward, and when I struck northern Montana, again came to my old stamping grounds and among my old friends. I met all kinds of queer characters with whom I had hunted and worked and slept and sometimes fought. From Helena, I went southward to Butte, reaching that city in the afternoon of May 27th. By this time, Seth Bullock had joined us, together with an old hunting friend, John Willis, a Donatello of the Rocky Mountains,—wholly lacking, however, in that morbid self-consciousness which made Hawthorne's 'faun' go out of his head because he had killed a man. Willis and I had been in Butte some seventeen years before, at the end of a hunting trip in which we got dead broke, so that when we struck Butte, we slept in an outhouse and breakfasted heartily in a two-bit Chinese restaurant. Since then I had gone through Butte in the campaign of 1900, the major part of the inhabitants receiving me with frank hostility, and enthusiastic cheers for Bryan.

"However, Butte is mercurial, and its feelings had changed. The wicked, wealthy, hospitable, full-blooded, little city, welcomed me with wild enthusiasm of a disorderly kind. The mayor, Pat Mullins, was a huge, good-humored creature, wearing, for the first time in his life, a top hat and a frock coat, the better to do honor to the President.

"National party lines counted very little in Butte where the fight was Heinze and anti-Heinze, Ex-Senator Carter and Senator Clark being in the opposition. Neither side was willing to let the other have anything to do with the celebration, and they drove me wild with their appeals, until I settled that the afternoon parade and speech was to be managed by the Heinze group of people, and the evening speech by the anti-Heinze people; and that the dinner should contain fifty of each faction and should be presided over in his official capacity by the mayor. The ordinary procession, in barouches, was rather more exhilarating than usual, and reduced the faithful secret service men very nearly to the condition of Bedlamites. The crowd was filled with whooping enthusiasm and every kind of whiskey, and in their desire to be sociable, broke the lines and jammed right up to the carriage. . . . Seth Bullock, riding close beside the rear wheel of my carriage, for there were hosts of so-called 'rednecks' or 'dynamiters' in the crowd, was such a splendid looking fellow with his size and supple strength, his strangely marked aquiline face, with its big moustache, and the broad brim of his soft dark hat drawn down over his dark eyes. However, no one made a motion to attack me. . . .

"My address was felt to be honor enough for one hotel, so the dinner was given in the other. When the dinner was announced, the Mayor led me in!—to speak more accurately, tucked me under one arm and lifted me partially off the ground so that I felt as if I looked like one of those limp dolls with dangling legs, carried around by small children, like Mary Jane in the 'Gollywogs,' for instance. As soon as we got in the banquet hall and sat at the end of the table, the Mayor hammered lustily with the handle of his knife and announced, 'Waiter, bring on the feed.' Then, in a spirit of pure kindliness, 'Waiter, pull up the curtains and let the people see the President eat';—but to this, I objected. The dinner was soon in full swing, and it was interesting in many respects. Besides my own party, including Seth Bullock and Willis, there were fifty men from each of the Butte factions.

"In Butte, every prominent man is a millionaire, a gambler, or a labor leader, and generally he has been all three. Of the hundred men who were my hosts, I suppose at least half had killed their man in private war or had striven to compass the assassination of an enemy. They had fought one another with reckless ferocity. They had been allies and enemies in every kind of business scheme, and companions in brutal revelry. As they drank great goblets of wine, the sweat glistened on their hard, strong, crafty faces. They looked as if they had come out of the pictures in Aubrey Beardsley's Yellow Book. The millionaires had been laboring men once, the labor leaders intended to be millionaires in their turn, or else to pull down all who were. They had made money in mines, had spent it on the races, in other mines or in gambling and every form of vicious luxury, but they were strong men for all that. They had worked, and striven, and pushed, and trampled, and had always been ready, and were ready now, to fight to the death in many different kinds of conflicts. They had built up their part of the West, they were men with whom one had to reckon if thrown in contact with them. . . . But though most of them hated each other, they were accustomed to take their pleasure when they could get it, and they took it fast and hard with the meats and wines."

The above description by the pen of my brother is the most vivid that could be given of a certain type of man of the West. The types were many. . . . The Sylvane Ferrises and the Will Merrifields were as bold and resourceful as these inhabitants of the city of Butte and its vicinity, but for the former, life was an adventure in which the spirit of beauty and kindness had its share in happy contrast to the aims and objects of the men described by my brother in this extraordinary pen-picture. The picture is so forcibly painted that it brings before one's mind, almost as though it were an actual stage-setting, this type of American, who would appear to be a belated brother of the men of the barbaric period of the Middle Ages in the Old World, in their case, however, rendered even more formidable by a New World enterprise and acumen, strangely unlike what has ever been produced before.

It was because of his knowledge of just such men, and of the fact that they knew, although his aims were so different and his ideals so alien to theirs, that the courage of his mental and physical equipment could meet them on their own ground, that

Theodore Roosevelt was respected and admired, although sometimes hated, by this type of humanity so opposed to the goals, actual and spiritual, for which he worked so faithfully during his whole valiant existence. They knew him for what he was, and feared him for the qualities which he possessed in common with them, and even more for the traits that they did not understand, and which, to them, made him inevitably and forever "The Mysterious Stranger."

VII

TWO RECREANT NEW YORK POLICEMEN

Who serves her truly, sometimes saves the state.
—Arthur Hugh Clough.

There is sprung up a light for the righteous; and joyful gladness for such as are true-hearted.—97th Psalm.

THE years between 1890 and 1896 were busy years, with devoted service as Civil Service Commissioner, winters at Washington and happy summers at Oyster Bay, when Theodore Roosevelt gave himself up to family joy and the activities of the growing children. In 1893 he writes most lovingly of my children and his—his never-failing sympathy in all the minor illnesses of my little family, expressed in the most affectionate terms, and the common sorrow which we both suffered in the loss of our devoted aunt, Mrs. James Gracie, fills many pages during those years. We met frequently during the summer-time, and when we met he shared with me his many Washington experiences, but the letters are largely to show me his loving interest in the many details of my family life.

In August, however, he goes a little more fully into some matters of public interest, and writes: "For the last fortnight, I have virtually been living with Cabot, for I take all my meals at his house, though I sleep at my own. [Mrs. Roosevelt and the children were at Oyster Bay.] After breakfast, an hour spent by Cabot and myself in gloomy discussion over the folly of the Mug-wumps and the wickedness of the Democrats, I go to the office and work until four or five o'clock, most of my work taking the light but not always agreeable shape of a succession of interviews of varying asperity with Congressmen; then I go to gruff old Olney's and play tennis with him and any other stray statesman, diplomat or military personage whom he has captured for an hour or two. Sometimes, Cabot and I dine alone; more often, we have in one or two of our cronies such as Tom Reed or Senator Davis of Minnesota. . . . I think the tariff deadlock will break in a day or two, when I shall be left alone here with so much work on hand, however, that I fear I shall not get away until the end of the month, when I shall go back to Sagamore and Edith and the blessed bunnies."

The intimacy with Senator Lodge, the charm of his library, where tradition and intellect always held sway, were amongst the most delightful associations that Washington gave to my brother during the many years spent there, both before the days of the White House and later under its roof.

Late in August of that year my brother Elliott died. My brother Theodore came to me at once and we did together the things always so hard to do connected with the death of those we love, and he writes me afterward: "The sadness has been tempered by something very sweet when I think of the way I was with you, my own darling sister." The quality of sharing, which, as I always say, was one of his most marked attributes, never showed more unselfishly than in times of sorrow. Almost immediately after the above letter, he encloses to me a clipping from the newspaper of Abingdon, Va., about my brother Elliott, who had lived there for some time in connection with the property of my husband in the Virginia mountains. No one, not even my brother Theodore himself, was ever more loved by those with whom he came in contact than was the "Ellie" of the early days in 20th Street, and later wherever he went he found rare and devoted friendship. *The Virginian* (the name of the Abingdon paper) says:

"The New York papers announce the death of Mr. Elliott Roosevelt. This gentleman has been a member of this community for the past two years, and although his stay was so brief, it was long enough for him to make his impress as a whole-souled, genial gentleman, courteous and kind at all times, with an ever ready cheer for the enterprising or help to the weak. His name was a byword among the needy, and his charities were always as abundant as they were unostentatious. He was public spirited and generous, this much we can truthfully say. His influence and his aid will be missed, and more frequently than is generally known among those to whom it was a boon."

After speaking of the enclosure, my brother continues: "My thoughts keep hovering around you, my darling sister, for I know how you loved Elliott; what a gallant, generous, manly boy he was. So many memories come back to me."

In 1895 he had been appointed police commissioner, and was already in the thick of the hard fight to reform the Police Department. He writes in August of that year: "Governor Hill and I have had two savage tilts. I have not the slightest idea of the ultimate results of our move on the excise question, but we have made a good fight against heavy odds." Perhaps, of all the pieces of work done by my brother, none stands out more clearly than the splendid achievement of remaking the Police Department into a fine working body, for which the whole city of New York had the utmost respect, and on which it leaned for safety and protection. I have but few letters from him during that period, for, much to our delight, he was once more in our midst, and many and many a time would I go down to the old Vienna bakery on the corner of 10th Street and Broadway, and he would come from Mulberry Street, where his office was, and together we would sit over the type of lunch he loved so well: either bread and milk or a squab and *café au lait*. I can still see Senator Lodge's expression when he joined us on one of these simple occasions, and asked in a somewhat saturnine manner whether any one *could get* a respectable lunch at the place we loved so well! What talks we had there over all the extraordinary situations that arose in the Police Department. There he described to me the delicious humor of the parade inaugurated by the German brewer societies as a protest against his enforcement of the law. They were parading to show their disapproval of him, but at the last moment, as a wonderful piece of sarcasm, they decided to invite him to review the parade, hardly thinking that he would accept the invitation. Needless to say, he *did* accept it, and leaning over from the platform where he had been invited to sit, he saw the mass of marching men carrying banners with "Down with Teddy," and various other more unpleasant expletives. One company, as it passed the reviewing-stand, called out: "Wo ist Teddy?" "Hier bin ich," called out the police commissioner, leaning over the railing and flashing his white teeth good-humoredly at the protesting crowd, who, unable to resist the sunshine of his personality, suddenly turned and, putting aside the disapproving banners, cheered him to the echo.

It was during that same time, the story ran, that two recreant policemen who left their beats at an inopportune moment were called to the realization of their misdemeanor by coming face to face, in a glass window-case, with a set of false teeth which, they explained, grinned at them with a ferocity so reminiscent of the strong molars of the police commissioner, that they almost fainted at the sight, and hastily returned to their forsaken duties. Many and many a settlement-worker told me in those days that they could go anywhere in the most dangerous parts of the city, during the administration of Theodore Roosevelt, and the police were always on hand, always ready to protect those who needed their care.

At that time also I was amused one day when he told me the story about his little Irish stenographer, a young girl whose knowledge of orthography was less than her sympathetic interest in the affairs of the police commissioner! He took a warm interest in the nice young Irish girl, hard worker as she was, an important factor in the support of a large family of younger children, and could not bear to dismiss her from his service, in spite of her alarming mistakes in spelling. He said he always had to look over her manuscript and correct it in spite of his many other cares, and he laughingly remarked that it was well he did, as having dictated the following sentence in connection with a certain policeman, "I was obliged to restrain the virtuous ardor of Sergeant Murphy, who, in his efforts to bring about a state of quiet on the streets, would frequently commit some assault himself," the young Irish stenographer, listening to the rapid dictation, spelled "some assault" "somersault," and, as my brother remarked, one could not but laugh at the thought of Sergeant Murphy performing somersaults like a circus clown on Mulberry Street, and, fortunately, the word caught the ever-watchful eye of the police commissioner before the report was printed, and, even in spite of the inconvenience, he set himself to work to improve the young stenographer's mistaken orthographic efforts.

In spite of his busy days and busy nights, he had time, as usual, to write to me when he thought that I needed his care or interest. I was far from well at the time, but was obstinately determined to go up to visit my boys at St. Paul's School, and he writes me: "Won't you let Douglas and me go up to St. Paul's, and you stay at home? If you will do this, I shall positively go for anniversary on June 2nd. I believe you should not go on these trips whether for pleasure or duty, and should take more care of yourself. Your loving and anxious brother."

He himself has given in his autobiography many incidents connected with his police commissionership.

The force were devoted to him, as were his Rough Riders later, largely on account of the justice with which he treated them, and the friendly attitude which he always maintained toward them. Otto Raphael, a young Jew, and a young Irishman called Burke were two of the men whom he promoted because of unusual bravery, and their loyalty and admiration followed him unswervingly. On the sad day when he was carried to the little cemetery at Oyster Bay, Burke—now Captain Burke—had been put in charge of the police arrangements for the funeral. As he stood by the grave, the captain turned to me, the tears streaming down his face but with a smile in his blue Irish eyes, and said: "Do you remember the fun of him, Mrs. Robinson? It was not only that he was a great man, but oh, there was such fun in being led by him. I remember one day when he was governor, and I was in charge of him, and I was riding by the side of his carriage down Madison Avenue, and he suddenly stuck his head out of the window and, 'Burke,' said he, 'we are just going to pass my sister's house. I want to get out and say "how do you do" to my sister.' 'I don't think you have time, governor,' I said, 'I am afraid you are late now.' 'Oh, now, Burke, I want you to meet my sister. Get somebody to hold your horse,' he said; 'it won't take a minute.' And with that he leaped out of his carriage and was ringing the front door-bell in a flash. I followed him and I heard him call out to you, Mrs. Robinson, that he had his friend Lieut. Burke with him, and could he bring him up-stairs to shake hands, and sure enough he did, and when I went down-stairs again I heard him telling you some story, and the two of you were laughing fit to kill. When I got back that night to my wife, I said: 'Susan, if you are ever downhearted, all you have to do is to go up to 422 Madison Avenue when the governor stops to see his sister, and hear them laugh.' "

The commissionership was a big job well done, and the city of New York could not but feel a sense of great regret when President McKinley promoted the active young commissioner to be assistant secretary of the navy in 1897. It was his pride and one of his greatest satisfactions in later years to feel that he was instrumental in preparing our navy for the war with Spain. For many years he had been convinced that the Spanish rule in Cuba should not continue; and the condition in Cuba, he felt, was too intertwined with the affairs of the United States to be differentiated from them. In the days of President Cleveland, my brother had felt that action should be taken, and in the same way he was convinced that Mr. McKinley was only putting off the evil day by not facing the situation earlier in his incumbency.

As was the case in almost every crisis which arose, either national or international, during my brother's life, he seemed to have a prescience of the future, and, therefore, he almost invariably—sometimes before other public men were awake to the contingency—sensed the need of taking steps to avert or meet difficulties which he felt sure would soon have to be faced.

The young assistant secretary of the navy was not very popular with the administration on account of the views which he felt it his duty honestly to express. On March 6, 1898, he writes to my husband: "Neither I nor anyone else, not even the President can do more than guess. We are certainly drifting towards and not away from war, but the President will not make war, and will keep out of it if he possibly can. Nevertheless, with so much loose powder around, a coal may hop into it at any moment. In a week or two, I believe, we shall get that report. If it says the explosion was due to outside work, it will be very hard to hold the country. [He refers to the blowing up of the battleship *Maine* in Havana harbor.] But the President undoubtedly will try peaceful means even then, at least, at first."

At the time of the writing of that letter, Mrs. Theodore Roosevelt had been very ill and was still very delicate, and my brother had not only the many worries of the department in which he was working, as he himself puts it, "like a fiend, for we have serious matters ahead," but he also had the great anxiety of her condition on his heart. On the 28th of March: "I have been working up to the handle here, and have about all I can do on hand now. I have very strong convictions on this crisis, convictions which, I fear, do not commend themselves to my official superiors." And again on April 2, 1898, he writes in full to my husband, who was always one of his most welcome advisers:

Navy Department, April 2, 1898.

Dear Old Man:

In one way I was very much pleased at receiving your letter, for it shows the thoughtfulness and affection you always feel for me. In another way your letter makes it very hard for me. All my friends have written me as you have, and yet I am convinced that you are all wrong. Do not misunderstand me. It may well be that I can't get down with an Expeditionary force even if, as I think unlikely, an Expeditionary force is started before next fall. Indeed I think I shall probably have to stay here, and I should certainly stay here until we got a successor broken in. But if I get a fair chance to go, or could make a fair chance, I conscientiously feel that I ought to go. My usefulness in my present position is mainly a usefulness in time of peace, because in time of peace the naval officers cannot speak freely to the Secretary and I can and do, both to the Secretary and President, even at the cost of jeopardizing my place. But in time of war the naval officers will take their proper positions as military advisers, and my usefulness would be at an end. I should simply be one of a number of unimportant bureau chiefs. If I went I shouldn't expect to win any military glory, or at the utmost to do more than feel I had respectably performed my duty; but I think I would be quite as useful in the Army as here, and it does not seem to me that it would be honorable for a man who has consistently advocated a warlike policy not to be willing himself to bear the brunt of carrying out that policy. I have a horror of the people who bark but don't bite. If I am ever to accomplish anything worth doing in politics, or ever have accomplished it, it is because I act up to what I preach, and it does not seem to me that I would have the right in a big crisis not to act up to what I preach. At least I want you to believe that I am doing this conscientiously and not from merely selfish reasons, or from an impulse of levity.

I shall answer Corinne in a day or two. April 13th I was to have been in Boston, but if we have trouble, I, of course, can't get away. I hope Corinne will stay over the following Sunday, so I may have a good chance to see her.

Faithfully yours.

The above is a most characteristic letter. Those who were nearest to him, like myself and my husband, and even Senator Lodge, were doubtful of his wisdom in leaving his important position (I mean important for the affairs of the country, not for himself) as assistant secretary of the navy to take active part in the war, should war come, but he himself knew quite well that being made of the fibre that he was, he must act up to what he had preached. Nothing is more absolutely Theodore Roosevelt, was ever more thoroughly Theodore Roosevelt, than that sentence. "I have a horror of the people who bark but don't bite. If I am ever to accomplish anything worth doing in politics, or ever have accomplished it, it is because I act up to what I preach, and it does not seem to me that I would have the right in a big crisis not to act up to what I preach. At least I want you to believe that I am doing this conscientiously and not from merely selfish reasons or from an impulse of levity." No sentence ever written by my brother more fitly expressed his attitude toward conviction and acting up to conviction.

VIII

COWBOY AND CLUBMAN

A RHYME OF THE ROUGH RIDERS

The ways of fate they had trod were as wide
As the sea from the shouting sea,
But when they had ranged them side by side,
Strenuous, eager, and ardent-eyed,
They were brothers in pluck, they were brothers in pride,
As the veriest brethren be.

They heard no bugle-peal to thrill
As they crouched in the tangled grass,
But the sound of bullets whirring shrill
From hidden hollow and shrouded hill;
And they fought as only the valiant will
In the glades of Guasimas.

Aye, they fought, let their blood attest!—
The blood of their comrades gone;
Fought their bravest and fought their best,
As when, like a wave, in their zealous zest
They swept and surged o'er the sanguine crest
Of the heights of San Juan.

So here's to them all—a toast and a cheer!—
From the greatest down to the least,
The heroes who fronted the deadliest fear,
Leader and lad, each volunteer,
The men whom the whole broad land holds dear
From the western sea to the east!

—Clinton Scollard, 1898.

THOSE April days of 1898 in Washington were full of an underlying current of excitement. Drifting toward war we certainly were, and within a very short few weeks the drift had become a fixed headway, and Captain Dewey, on the receipt of a certain telegram from a certain acting secretary of the navy, was to enter Manila Bay, and by that entrance, and by the taking of Cavite, to change forever the policy of the United States. Theodore Roosevelt had been criticised for the amount of ammunition used in practice by the gunners of the navy during the past spring. He knew only too well that the real extravagance in either army or navy comes from lack of foresight, and the fine marksmanship of the sailors and marines was to prove a feather in the cap of the young assistant secretary.

Everything was bustle and hurry toward the end of April. Within a few days the assistant secretary was to become the lieutenant-colonel of the Rough Riders, or, as they were at first called, The First U. S. Volunteer Cavalry. Mr. McKinley offered to Mr. Roosevelt the colonelcy of the regiment, but he, with modesty and intelligence, refused the offer, knowing that he was not as well fitted by experience for the position as was his friend, Mr. McKinley's physician, that gallant surgeon in the army, Leonard Wood, who had had as a younger man so much experience in the campaign against Geronimo. The two young men, within a year of each other in age, had been friends for some time, having many tastes in common, and the same stalwart attitude of unswerving Americanism. Their friendship had been cemented during the spring of 1898 by the fact that they felt that their views in connection with the mistakes of Spain in Cuba were very sympathetic. On the long tramps which they took together on those spring afternoons, they discussed the all-important question over and over again, and also discussed the possibility of raising a regiment of men from the fearless, hardy cowboys and backwoodsmen of the West. It was no sooner known that Leonard Wood and Theodore Roosevelt were about to raise a regiment to go to Cuba than every sort and kind of individual flocked to their standard. The mobilization of the regiment took place in San Antonio, Texas.

My brother writes to me on May 5, 1898, from Washington: "You could not give me a more useful present than the watch. It was exactly what I wished. Thank old Douglas too, for the watch and for his many many kindnesses. I hope to leave to-morrow, but Wood, who is now in San Antonio, may keep me here a day or two longer to hurry up the shipment of the troops, rifles, etc. I much want to get with the regiment to help get it into shape, but there will be many tedious and irritating delays, of course. I have about twenty-five 'gentlemen rankers' going with me from the Knickerbocker Club, and twelve clean-cut stalwart young fellows from Harvard,—such fine boys. I feel rather like a fake at going, for we may never get down to Cuba at all, and if we do, I do not think we shall see very serious campaigning, while proper care will prevent the serious risk of disease."

And again on May 8:

"Kenneth turned up just in time. [Referring to my husband's young Scotch cousin, Kenneth Douglas Robinson, associated with my husband in business, who was confident that he was doing the right thing to follow his hero, Theodore Roosevelt, into the Spanish War.] I enlisted him and sent him off with Bob Ferguson [another Scotch friend] and the rest. . . ."

And again on May 12, after I had sent him a poem, he writes:

"My own darling sister:—I loved tne poem and I loved your dear letter; it made me sure that you really knew just how I felt about going. I *could not* stay; that was the sum and substance of it;—although I realize well how hard it is for Edith, and what a change for the worse it means in my after life. It will be bitter if we do not get to Cuba, but we shall have to take things as they come. Your own brother."

I had doubted whether it was his duty to go to Cuba, feeling it might be even more his duty to remain in his important and difficult position of assistant secretary of the navy, but Theodore Roosevelt would not have been his true self unless he had practised what he had preached so vigorously.

Kenneth Robinson writes on May 17 from San Antonio:

"Theodore has been drilling us the last few days. The men always do their best when he is out. He would be amused indeed if he heard some of the adjectives and terms applied to him, meant to be most complimentary but hardly fit for publication. We certainly are a curious aggregation,—cavalry men, cowboys, college men, etc."

And Bob Ferguson, our very dear friend who had made America his home, and was like a member of our family, writes early in June:

"You should see some of the broncho busting that has been going on daily in camp;—the most surprising horsemanship, and though it cost about a man a day at first, knocked clean out, the busted-rate is now diminishing. The men, as you can imagine, are well satisfied with their commanders; Theodore has a great hold on them, and before long he will be able to do anything he likes with them. The Army officers said they had never seen such a body of men. One of the troops from Arizona came almost entirely from one large ranch; they all know each other and will fight shoulder to shoulder. Our own troop—'K' was rather a gay affair at first, a little gang of Fifth Avenue 'Dudes' having constituted themselves as leaders before Theodore arrived, but now it has a large number of first rate cow-punchers and sheriffs drafted into it, and has been increased one-third beyond its normal strength. We are more or less intelligent, and are looked to as the possible crack troop."

It is interesting to look back and remember that that Company "K" was indeed a "crack troop," and the writer of the above lines became one of its most gallant officers. What a body of men they were! The romance of mediæval days was reborn in that regiment, and the strange part of it all was that they had so much of chivalry about them, in spite of the roughness of the cowboys, in spite of the madness of the bronco-busters, in spite, perhaps, of another type of madness injected into the regiment by the Fifth Avenue "Dudes"; still, that body of men, as a whole, stood out for gallantry and courage, and gentleness of spirit wherever gentleness of spirit was needed in the hard days to come. There was a poem written at that time "The Yankee Dude'll Do," and I remember the little thrill with which I read it, realizing how the names that up to that time had been connected with rather gay and useless lives became bywords for hard, persistent work "to make" good in the various companies.

Theodore himself writes to me on June 7 in camp near Tampa, Florida:

"First Regiment, U. S. Volunteer Cavalry.

"We are on the point of embarking for Cuba. Yesterday I thought I was going to be left, and would have to stay on this side during the first expedition for they intended to take but four troops. Now, however, they intend to take eight, and unless the transports give out, I shall go. I need not say how rejoiced I am, for I could not help feeling very bitterly when it seemed that I would be left. This really is a fine regiment, and Count Von Goetzen and Capt. Lee, the German and English Military Attachés, watched our gun drill yesterday in camp with General Sumner, and all three expressed what seemed to be sincere astonishment and pleasure at the rapidity with which we had got the men into shape. I wish you could see how melancholy the four troops that remain behind feel; it is very hard on them. I had the last two squadrons under my care on the harassing journey on the cars and it was no slight labor. How I would like to have Douglas as an officer in this regiment with me. He would take to it just as I do.

"Well, if our hopes are realized, we sail tomorrow for Cuba, but nobody can tell how many of us will get back, and I don't suppose there is much glory ahead, but I hope and believe we shall do our duty, and the home-coming will be very very pleasant for those who do come home."

How my heart ached as I read those last words and realized that the chances, in all probability, were strongly against his coming home again.

On June 12:

On board U. S. Transport *Yucatan.*

Darling Corinne:

I suppose it is simply the ordinary fortune of war for the most irritating delays to happen, but it seems to me that the people at Washington are inexcusable for putting us aboard ship and keeping us crowded to suffocation on these transports for six days in Tampa Harbor, in a semi-tropical sun. The men take it with great resolution and good humour, but if we are kept here much longer, it cannot fail to have a bad effect upon them. We have been dismounted, but I care nothing for that if only we are sent, and given a chance to get into the game. I wish you could see or could have seen us at some of the crises when, for instance, we spent all night standing up opposite a railway track, waiting for a train to come, and finally taking coal cars in the morning.

On the 14th he writes to my husband:

"We are about to sail and as we are at the mouth of the harbor, it is hardly likely that we can be recalled. . . . It has been most interesting even when the work was irritating and full of worry. The regiment is a wonderful body of men and they have taken to discipline with astonishing readiness and are wild with eager enthusiasm. Those of us who come out of it safe will be bound together all our lives by a very strong tie. You may rest assured I haven't the slightest idea of taking any risk I don't feel I absolutely must take."

There was no doubt of the strong tie that bound the Rough Riders, as they were later called, together. We always teased my brother when, as President, he would suddenly announce that "Happy Jack of Arizonia," or some such erstwhile comrade, was eminently fitted for a position for which the aforesaid "Happy Jack" did not seem to have strong qualifications. How they loved their leader, and how that love was returned! Whenever my brother spoke of his "regiment" a note of tenderness came into his voice such as might be heard in the voice of a woman when speaking of her lover.

That same day, June 14, Bob Ferguson wrote to me:

"Theodore is absolutely radiating. He just lent me 'Vanity Fair' in return for a box of peppermints, and it has been queer just at this moment to read about old Curzon street and the Brussels' Ball; but Becky made us laugh more than ever after reading nothing but Tactics or a local newspaper for several weeks. . . . This country is becoming the laughing-stock of the world at present, and the German experts really do not believe the United States can fight. It will bring on big world complications unless they show their power soon."

The above opinion is interesting in the light of what the German experts again felt about the United States before we entered the Great War in 1917!

On June 15 a letter dated in the Gulf of Mexico runs as follows:

"We are steaming southward through a sapphire sea, wind-rippled under an almost cloudless sky. There are some forty-eight craft in all, in three columns,—the black hulls of the transports setting off the gray hull of the man-of-war. Last evening, we stood up on the bridge and watched the red sun sink and lights blaze up on the ships for miles ahead, while the band played piece after piece from the Star Spangled Banner (at which we all rose and stood uncovered) to The Girl I Left Behind Me. It is a great historical expedition and I thrill to feel that I am part of it. If we fail, of course, we share the fate of all who do fail, and if we are allowed to succeed, for we certainly shall succeed if allowed, we have scored the first great triumph of what will be a world movement. All the young fellows have dimly felt what this means, though the only articulate soul and imagination among them belong, rather curiously, to Ex-sheriff Capt. Buckey O'Neil of Arizona."

The above Buckey O'Neil, leaning over the rail at sunset, would often quote Browning, my brother used to tell me, or

Whitman, or even Shelley. He was a real "Bret Harte" character, and one of my brother's greatest griefs in the days to come was that that gallant officer was amongst the first to fall. He had just exposed himself to Spanish fire somewhat unnecessarily, and my brother said to him: "Get down, Buckey; I cannot spare you." The other laughingly replied, "There isn't a bullet made that can kill me, Colonel," and literally, as he spoke, a stray shot struck him and he fell dead across my brother's knees. But to return:

June 20, 1898—Troop Ship near Santiago.

All day we have steamed close to the Cuban coast; high barren-looking mountains rise abruptly from the shore, and at this distance look much like those of Montana. We are well within the tropics and at night, the Southern Cross is low above the horizon. It seems too strange to see it in the same sky with the friendly Dipper.

And then later:

June 25, 1898—Las Guasimas—

Yesterday we struck the Spaniards and had a brisk fight for two and a half hours before we drove them out of their position. We lost twelve men, killed or mortally wounded, and sixty, severely or slightly wounded. Brodie was wounded,—poor Capron and Ham Fish were killed; one man was killed as he stood beside a tree with me, another bullet went through a tree behind which I stood and filled my eyes with bark. The last charge I led on the left using a rifle I took from a wounded man. Every man behaved well; there was no flinching. The fire was very hot at one or two points where the men around me went down like nine-pins. We have been ashore three days and were moved at once to the front without our baggage. I have been sleeping on the ground in a mackintosh, and so drenched with sweat that I have not been dry a minute day and night. The marches have been very severe. One of my horses was drowned swimming through the surf. It was a fierce fight; the Spaniards shot well, but they did not stand when we rushed.

We received the details of the fight of Las Guasimas on the 4th of July, I remember, and all night long I sat on my piazza on Orange Mountain, thinking, with a strange horror, of the danger in which my brother had been and still was.

On June 27, 1898, another letter, this time dated Santiago:

"We have a lovely camp here by a beautiful stream which runs through jungle-land banks. The morning after the fight, we buried our dead in a great big trench, reading the solemn burial service over them, and all the regiment joined in singing 'Rock of Ages.' The woods are full of land crabs, some of which are almost as big as rabbits; when things grew quiet, they slowly gathered in gruesome rings around the fallen."

Bob Ferguson also adds interesting evidence to the courage of the First Volunteer Cavalry under fire.

Las Guasimas—June 25, 1898.

Theodore and Wood are more than delighted with the conduct of the men. You never heard such a hail of shot. The enemy, of course, knew when we would be in the jungle, and we could only guess their whereabouts. Their volleys opened up from all directions. Theodore did great work skipping from one troop to another, and directed them as they were deployed, but we can only trust that this kind of thing won't happen too often, for fear of results. It was, in fact, a surprise party, however, an expected one. Our men rushed into a known ambush with the careless dash of the cow-puncher. Once in, they literally had to hug the ground while the trees above and beside them were torn to shreds. . . . Theodore has marked the Spaniard all right—and the name of his regiment will never be spoken of any too lightly. They really did not understand fear and would willingly repeat the dose tomorrow. Poor Ham Fish,—

he was such a good-hearted, game fellow, and I got to like him ever so much on the way down;—it is more than much now!— The Spaniards showed any amount of skill in their tactics, and only the extraordinary grit of our men undid their calculation, together with the good work of a parallel column of Regulars, who cleared the Spaniards off a flanking ridge in the forest in the finest style—otherwise they could have out-flanked us on either side and given us Hell in open sight. So far, it seems like fighting an army of invisible Pigmies. . . . Kenneth was awfully good yesterday after the fight. He was the first to volunteer to help the wounded when the entire troop was too exhausted to move;—he carried them for hours until his back gave out. . . . We really did splendidly yesterday. The Regulars are to have their turn now. We have been blooded ourselves. We lost too many officers. One little fellow, shot right through both hips, was the greatest little sport. He refused to be attended to until others were made comfortable, and he lay and smoked his pipe patiently. One man walked to the hospital with five wounds:—in the neck, right shoulder, right hand, left thigh, and one other.

It is a matter of interest to print the above extracts, for even when my brother wrote his book called "The Rough Riders," he could not give quite the spirit which the letters, penned at the moment of the happenings, can so fitly interpret. Bob Ferguson again, on July 5, gave an important description of my brother:

Before Santiago, July 5, 1898.

We have been having the devil of a fine time of it, shooting Spaniards, and being "stormed at by shot and shell." When I caught up with Theodore, the day of his famous charge, (having been held in the reserve line until tired of being pelted at from a distance) "T" was revelling in victory. He had just "doubled up" a Spanish officer like a jack-rabbit, as he retreated from a block house. . . . That same evening, having reached the most advanced crest possible, with about 300 men, and having the whole Spanish Army firing at us from their entrenchments around the city, the summit of our ambition was almost reached.

Theodore moved about in the midst of shrapnel explosions like Shadrach, Meschach & Sons in the midst of the fiery furnace, unharmed by the vicious Mauser balls or by the buzzing exploding bullets of the Irregulars. . . . Theodore preferred to stand up or walk about snuffing the fragrant air of combat. I really believe firmly now, that they cannot kill him. It looks, too, somewhat as if they would not get a chance for a spell, for our lines are around the Spanish Dog's throat, and he will be smothered by our fire in a moment should the fight open once more. It would seem a shame now to have to damage them any more, for they say the streets are full of wounded and spent balls shower among them. . . . Theodore has sure made his mark on the Spaniard,—and the Rough Riders [the regiment had already ceased to be called the First Volunteer Cavalry, and was never again known as anything but the Rough Riders] will *remain*—pitching bronchos and all, afoot or on horseback! . . . The "bob whites" whistle all around these plantations, and transport one straight back to Sagamore Hill on a summer's day. The mountains here are glorious; the valleys, a dream of drooping palms, and dark, cool, shaded mangroves clustered; soft bamboo waves near the creeks and smiling ridges, once all under cultivation.

My brother himself, in a letter dated from Santiago, July 19, 1898, writes:

"Darling Corinne:—'Triumph tasted'!—for that, one will readily pay as heavy a price as we have paid; but it is bitter to think that part of the price was due to the mismanagement of those in authority. The misery has been fearful. Today, out of my four hundred odd men in camp, one hundred and twenty-three are under the doctor's care. The rest of the six hundred with whom I landed are dead or in the rear hospitals. I cannot explain the breakdown of the transportation service, the commissariat, or the hospital service."

I quote the above letter for the special purpose of recalling to my readers the fact that Colonel Roosevelt was much criticised later for instigating the writing of a "round-robin" letter in the summer, urging the authorities to bring home the regiments after the victory was won. Due to the "breakdown" which he describes, the men were dying like flies, and had that "round robin" (severely censured by my brother's enemies) not been written, had the authorities at Washington not decided to follow the suggestions of Theodore Roosevelt and order our gallant men back from their death-trap, very few of that expedition to Cuba would have lived to tell the tale. At the end of the above letter, after describing in full the sufferings of the men because of lack of care, he says:

"They have been worn down by the terrific strain of fighting, marching, digging in the trenches, during the tropical midsummer; they have been in the fore-front, all through, they never complained though half-fed and with clothes and shoes in tatters; but it is bitter to think of the wealth at home, which would be so gladly used in their behalf if only it could be so used. They are devoted to me, and I cannot get their condition out of my thoughts. If only you could see them in battle, or feeding these wretched refugee women and children, whose misery beggars description. [Did I not say that these wild, strong men of the West were gentle in heart as well as fierce in courage!]

"Well, it is a great thing to have led such a regiment on the crowning day of its life. Young Burke [Eddie Burke] is well and is a first-class man and soldier. I like and respect him. Bob earned his promotion. The New York men have stood the strain well. I felt dreadfully about Kenneth's wound that day, but I was near the line, with my men, nearest the Spaniard, and I could not have gone back or held back for my own son. No man was ahead of me when we charged or rushed to the front to repel a charge; and indeed, I think my men would follow me literally anywhere. In the hard days I fared absolutely as they did, in food and bedding,—or rather, the lack of both. Now, yellow fever has broken out in the Army and I know not when we shall get away, but whatever comes, it is all right and I am content. Love to little Teddy and all the others. Your brother."

The same day he wrote my husband:

"Two of our men have died of yellow fever. We hope to keep it out of camp, and if we succeed, I trust we shall soon get to Porto Rico. Whatever comes, I cannot say how glad I am to have been in this. I feel that I now leave the children a memory that will partly offset the fact that I did not leave them much money. I have been recommended for the Colonelcy of this regiment, and for the medal of honor. Of course, I hope to get both, but I really don't care very much, for the *thing itself* is more important than the reward, and I have led this regiment during the last three weeks, the crowning weeks of its life. There is nothing I would have exchanged for having led it on horseback, where, first of all the army, we broke through the enemy's entrenchments. By the way, I then killed a Spaniard myself with the pistol Will Cowles raked up from the *Maine*. Of the six hundred men with whom I landed, less than three hundred are left; the others are dead or in the hospital; the mismanagement has been beyond belief."

Alas, how sad it seems that the mismanagement should have been beyond belief at such a time!

On July 27 a letter dated "First Regiment, U. S. Volunteer Cavalry, in camp near Santiago de Cuba," was received by my husband. A very characteristic letter it was, full of the joy of a fight well fought, and full also, of that tremendous human sympathy with his men, combined with an intelligent practicality which resulted later in the "round robin," requesting that the men who had fought so bravely, should not be allowed to die of disease unnecessarily by being retained for no good reason in the broiling heat of a Cuban summer.

"Dear Douglas," he writes, "we had a bully fight at Santiago, and though there was an immense amount that I did not exactly enjoy, the charge itself was great fun. Frankly, it did not enter my head that I could get through without being hit, but I judged that even if hit, the chances would be about 3 to 1 against my being killed.

"As far as the political effect of my actions;—in the first place, I never *can* get on in politics, and in the second, I would rather have led that charge and earned my colonelcy, than serve three terms in the United States Senate. It makes me feel as though I could now leave something to my children which will serve as an apology for my having existed. [How much his existence needed an apology!] In spite of the strain, and the anything but hygienic conditions under which we have lived, I am in very good health. If we stay here all summer, we shall have yellow fever among us, of course, but I rather think I will pull through that too. I wish they would let us go to Porto Rico, or if not, then let me get all my regiment together in Maine or somewhere like that and get them in trim for the great campaign against Havana in the Fall. I wish you could see these men. I am as proud of them as I can be, and I verily believe they would go anywhere with me. They are being knocked down right and left, however, with the fever. I shan't take any risks unless I really think I ought to, and now, I begin to believe that I am going to get home safely."

A letter from Bob Ferguson about the same time backs up his future position in regard to moving the men, and reiterates:

"It was a glorious spin, over trenches and barbed wires instead of oaken panels, however. One never expects to see the like again;—Corinne and Anna must have suffered terribly from Theodore's wild, whirlwind career! His courage all through was so simple and so true to him. The Spaniards laughed at the Cubans, and said they had no fighting to do until the Americans came;—they 'kept on coming.' One officer told Colonel Wood that the Americans were 'magnanimous, brave, and ferocious.' If Cervera had stayed in harbor with his ships, we would have been in the devil of a hole between starvation and fever. It is lucky things went as they did."

And again, on August 6, he writes to me:

"These dreary Cuban days and dark and dismal nights are drawing to a close for the time,—Thank the Lord and Theodore. [The much-criticised "round robin" had had its effect.] It is hardly fair to damn this country that way, however, for in reality, it is most inexplicably beautiful. In the sunshine of the morning, when once in a while an almost refreshing breeze comes, then the tropical valleys bask and smile in the most enticing luxuriance, and entrance one into lazy dreams of fairy-land. The mass of the scarlet acacia, the trails of morning-glories, and lilies, and the hot growth of all kinds,—above all, the graceful and kingly royal palm and his harem, the slender, tall, clustering bamboos,—are all lovely. These things by moon-light were simply inexpressible; however, the real side of nature is deadly sun, over-whelming, drenching rain, dark, drizzly mist and dew, fever, malaria, filth, disgust with everything. Well, this is at an end now, and almost time it were, for there would not be many left to tell the tale if left here all summer as the President and Secretary proposed to leave us only a couple of days ago, but Theodore 'sicked one' as your Stewart's whole pack of pup-dogs could not commence to do. If we take a final fall, it will be at Havana in the autumn and not with yellow fever, if we can help it, here at Santiago. You all had a dreadful time of it, probably far worse than we merry men of the Greenwood. Honestly, while it is all going along and when there is an advance, the spirits rise amazingly and one trips forward as gaily as in Sir Roger or any other airy measure. That, however, is the one really satisfactory sensation. Lying passive in reserve, and being searched and found by the long-range mausers and shrapnel in the bushes, is not so cheerful an occupation; in fact, it is a low proceeding altogether.

"Whooping along from time to time 'thoro bush—thoro brier,' with a wildish throng, firing, cheering, laughing, and running,—that, is a very different story, and holding the advance point in spite of orders to retire (!) is another thing to make even novices chuckle inwardly when they once feel they can do it,—but Theodore was the sparkle to all that fun.

"I could make your flesh creep, however, with horror; meanwhile, you can picture to yourself in pleasant nightmares, flocks of vultures and buzzards, the dead and wounded lost in the tangled growth,—and swarms of crabs,—great big land crabs with one, enormous, lobster-like claw, creeping, rustling, scuffling thro' the dried aloes and palmettoes. . . . War never changes its hideous phantasms. The heroism of even modern men (and none the less of the women who let them go) is the one thing to glory and hope in. We pack up tonight. My love to all."

And so ended the brief and glorious career of the Rough Riders, a career which has about it a touch of Roland and Robin Hood. These letters, written *at the time*, are valuable refutations of some bruited questions, and the very people who criticised certain actions of my brother, *at the time*, would be the first, I verily believe, now, to wish they had withheld their criticism.

The depleted regiment, emaciated beyond words, returned to Montauk Point on Long Island, and my husband and I came down from the Adirondack Mountains to meet them at Camp Wyckoff. What a night we spent in a Red Cross tent at the camp! How we talked! How good it was to greet the gallant men again, so many of whom we knew and loved, and how infinitely interesting to come in contact with the wild Westerners about whose courage and determination my brother had written such glowing accounts.

In the last letter my brother wrote to my husband from Santiago, the sentence "As for the political effect of my actions,

I never can get on in politics" was soon to be refuted, for hardly had he arrived at Montauk than the politicians flocked surreptitiously to sound him as to the possibility of his running for governor of New York State, but that's another story!

The throb of parting from their leader was soon to be experienced by the gallant men who had followed Theodore Roosevelt so eagerly in the Cuban jungles. Picturesque to the end, the mustering out of the Rough Riders, under blue autumnal skies at Montauk Point, was the culmination of its romantic career, and many a ferocious fighter and wild bronco-buster turned from the last hand-clasp of his colonel with tears in the eyes which had not flinched before the fiercest Spanish onslaught.

IX

THE ROUGH RIDER STORMS THE CAPITOL AT ALBANY

THE MAN WHO CAN

(Old Saxon for "The King")

WRITTEN OF THEODORE ROOSEVELT

How shall we know "the man who can"?
(That was the Saxon phrase, they say.)
Nay, perchance we shall find the man
Close to our hearts and lives to-day!

Soldier and patriot, strong of hand,
Keen of vision to know the time,
Quick and true to the hour's demand,
Poet, too, without rune or rhyme!

Poet, because through mists of sin
He finds the best as it yet shall be.
Faces evil, yet dares begin
To *live* the good that his soul can see.

Speech like an arrow, swift and straight,
Strength that smites to the core of wrong;
Smile that mocks but an adverse fate,
Heart of a boy, that leaps to song.

Honor scornful of life or place,
Courage brightest in sordid strife;
Such is the man whose first, best grace
Was the simple crown of a stainless life!

—Marion Couthouy Smith.

IT could not have been a pleasant thought to Mr. Thomas Platt (the acknowledged Republican boss of New York State, and a most interesting and unusual personality) when he realized that the tremendous popularity of the colonel of the Rough Riders would force him to accept the suggestion of some of the Republican leaders that this same colonel should be the Republican nominee for governor that autumn of 1898. The dash of the Rough Riders up San Juan Hill was not more strenuous than Theodore Roosevelt's sudden and unexpected storming of the Albany Capitol. What an autumn it was! Every imaginable obstacle was put in the way of his success. He was accused of not having paid his taxes; he was bitterly impugned by a certain number of his former friends and adherents—Independents—who did not believe that he should accept the "regular" nomination, and many and varied were the battles fought about and around his personality.

The whole campaign had to be arranged so suddenly and hurriedly that all kinds of amusing, although sometimes unpleasant, contretemps occurred. One remains clearly in my mind. There was to be held near Troy a country fair. Its date had apparently not been determined upon before my brother had agreed to speak at what promised to be a large colored meeting the evening of the same day on which the fair was to be held. My brother had not expected to have to go to the fair, but a sudden summons came, saying that it was very important that he should appear and make an out-of-door speech to a large concourse of up-state farmers. He was torn from Oyster Bay at an abnormally early hour and dashed up to Troy. Meanwhile, the newspapers of Albany and Troy had announced that he could not be present owing to his engagement for the evening in New York. The consequence was that the attendance at the fair at the time he was supposed to speak was almost nil, and he returned to New York much depressed at the apparent lack of interest. I came in from my country home to dine with him and go to the colored meeting. The colored people were especially enthusiastic about my brother's candidacy, because the Tenth Regiment of regulars, a colored regiment, had stormed San Juan Hill side by side with the Rough Riders. The meeting scheduled had been widely heralded, and we started for the hall with the conviction that although the *day* had been a failure the *night* was going to justify our highest expectations. Arriving at the hall, one old man with a long gray beard, sitting in the front seat, was apparently the total of the great audience that had been promised. My brother and I waited in the little room near the platform, anxiously peering out every now and then, hoping that the hall would soon be filled to overflowing, but no one came, and after an hour and a half of disheartening disappointment, we shook hands warmly with the faithful elderly adherent—who had remained silently in his seat during this period of waiting—and left the hall. My brother, in spite of distinct distress of mind, turned laughingly to me as we walked rapidly away and said, quoting from Maria Edgeworth's immortal pages: "Little Rosamund's day of misfortunes!" The next day the morning newspapers announced that the evening newspapers had given the misinformation that the Republican candidate for governor would not be able to return from the Troy fair in time for the colored meeting, an announcement which had so discouraged the colored folk that only one old man had been true to his colors!

From that day on, through the strenuous campaign, my brother was known by the family entirely as "Little Rosamund."

Another evening comes back to my mind. My husband and my brother had left me in my country home on the hill at Orange, and they were supposed to return at eleven o'clock that night. The last train arrived and my carriage returned from it empty. I was worried, for they were so thoughtful that I felt they would surely have telephoned to relieve my possible anxiety, and when at twelve o'clock the telephone-bell rang, I ran to the instrument expecting to hear a familiar voice, instead of which "I am a *World* reporter" was what I heard, "and I would like to know where Colonel Roosevelt and Mr. Douglas Robinson are." "I cannot give you any information," I replied discreetly, and more truthfully than usual, I confess. "It is very strange," said the voice—a distant unknown voice at twelve o'clock at night, when you are the sole occupant of a remote country house, always has a somewhat eerie effect—"for we have traced them up to within the last hour and we cannot find them anywhere." A slight wave of apprehension passed over me, but at the same time I was sufficiently confident of my two stalwart gentlemen not to have any serious fear concerning their whereabouts, and suddenly seized with an irresistible desire to be "funny"—a perfectly inexcusable inclination in a political campaign—I said to the reporter: "Wait one moment, please. Should you by any chance discover the whereabouts of Colonel Roosevelt and Mr. Robinson, would you be kind enough to let *me* know where they are?" I have always remembered the sound of the distant laugh of the man as I hurriedly put down the telephone-receiver, fully realizing my mistake in becoming jocose, and sure enough the next morning, in large headlines, appeared on the front page of the *World*: "Mrs. Douglas Robinson has no knowledge where Colonel Roosevelt and Mr. Douglas Robinson have spent the night."

Another incident that comes back into my memory was an evening in Chickering Hall, almost immediately before Election day, at which many well-known speakers were to make their plea for the election of Theodore Roosevelt, and at which, also, that most brilliant of speakers and charming of men, Mr. Joseph H. Choate, was to bring the evening to a climax. As Election day drew near, the great boss of Tammany Hall, Richard Croker, forsook his usual methods of strict silence, and began to be loquacious. Croker, when running a candidate, was always very careful indeed to keep the mystery of the Wigwam (Tammany) wrapped closely about him, but as the fight waxed hot and heavy, he lost his control and said many a foolish thing, and the Republican papers jubilantly announced that when Croker began to talk, it meant that he knew that his cause was lost.

At the meeting at Chickering Hall, when Mr. Choate rose to make the final speech of the evening, he said:

"Ladies and gentlemen, it is late; you have heard many

speakers and I shall be brief. All that I wish to do is to recall to your minds a certain Bible story—you may not have the incident clear in your memory. I refer to the story of Balaam and his ass!" Here the learned speaker paused and his audience concentrated their attention upon him, somewhat puzzled as to what he was about to say. He continued: "You may remember that Balaam was riding upon the ass through a dark forest, and that suddenly the ass stopped, and even more suddenly, *the ass spoke!*" Mr. Choate paused again, and the audience suddenly rippled out their mirth and their realization that the "ass" who spoke had a distinct reference to the utterances of Croker. As the laughter grew louder, Mr. Choate suddenly lifted his hand in the most impressive manner, and continued in a serious tone full of dramatic power: "But, ladies and gentlemen, you have perhaps forgotten *why* the ass spoke. The reason that he did so was because directly in his path, in shining garments, stood a young man with a flaming sword in his hand!" As one man the audience rose to its feet! Simultaneously, a great cheer rose to the lips of every one present, for the figure of speech had done its work, and each person in the house visualized the figure of Theodore Roosevelt, ardent and young, courageous and honest, truly "a young man with a flaming sword in his hand!"

Election day came and with it an overwhelming victory for the man who so lately had written to Douglas Robinson: "As for the political effect of my actions, I never can get on in politics."

During his incumbency as governor of New York State he always made his headquarters either at the house of my sister, Mrs. Cowles, or at my house, and many were the famous breakfast-parties at 422 Madison Avenue in those strenuous days. He was criticised for breakfasting with Mr. Platt and Mr. Odell (Mr. Platt's associate boss), but almost all of those much-discussed meals took place at my own house, and many a time Messrs. Platt and Odell had the unusual experience of finding that they were apparently expected to sit upon one chair, as my brother had invited so many more people to breakfast than could possibly be seated at my comparatively small table. After breakfast was over, Mr. Platt would say in a rather stern manner, "And now, Governor Roosevelt, I should like to have a private word with you," and my brother would answer, "Why, certainly, Mr. Platt, we will go right up to my sister's library—good-by, gentlemen," turning to his other guests, and then to Mr. Platt again, "We shall be quite private except for my sister. I always like to have her present at all my conferences. She takes so much interest in what I am doing!" This with a humorous side-glance at me, knowing how irritating my presence was to the gentleman in question. I can bear witness to the fact that through those many conferences my brother's courtesy to the brilliant older man never failed, nor did he ever lose his independent outlook or action. My brother's effort to work with Mr. Platt rather than against him also never failed, and many a time I have heard him say: "Mr. Platt, I would rather accept your suggestion of an appointee than that of any one else *if* you will suggest as good and honorable a man as any one else. I *want* to work with you and I know that your great information about Republican affairs is of enormous value to me, but I must reserve my own power of decision in all matters, although I hope always to be in accord with you."

The Rough Riders were always turning up on every occasion, or if they did not actually turn up in *propria persona*, strange letters on many and varied subjects came to my house from them. Amongst these letters one arrived when my brother was breakfasting with me one morning at my house. The mail that morning was unique in more ways than one, for another letter arrived with no name and no address on it. Instead of name and address there was a drawing of a large set of teeth, and on the reverse side of the envelope was written: "Please let Jack Smith, 211 W. 139th Street, know whether this letter reaches its destination. It is a bet and a lot of money hangs in the balance"! Those strong white teeth, which had been the terror of the recreant policemen, were quite as much a factor at the Capitol on the hill at Albany.

In the same mail, as I said, came a very characteristic epistle from a Rough Rider, which ran as follows:

"Dear Colonol: Please come right out to Dakota. They ain't treatin me right out here. The truth is, Colonel, they have put me in jail and I ain't ought to be here at all, cause what they say ain't true, Colonel. They say that I shot a lady in the eye and it ain't true, Colonel, for I was shootin at my wife at the time.—I know you will come and get me out of jail right off, Colonel,—please hurry. J. D."

How my brother laughed as he turned the manuscript over to me, and said: "They are the most unconscionable children that ever were, but oh what fighting men they made!"

Another amusing incident occurred at the house of my sister, where we were all lunching one day, having one of our merry family reunions to meet the governor. My sister had just returned from Europe with a "perfect treasure" of an English butler, who had not yet become entirely accustomed to the vagaries of the Roosevelt family! We were in the midst of a specially merry argument when the door-bell rang and the butler left the dining-room to answer the bell. In a few moments he returned with a somewhat puzzled expression on his face, and leaning over my brother's chair, he said in a stage whisper: "There is a —— there is a —— *gentleman* in the hall, sir —— he says, sir, that his name, sir, is —— *Mr.* 'Happy Jack' of Arizona." "Why," said my brother, leaping to his feet, "I didn't know that 'Happy Jack' was in New York," and he hurriedly left the room to welcome his precious Rough Rider. In a few moments he came back literally doubled up with laughter, and burst out: "You know, there has been a great deal in the newspapers about the trouble that I have had with importunate office seekers, who have forced themselves, in a very disagreeable way, into the executive mansion at Albany. Dear old

'Happy Jack' read, way out in Arizona, about the annoyance I was having with these people, and he just packed his kit and came all the way from Arizona to offer to be 'bouncer-out' of the executive mansion! Wasn't that fine of 'Happy Jack'!"

Several years later, when my brother was President of the United States, I was in England and I spent a week-end with the St. Loe Stracheys in Surrey, where Lord and Lady Cromer were also passing Sunday. Lord Cromer having, as a young man, visited our Western plains and prairies, adored the stories of the Rough Riders, and especially the incident of "Happy Jack's" desire to become "bouncer-out" of the executive mansion. He loved the story so much that he insisted upon my telling it to another English peer, in whom the sense of humor was less striking than in Lord Cromer. I shall never forget the dreary sensation of struggling to tell Earl S—— that particular story. We were at a rather dreary garden-party, and Lord Cromer had presented his friend for the special purpose of having me tell this Rough Rider story. Much against my will, I acceded to his request, and the story seemed to get longer and longer and duller and duller in the telling. Having mentioned the "perfect treasure" of a butler in the beginning of the tale, that seemed to be the rudder to which Earl S—— clung through the involutions of Rough Riderism, and as I stumbled on to the ever-lengthening end of that unfortunate anecdote, the English peer in question turned to me as I fell into silence and said, coldly and courteously: "Is that all?" "Yes," I said hastily, "quite all." "Oh!" said my companion, with a sigh of relief, and then feeling that he had not been quite sufficiently sympathetic, he added courteously: "And did the butler stay?" When I returned with this sequel to the story of "Happy Jack" of Arizona and recounted it to my brother, he laughed immoderately and said: "I know you must have suffered telling the story, but that postscript to the story is worth all the pain you suffered."

One afternoon in May, I think in the year 1900, my brother telephoned me that he wanted to bring several men to dinner the following day, amongst others, Mr. Winston Churchill, of England, now so well known all over the world, but then still very young, though having had many experiences as a writer in connection with the Boer War. He was making a speaking tour in America. As usual, the little party grew, and when we assembled at dinner the following evening, dear old General Wheeler (Fighting Joe), Mr. St. Clair McKelway, of the Brooklyn *Eagle*, and one or two others, I remember being very much interested in Mr. Churchill's method of probing Governor Roosevelt's mind. The young Englishman, of mixed parentage, had on his American side a certain quality unusual in the average Englishman, and the rapid fire of his questioning was very characteristic of the land of his mother's birth, while a certain "sureness" of point of view might be attributed to both countries. At one period during the dinner he referred to a certain incident that had occurred in Africa, and relegated it to the action which took place at Bloemfontein. My brother very courteously said: "I beg your pardon, but that particular incident took place, if I am not mistaken, at Magersfontein." The young Englishman flushed and repeated with determination that it had occurred at Bloemfontein, and added the fact, which was already known to us, that he had been there. My brother again, his head a little on one side, and still most courteously, reiterated: "I think, Mr. Churchill, if you will stop and think for a moment, you will remember that I am right in this instance, and that that incident took place at Magersfontein." Mr. Churchill paused a moment in the ever-ready flow of his talk and then suddenly, with a rather self-conscious frown, said: "You are right, governor, and I am mistaken. It did occur at Magersfontein." This anecdote I give simply to show, what is known by all who were intimate with my brother, namely, the extraordinary accuracy with which he followed the affairs of the day, and the equally extraordinary memory which retained the detail of individual occurrences in a most unusual manner. In the soft spring air we sat later in the evening by the open window while General Wheeler, son of the South, veteran of the Civil War, and Theodore Roosevelt, son of the North, who had so lately led his famous regiment through the Cuban jungles in close proximity to General Wheeler, told story after story of the way in which, shoulder to shoulder, they had buried the old differences in the new co-operation.

In May, 1899, I received one of the comparatively few letters which came to me while my brother was governor, for we met so frequently that we rarely wrote. The following letter, coming as it did at the end of his first year of service as governor of New York State, is of special interest.

"Darling Corinne," he says, "your letter touched me deeply. It was so good to catch a glimpse of you the other day. I have accomplished a certain amount for good this year. I want to see you and go over it all at length with you. In a way, there is a good deal that is disappointing about it because I had to act, especially towards the end, *against* the wishes of the machine people who have really given me my entire support, and *with* the reformers, labor and otherwise, who are truly against me whenever it comes down to anything really important to me. We have just returned from a really delightful driving trip to a quaint, clean, little inn at Crooked Lake, some eighteen miles off. We drove out there Saturday with every child except Quentin, and back again on Sunday. Everything went off without a hitch and Edith and I enjoyed it as much as the children. . . . My love to Douglas and to blessed little Corinne. Ever yours, T. R."

Nothing was more discouraging to my brother during his long and varied career than the fact that the so-called reformers were frequently so visionary that they were rarely, if ever, to be counted upon where an effort to achieve a distinct practical purpose was concerned, but the disappointments which he perpetually endured from this attribute never induced him to yield to the machine politicians unless he felt that by so doing he could achieve the higher end for which he always worked.

A little later in May of that same year, 1899, he writes me in patient answer to various questions: "In reference to my attitude on the bills that have not passed, there are hundreds of people to whom, if I had time, I should explain my attitude, but I have not the time. I have the gravest kind of doubts, for instance, as to the advantages to the State of our High School system, as at present carried out. . . . I strongly believe that there has been a tendency amongst some of the best educators recently to divert from mechanical trades, people who ought, for their own sake, to keep in at the mechanical trades." He was always so willing to answer my questions, even when pressed by many harassing affairs.

From Oyster Bay, on July 17, 1899, he writes as one freed temporarily from the cares of state, and speaking of my eldest boy, who was then sixteen, he says: "I am afraid it is dull here for Teddy. You see, we have no one here quite his age and he has passed the time when such a simple pleasure as a scramble down Cooper's Bluff appears enthralling, although I take him down it nevertheless. He is a very fine fellow. . . . I have been giving him information about his hunting trip." Again the painstaking effort to be helpful to me and mine, and, indeed, all those who needed his help or advice.

On December 18, having returned to Albany, he plans a hurried trip to New York, and writes characteristically: "On Thursday, December 21st, may I have dinner at seven o'clock? If you are going out, do remember, that seriously, I am quite as happy with bread and milk as with anything else. Ever yours, Theodore Roosevelt." What could be more unusual than the governor of New York State being "quite as happy with bread and milk as with anything else"! And I really think he was rather happier with bread and milk than with anything else, much to the occasional discomfort of the fastidious companions who sometimes ran across his rather primitive path.

My last letter of that year, and, indeed, of the period during which he was governor, was late in December, 1899, and it ran as follows: "On Saturday I find Senator Platt wants me to breakfast with him at the Fifth Avenue." That was one of the rare occasions when the unfortunate senator induced the governor to part from his sister, and the inevitable presence of that sister at the conferences which Senator Platt quite naturally preferred to have alone with the governor. The letter continues: "On Friday, at half past eight, General Greene, Mr. F. S. Witherbee, Mr. Fox and Mr. MacFarlane will give you the unexpected pleasure of breakfasting with you. Is this all right?" Needless to say, it *was* all right; only, if I remember correctly, a large number were added equally unexpectedly to the four above-mentioned gentlemen. Those breakfasts were the most delightful of meals. My brother's friend Professor William M. Sloane in later days was frequently a member of the breakfast-parties at my house, and he used, laughingly, to remark that he wondered why we were all bidden so promptly at half past eight when the gentleman who so sternly called others from their comfortable beds on cold winter mornings at that matutinal hour seemed always able to sit over the breakfast-table until about eleven! That, however, was not the case in those early gubernatorial days, for the young governor was pressed with too many affairs to yield to his Southern inclination to "brood" over the breakfast-table.

In later days at the rare periods of comparative leisure, between 1910 and 1912, the "half-hours at the breakfast-table" were prolonged into several whole hours, and many a time my friend Mrs. Parsons and I have listened to the most enchanting discussions on the part of Colonel Roosevelt and Professor Sloane, dealing occasionally with Serb or Rumanian literature or the intricacies of Napoleonic history.

One luncheon during the time that my brother was governor stands out clearly in my mind, owing to an amusing incident connected with it. My dining-room at 422 Madison Avenue was small, and fourteen people were the actual limit that it could hold. One day, he having told me that he was bringing ten people to lunch, and realizing his hospitable inclinations, I had had the table set for the limit of fourteen. We were already thirteen in the sitting-room when the door-bell rang and, looking out of the window, he turned to me with a troubled expression and said: "I think I see two people coming up the front steps, and that will make fifteen." I suddenly decided to be unusually firm and said: "Theodore, I have not places for fifteen; you said there would only be ten. I am delighted to have fourteen, but you will have to tell one of those two people that they will have to go somewhere else for lunch." He went out into the hall, and in a moment returned with one of his beloved Rough Riders and an air of triumph on his face. I whispered, "Were there really two, and who was the other, and what has happened to him?" and he whispered back, like a child who has had a successful result in some game, "Yes, there were two—the other was the president of the University of ——. I told them they had to toss up, and the Rough Rider won"—this with a chuckle of delight!

X

HOW THE PATH LED TO THE WHITE HOUSE

Frédéric Mistral, the Provençal poet, said of Theodore Roosevelt:

C'est lui qui donne une nouvelle espérance à l'humanité.

TOWARD the spring of 1900, while my brother was in his second arduous year of activity as governor of New York State, he came one afternoon to my house, as he frequently did, for he made headquarters there whenever he was in New York. I remember I was confined to my room with an attack of grippe. The door-bell rang in the rapid, incisive way which always marked his advent, and in a moment or two I heard him come bounding up the stairs to my bedroom. He seemed to bring the whole world of spring sunshine into the room with him, and before I could say anything to greet him he called out: "Pussie, haven't *we* had fun being governor of New York State?" I remember the grippe seemed to leave me entirely. My heart was full of that elation which he alone could give by his power of sharing everything with me. He sat down in a rocking-chair by me and began to rock violently to and fro, every now and then receding almost the whole length of the room as he talked, and then rocking toward me with equal rapidity when he wished to emphasize some special point in his conversation. When he stopped for breath, I said laughingly, but with a certain serious undertone in the midst of my laughter: "Theodore, are you not going to take a complete rest *some time* this summer? You certainly need it. It has been year after year, one thing after another, more and more pressing all the time—civil service commissioner, police commissioner, assistant secretary of the navy, lieutenant-colonel, then colonel of the Rough Riders, and all that that campaign meant, and now nearly two years of hard work as governor of New York State. Surely, you must take some rest this summer."

He looked back at me rather as one of my little boys would look if I spoke to them somewhat harshly, and answered in a very childlike way: "Yes, of course you are right. I do mean to take a rest of *one whole* month this summer." I said: "That isn't very much—one month, but still it is better than nothing. Now, do you really mean that you are going to rest for one whole month?" "Yes," he answered, as if he were doing me the greatest possible favor, "I really mean to rest one whole month. I don't mean to do one *single* thing during that month—except write a life of Oliver Cromwell." How I laughed! What an idea of complete rest—to write a life of Oliver Cromwell! And write a life of Oliver Cromwell he did during that period of complete rest, but before he was able to do it there came many another stirring event and change in the outlook of his existence.

Messrs. Platt and Odell, supposedly the arbiters of the fate of every New York State governor, agreed that two years of Theodore Roosevelt in the Executive Mansion at Albany was quite enough, and that come what might, he should not have another term, and so they bent all their subtle political acumen toward the achievement of their wish to remove him. They would, however, have been thwarted in their purpose had not the Western part of our country decided also that Theodore Roosevelt's name was necessary on the presidential ticket, to be headed, for a second time, by William McKinley.

The young governor, deeply absorbed in the many reforms which he had inaugurated in the Empire State, was anything but willing to be, as he felt he would be, buried in Washington as vice-president, but as the time drew near for the Republican Convention of June, 1900, more and more weight was thrown in the balance to persuade him to accept the nomination.

I have frequently said in these pages that one of the most endearing characteristics of my brother was his desire to have my sister and myself share in all of his interests, in his glory, or in his disappointments, and so, when the convention at Philadelphia met, and as the contending forces struggled around him, he telegraphed to my husband and myself, who were then at our country home in New Jersey, and begged us to come on to Philadelphia, and be near him during the fray. Needless to say, we hurried to his side.

I shall always remember arriving at that hotel in Philadelphia. How hot those June days were, and how noisy and crowded the corridors of the hotel were when we arrived! Blaring bands and marching delegations seemed to render the hot air even more stifling, and I asked at once to be shown to the room where Governor Roosevelt was. A messenger was sent with me, and up in the elevator and through circuitous passages we went, to a corner room overlooking a square. We knocked, but there was no answer, and I softly opened the door, and there sat my brother Theodore at a distant window with a huge volume upon his knees. The soft air was blowing in the window, his back was turned to the door, and he was as absolutely detached as if vice-presidential nominations, political warfare, illicit and corrupt methods of all kinds in public life were things not known to his philosophy. I tiptoed up behind him and leaned over his shoulder, and saw that the great volume spread out before him was the "History of Josephus"! I could not but laugh aloud, for it seemed too quaint to think that he, the centre of all the political animosity, should be quietly apart, perfectly absorbed in the history of the Jews of a long-past day. As I laughed, he turned and jumped to his feet, and in a moment Josephus was as much a thing of the past as he actually was, and Theodore Roosevelt, the loving brother, the humorous philosopher, the acute politician, was once more in the saddle. In a moment, in a masterly manner, he had sketched the situation for me: 'Yes, Platt and Odell did want to eject him, that was true, but it wasn't only that. The West felt strongly, and the Middle West as strongly, that his name was needed on the presidential ticket. No, he didn't want to give up a second term as governor of New York State; he hated the thought of a vice-presidential burial-party, but what was he to do? He didn't really know himself.'

At that moment, without any ceremony, the door was thrown open, and in marched the delegation from Kansas. Fife and drum and bugle headed the delegation with more than discordant noises. Round and round the room they went, monotonously singing to the accompaniment of the above raucous instruments: "We want Teddy, we want Teddy, we want Teddy." My brother held up his hand, but nothing seemed to stop them. Over and over again they filed solemnly around that sitting-room, and finally, forming in a straight line, they metaphorically presented arms, and stood for a moment silently before him. He stepped nearer to them and, with a somewhat anxious tone in his voice, said: "Gentlemen of Kansas, I know that you only want what is best for the country, and incidentally what you think is best for me; but, my friends, I wish you would withdraw your desire that I should be the candidate for the vice-presidency. I *want* another term as governor of New York State. I have initiated a good many reforms that I think would help my native state. I have made many appointments, and the people I have appointed would feel that I have gone back on them if I can't be there to help them with their work. I am sure I could be of more use to my country as governor of New York State than as vice-president. I wish you would change your minds and help me to do the thing which I think is the best thing to do." The delegation from Kansas looked the pleader gently but firmly in the eye. The fife and drum and bugle struck up its monotonous sound again. The leader of the Kansas delegation turned, and, with all his followers, once more they marched slowly and steadfastly around that room, making no answer to Governor Roosevelt except the indomitable refrain of "We want Teddy, we want Teddy, we want Teddy," which sounded for a long while down the corridor.

As we listened to their retreating footsteps, he turned to me with a look of mingled amusement and despair in his eyes, and said: "What can I do with such people? But aren't they good fellows!"

And so, as is now well known to history, the Kansas delegation and other like delegations had their way. Mr. Platt and Mr. Odell thought *they* had *their* way too, and at one of the most exciting conventions at which I have ever been present—dominated in masterful fashion by the unique personality of Mark Hanna—Theodore Roosevelt was made the nominee for the second place on the ticket of the Republican party of 1900. One little incident occurred the next morning which I have always felt had a certain prophetic quality about it. An article appeared in one of the Philadelphia papers, signed by that inimitable humorist, the brilliant philosopher, Peter Dunne, alias "Mr. Dooley." I wish I could find the article—I kept it for a long while—but this is about the way it ran:

"Tiddy Rosenfeldt came to the Convintion in his Rough Rider suit and his sombrero hat and his khaki clothes, trying to look as inconspichuous as possible, and as soon as he got there Platt fill on his chist and Odell sat on his stummick and they tried to crush him and squeeze the life out of him. And they *think* they have done it, and perhaps they have, but, Hinnessey, they needn't be quite so sure, for Tiddy Rosenfeldt will get somewhere no matter what happens, *even though the path lies through the cimitery!*"

Whether "Mr. Dooley" simply meant that as vice-presidents had always been supposed to be dead men as far as future preferment was concerned, or whether, with prophetic touch, he visualized the horror that was to come, and the way in which Theodore Roosevelt's path to a higher position actually did lie "through the cemetery," I know not, but those were approximately the very words which appeared in that Philadelphia newspaper the morning after Roosevelt was nominated as candidate for vice-president on the McKinley ticket.

Later in the autumn he started on one of the most strenuous campaigns of his life, and swung around the country asking for Republican support for William McKinley's second term. Just before Election day he was to return to New York to make his final address at Madison Square Garden. As usual, he was to spend the night before and the night of the meeting at my house. Just before he was to arrive I received a telegram saying that his voice was entirely gone from the strain of weeks of speaking, and would I please have a throat doctor at the house on his arrival to treat his throat. Of course I arranged that this should be done, and he arrived, bright and gay, although distinctly hoarse. The doctor treated him, and he was ordered to keep perfectly still during the evening. We went up to the library after dinner, and I said to him: "Now, Theodore, we must only have a few minutes' talk, and then you must go to bed." "But," he said, "I must tell you a few of the very funny incidents that happened on my trip." And with that he began—my husband and I feeling very conscience-stricken, but so fascinated that we had not the strength of mind to stop him. Suddenly, to our perfect surprise, the early morning light crept in through the windows, the milk-wagons began to rattle in the streets, and we realized that the dawn of another day had come, and that the future vice-president had outraged his doctor's orders and had talked all night long! And such stories as they were, too; I shall never forget them. One after another, he pictured to us the various audiences, the wonderful receptions, the unique chairmen of the different meetings. There was always a "bellowing" chairman, as he expressed it, or else one whose ineffectual voice did not reach even the first circle of the huge audiences that gathered everywhere to hear him. Out in the Far West eight-horse vehicles would meet the trains on which the nominees travelled, and inadvertent bands would blow in the ears of "shotgun" teams that had never been hitched up before, with such astounding results as the complete loss of the whole team at once, which necessitated the dragging of the carriage by ardent cowboy admirers, or, worse luck, eventuated in terrifying runaways, which, however, never seemed to produce anything but casual discomfort.

Mr. Curtis Guild, of Boston, and Judge John Proctor Clarke accompanied Governor Roosevelt on this trip, and on one occasion the aforesaid "bellowing" chairman introduced my brother as "one whose name was known from shore to shore and whose life story was part of every fireside, and whose deeds were household words from the Atlantic to the Pacific." Finding that this introduction was greeted with vociferous applause, he then made use of the same extravagant exaggeration in introducing Mr. Guild. The only trouble in the latter case was that, after stertorously repeating the aforesaid introduction, the chairman suddenly forgot the name of the second speaker, "so well known from the Atlantic to the Pacific," and turned with solemn disapproval to the refined New England statesman, whispering hoarsely: "What in h— is your name, anyway?"

Such were the tales with which he regaled us that too-short night in November, 1900. Any other man, having so disobeyed the doctor's stern commands to refrain from using his voice, would have been punished the following evening by not having any voice at all; but, on the contrary, his tones were clear and strong, his personality vital and inspiring, as he leaned from the platform toward the thousands of cheering human beings in the great Madison Square Garden, to put the finishing touch on that stirring campaign for the second nomination of McKinley.

The inauguration in Washington, in March, 1901, had a peculiar charm about it. Perhaps one felt this charm especially because of the youth of the Vice-President and of his wife, and because of the contrast between those two happy young people and the more serious President, weighed down as he was with many cares, the greatest of which was his loving anxiety for his fragile little wife.

Because we were the sisters of the Vice-President, Mrs. McKinley sent for my sister, Mrs. Cowles, and me just after the inauguration, and I remember very well the touching quality of that dainty personality, in whose faded face was the remains of exquisite beauty. She received us up-stairs in her bedroom, and by her side was a table on which was a little Austrian vase in which bloomed one superb red rose. As we sat down she pointed to the rose with her delicate little hand, and said softly: "My dearest love brought me that rose. He always brings me a rose every day, Mrs. Robinson." And then, a faint smile flitting over her face, she said: "My dearest love is very good to me. Every evening he plays eight or ten games of cribbage with me, and I think he sometimes *lets* me win." I remember the feeling in my heart when she spoke those words, as I thought of the man in the White House, oppressed with many cares; even, perhaps, at the time when the shadow of the war with Spain hung over his troubled head, sitting down with gentle affection and quiet self-control to play "eight or ten games of cribbage," "one for his nob, and two for his heels," with the pathetic little creature from whom the tender love of his early youth had never swerved.

The scenes outside of the White House connected with the young Vice-President were very different. In the home of my sister, Mrs. Cowles, where we all stayed for the inauguration, quaint happenings occurred. A certain Captain ——, a great admirer of my brother, telegraphed that he was sending from Thorley's florist shop in New York a "floral tribute" to be erected wherever the Vice-President was staying. My sister's house was moderate in size, but that made no difference to Captain ——. That "floral tribute" had to be erected. It cost, if I remember rightly, in the neighborhood of three thousand dollars. (My brother laughingly but pathetically said it was about half of his income at the time, and he wished the tribute could have been added to the income.) It had to be erected, and erected it was. It arrived in long boxes, painfully suggestive of coffins, much to the delight of the young members of the family, who were also staying with my always hospitable sister. There, for a whole day, three men worked haggardly building the "tribute," until the whole front room of my sister's house (which was much in demand for large numbers of delegations who wished to pay their respects to my brother) was filled in every nook and cranny by this enormous and marvellous structure, which reached from wall to wall and up to the ceiling. The overworked and tired men who created it were so exhausted by the questions of the small members of the Roosevelt and Robinson family that toward the end of the afternoon they sent word to Mrs. Cowles that unless those children were sent out of the house, that "tribute" would never be finished. Finished it was, however, and we were almost suffocated by the sweetness of its scents, and it was all that we could do, in spite of our spontaneous gaiety, to rise above the semifunereal feeling that this mass of conventional flowers produced upon the atmosphere of the whole house.

The inaugural ball was really a charming sight, but was shadowed for the presidential party by the fact that Mrs. McKinley was not well a short while before it took place. She was able to be present, however, in her box, but the shade of sadness was heavy on the President's face; and the people, for that very reason, turned with peculiar pleasure to the care-free younger couple, who were asked to come down from the box, and to walk in stately fashion once around the room, to the infinite admiration of the many interested observers.

After the inauguration my brother retired quietly to Oyster Bay, and it was from there on April 15, 1901, that he wrote me one of his most characteristic notes. At that time, as in the days of his governorship, he would frequently notify his friends to meet him and lunch with him at my house, much to my delight. On this particular occasion, he had invited so incongruous an assortment of people that he decided that one or two more equally incongruous would be advisable, and writes as follows: "Darling Corinne: Inasmuch as we are to have Cocky Locky, Henny Penny and Goosey Poosey at lunch, why omit Foxy Loxy? I am anxious to see Dr. R—— and I do hope you will ask him to lunch on Thursday also. Ever yours, T. R."

That lunch-party proved to be a great success, as did various others later; and then came a moment, for me, of serious anxiety when my eldest boy was stricken with diphtheria in college. At once many loving letters came from Oyster Bay—and later, when the young freshman had recovered from his illness, and I was at my home on Orange Mountain, the newly inaugurated Vice-President acceded to my wish that he should come to my home, where my husband and I had lived all our young married life, and be the hero and excitement of the neighborhood at a reception on my lawn. It proved a hot day in July, but his pleasure in meeting all my friends was unabated, and he took special interest in my butcher and grocer and fish man and ice man, and the kindly farming people who had been devoted to my husband's mother as well as to me for many years. At the end of the day he resuscitated with tender care an old veteran of the Civil War, who had stumbled up the hill in the blinding heat to pay his respects to the colonel of the Rough Riders, now Vice-President of the United States.

That same summer he engineered a sailing trip for his little boys and mine, and writes me in answer to a request from me to know how much I owed for the trip: "About $12 would cover completely your boys' share of the expenses. It is just like you to want to pay it, but I would like to feel that for this trivial matter your two boys were my guests. So if you don't mind, I am going to ask you to *sacrifice* your feelings. As I have told you the extent of the obligation, and it is surely *not* heavy, let me continue to stand as the munificent host!"

Once that summer during his "month's rest," of which I have already spoken at the beginning of this chapter, I spent a night at Sagamore Hill, and my sister-in-law, Mrs. Roosevelt, said to me that she was anxious about my brother. The "rest" did not quite agree with him, and the prospect of a more or less sedentary life in his new position weighed on the active initiative of his mind.

A little later they went to a hunting-lodge in the Adirondacks, and all the world knows what happened on September 6, 1901. Then came the great anxiety as to whether Mr. McKinley would recover from the assassin's onslaught, and on September 14, he succumbed to the weakness engendered by his wound. While the dramatic drive from the Adirondack Mountains, where Theodore Roosevelt was found, was in process, I, the only member of the Roosevelt family near New York, was inundated in my Orange Mountain home by reporters. That evening after receiving a number of reporters and giving them what slight information I could give, I said that I could not stand the strain any longer, that I could not be interviewed any more, and with the dear cousin, John Elliott, who had been our early childhood companion, and who happened to be visiting me, I went into my writing-room, shut the door to the world outside, and a strange coincidence occurred. My sister-in-law, Mrs. Theodore Roosevelt, had shortly before returned to me a number of childhood letters which we had exchanged, first as little children, and then as growing girls, for we had always been very intimate friends. These letters were in a box on my writing-table, and I said to my cousin John: "Let us forget all these terrible things that are happening, and for a moment, at least, go back into our merry, care-free past. Here are these letters. I am going to pick one out at random and see how it will remind us of our childhood days."

So speaking, I put my hand into the box and proceeded to draw out a letter. Curiously enough, as I opened the yellow envelope and the sheets fell from it, I saw that it was dated from Washington in 1877, and looking more closely I read aloud the words:

"Dearest Corinne: Today, for the first time, I went to the White House. Oh, how much I wished for you. It seemed so wonderful to me to be in the old mansion which had been the home of President Lincoln, and which is so connected with all our country's history. It gave me a feeling of awe and excitement. I wish you could have been here to share the feeling with me, for I don't suppose it is likely that we shall ever be in the White House together, and it would have been so interesting to have exchanged our memories of things that had happened in that wonderful old house. But how unlikely it is that you or I shall ever come in contact with anything connected with the White House."

As I read these words, I exclaimed with astonishment, for it did seem a curious freak of fate that almost at the very moment that I was reading the lines penned by the girl of fifteen, an unexpected turn of the wheel had made that same young girl the lady of the White House.

XI

HOME LIFE IN THE WHITE HOUSE

Uncrowned the brow,
Where truth and courage meet,
The citizen alone confronts the land.

. . . .

A man whose dreamful, valiant mind conceives
High purpose, consecrated to his race.

—Margaret Ridgely Partridge.

THE deed of the cowardly assassin had done its work. William McKinley was dead; the young Vice-President had made the hazardous trip from the heart of the Adirondack Mountains, had taken the solemn oath in Buffalo, had followed the body of his chief to the final resting-place, and had returned to Washington. From Washington he telegraphed to my husband and myself, with the thought which he always showed, and told us that as Mrs. Roosevelt was attending to last important matters at Sagamore, she could not be with him the day he moved into the White House, and that he was very anxious that not only my sister, Mrs. Cowles, and her husband, but that we also should dine with him the first night that he slept in the old mansion. So we went on to Washington, and were with him at that first meal in the house for which he had such romantic attachment because it had sheltered the hero of his boyhood and manhood, Abraham Lincoln. As we sat around the table he turned and said: "Do you realize that this is the birthday of our father, September 22? I have realized it as I signed various papers all day long, and I feel that it is a good omen that I begin my duties in this house on this day. I feel as if my father's hand were on my shoulder, and as if there were a special blessing over the life I am to lead here." Almost as he finished this sentence, the coffee was passed to us, and at that time it was the habit at the White House to pass with the coffee a little boutonnière to each gentleman. As the flowers were passed to the President, the one given to him was a yellow saffronia rose. His face flushed, and he turned again and said: "Is it not strange! This is the rose we all connect with my father." My sister and I responded eagerly that many a time in the past we had seen our father pruning the rose-bush of saffronia roses with special care. He always picked one for his buttonhole from that bush, and whenever we gave him a rose, we gave him one of those. Again my brother said, with a very serious look on his face, "I think there is a blessing connected with this," and surely it did seem as if there were a blessing connected with those years of Theodore Roosevelt in the White House; those merry happy years of family life, those ardent, loving years of public service, those splendid, peaceful years of international amity—a blessing there surely was over that house.

Nothing could have been harder to the temperament of Theodore Roosevelt than to have come "through the cemetery," as Peter Dunne said in his prophetic article, to the high position of President of the United States. What he had achieved in the past was absolutely through his own merits. To him to come to any position through "dead men's shoes" was peculiarly distasteful; but during the early years of his occupancy of the White House, feeling it his duty so to do, he strove in every possible way to fulfil the policies of his predecessor, retaining his appointees and working with conscientious loyalty as much as possible along the lines laid down by President McKinley.

That first winter of his incumbency was one of special interest. Many were the difficulties in his path. England, and, indeed, all foreign countries were watching him with deep interest. I realized that fact in a very special way as that very spring of

1902 I took my young daughter abroad to place her at a French school directed by Mademoiselle Souvestre in England. It was the spring when preparations were being made for the coronation of King Edward VII, and because of the fact that I was the sister of the President of the United States, I was received with great courtesy. Our dear friend Mr. Joseph H. Choate was then ambassador to England. Mrs. Choate presented me at court, and the King paid me the unusual compliment—out of respect to my brother—of leaving the dais on which he and the Queen stood, and came forward to greet me personally in order to ask for news of my brother. Special consideration was shown to me in so many ways that when Mr. Robinson and I were visiting Edinburgh, it seemed in no way unusual that we should be invited to Holyrood Castle to the reception given by the lord high commissioner, Lord Leven and Melville. It so happened that we were in Edinburgh during that week of festivity when the lord high commissioner of Scotland, appointed as special representative of the King of Great Britain, holds court in the old castle as though he were actually the King.

We had dined with friends before the reception, and were therefore late in reaching the castle, and were literally the last people at the end of the long queue approaching the dais on which Lord and Lady Leven and Melville stood. As King Edward had himself stepped forward to meet me in Buckingham Palace, I was not surprised when Lord Leven and Melville stepped down from the dais, and I expected him also to ask news of my brother, the President of the United States, as King Edward had done, but to my great surprise, and be it confessed intense pleasure, I heard the lord high commissioner speak as follows: "Mrs. Douglas Robinson, you have been greeted with special courtesy in our country because of your distinguished brother, the President of the United States, but I am greeting you with even greater interest because of your father, the first Theodore Roosevelt. You probably do not remember, for you were a little girl at the time, that a raw-boned young Scotchman named Ronald Leslie Melville came long ago to New York and was much at your home, having had letters of introduction to your father as one of the men best fitted to teach him the modern philanthropic methods used in America. Only to-day," he continued, "I told the children of Edinburgh, assembled, as is the custom, to listen to the lord high commissioner, that the father of the present President of the United States was the first man who taught me to *love* my fellow men."

My heart was very full as I made my courtesy and answered the lord high commissioner. Before he let me pass on he said, with a charming smile: "If you and Mr. Robinson will come to-morrow to lunch with us quietly I will take you to Lord Darnley's room, which is my dressing-room during the week of Holyrood festivities, and on my dressing-table you will see the photograph of your father, for I never go anywhere without it." I accepted the invitation gladly, and the next day we went to Holyrood Castle, lunched informally with the delightful chatelain and chatelaine, and I was taken, as the former promised, to see Lord Darnley's room, where my father's face smiled at me from the dressing-table. My brother loved to hear me tell this story, and I feel that it is not amiss to include it in any recollections concerning my brother, for he was truly the spirit of my father reincarnate.

In May, 1902, Mrs. Roosevelt writes that "Theodore" is just about to leave for a hunting trip, which she hopes will "rest" him. (The rest the year before, of writing a life of Oliver Cromwell, had not been made quite strenuous enough for a real rest!) Later he returned and made a famous speech in Providence, a speech epoch-making, and recognized as such by an English newspaper, *The Morning Post* of August 27, 1902, a clipping from which I have at hand, and which runs as follows:

"Our New York correspondent announced yesterday that President Roosevelt's great speech at Providence on the subject of 'Trusts' is regarded on all sides and by both parties as an absolutely epoch-making event. This is not surprising to those who have studied the conditions of American politics, and the merits of the particular economic question involved, so far as they are intelligible to us, or last but by no means least, the character and personality of President Roosevelt. It would now seem that the people of the United States are at the parting of the ways between the corrupt, old political system and a newer, manlier, honester conception of public rights and duties."

Perhaps this sentence foreshadows more than any other contemporary expression the enormous instrument for honesty in high places in the history of his country which it was Theodore Roosevelt's destiny to be.

Mingled with these great cares and far-reaching issues came, later, brighter moments, and it was about that time that during an interval of play at Oyster Bay, he started the custom of his famous "obstacle walks." He would gather all the little cousins and his own children and mine, if I could bring them down for a week-end, on Sunday afternoon at Sagamore Hill (even an occasional "grown person" was considered sufficiently adventurous to be included in the party), and would start on one of the strenuous scrambles which he called an "obstacle walk." It was more like a game than a walk, for it had rules and regulations of its own, the principal one being that each participant should follow the presidential leader "over or through" any obstacle but never "around." There were sometimes as many as twenty little children as we stood on the top of Cooper's Bluff, a high sand-bank overlooking the Sound, ready for the word "go," and all of them children were agog with excitement at the probable obstacles in their path. As we stood on the brink of the big sand-bank, my brother would turn with an amused twinkle in his eye and say: "There is a little path down the side, but I always jump off the top." This, needless to say, was in the form of a challenge, which he always accompanied by a laugh and a leap into the air, landing on whatever portion of his body happened to be the one that struck the lower part of the sand-bank first. Then there would be a shout from the children, and every one would imitate his method of progress, I myself, generally the only other grown person, bringing up the rear rather reluctantly but determined not to have to follow the other important rule of the game, which was that if you could not succeed in going "over or through" that you should put your metaphorical tail between your physical legs and return home. You were not jeered at, no disagreeable remark was directed at you, but your sense of failure was humiliation enough.

Having reached the foot of the bank in this promiscuous fashion, we would all sit on stones and take off our shoes and stockings to shake the quantities of sand therefrom, and then start on the real business of the day. With a sense of great excitement we watched our leader and the devious course he pursued while finding the most trying obstacles to test our courage. I remember one day seeing in our path an especially unpleasant-looking little bathing-house with a very steep roof like a Swiss chalet. I looked at it with sudden dismay, for I realized that only the very young and slender could chin up its slippery sides, and I hoped that the leader of the party would deflect his course. Needless to say, he did not, and I can still see the somewhat sturdy body of the then President of the United States hurling itself at the obstruction and with singular agility chinning himself to the top and sliding down on the other side. The children stormed it with whoops of delight, but I thought I had come to my Waterloo. Just as I had decided that the moment had come for that ignominious retreat of which I have already spoken, I happened to notice a large rusty nail on one side of the unfinished shanty, and I thought to myself: "If I *can* get a footing on that nail, then perhaps I *can* get my hands to the top of that sloping roof, and if I *can* get my hands there, perhaps by Herculean efforts I too can chin myself over the other side." Nothing succeeds like success, for having performed this almost impossible feat and having violently returned into the midst of my anxious group of fellow pedestrians, very much as the little boy does on his sled on the steepest snow-clad hill,

I was greeted with an ovation such as I have never received in later life for the most difficult achievement, literary or philanthropic! From that moment I was regarded as one really fit to take part in the beloved "obstacle walks," which were, I cannot help but think, strong factors in planting in the hearts and characters of the children who thus followed their leader, the indomitable pluck and determination which helped the gallant sons and nephews of Theodore Roosevelt to go undauntedly "over the top" on Flanders Field.

"Over or through, never around"—a good motto, indeed, for Young America, and one which was always exemplified by that American of Americans, my brother, Theodore Roosevelt.

At the end of October that year, his affectionate concern for me (for I was delicate at the time) takes form in a lovely letter in which, after giving me the best of advice, and acknowledging humorously that no one ever really took advice offered, he says: "Heaven bless you always whether you take my advice or not." He never failed to show loving and tender interest in the smallest of my pleasures or anxieties, nor did he and Mrs. Roosevelt ever fail to invite, at my instigation, elderly family friends to lunch at the White House, or gladly to send me autographs for many little boys, or checks to "Dolly," the nurse of his childhood, whose advanced years I superintended.

In April, 1903, he started on a long trip, and at that time felt that, as the years of his inherited incumbency were drawing to a close, he could forward his own gospel. A humorous reference comes in a letter just before he starts, in which he says: "I was immensely amused with Monroe's message [my second son, then at St. Paul's School] about boxing and confirmation, the one evidently having some occult connection with the other in his mind. Give him my love when you write. . . . Well, I start on a nine-weeks' trip tomorrow, as hard a trip as I have ever undertaken, with the sole exception of the canvass in 1900. As a whole, it will be a terrific strain, but there will be an occasional day which I shall enjoy."

Again, as he actually starts on that "hard" trip, he sends me a little line of never-failing love. "White House, April 1, 1903. [This in his own writing.] Darling Pussie: Just a last line of Good-bye. I am so glad your poor hand is better at last. Love to dear old Douglas. The house seems strange and lonely without the children. Ever yours, T. R." Those little notes in his own dear handwriting, showing always the loving thought, are especially precious and treasured.

After that exhausting journey, replete with many thrilling experiences, he returns to Oyster Bay for a little rest, and writes with equal interest of the beautiful family life which was always led there. My boy Stewart was with him at the time, and he speaks of him affectionately in connection with his own "Ted," who was Stewart's intimate friend:

"Stewart, Ted and I took an hour and a half bareback ride all together. Ted is always longing that Stewart should go off on a hunting trip with him. I should be delighted to have them go off now. Although I think no doubt they would get *into* scrapes, I have also no doubt that they would get *out of* them. We have had a lovely summer, as lovely a summer as we have ever passed. All the children have enjoyed their various activities, and we have been a great deal with the children, and in addition to that, Edith and I have ridden on horseback much together, and have frequently gone off for a day at a time in a little row boat, not to speak of the picnics to which everybody went.

"In the intervals I have chopped industriously. I have seen a great many people who came to call upon me on political business. I have had to handle my correspondence of course, and I have had not a few wearing matters of national policy, ranging from the difficulties in Turkey to the scandals in the Post Office. But I have had three months of rest, of holiday, by comparison with what has gone before. Next Monday I go back to Washington, and for the thirteen months following, there will be mighty little let-up to the strain. But I enjoy it to the full.

"What the outcome will be as far as I am personally concerned, I do not know. It looks as if I would be renominated; whether I shall be re-elected I haven't the slightest idea. I know there is bitter opposition to me from many sources. Whether I shall have enough support to overcome this opposition, I cannot tell. I suppose few Presidents can form the slightest idea whether their policies have met with approval or not. Certainly *I* cannot. But as far as I can see, these policies have been right, and I hope that time will justify them. If it doesn't why I must abide the fall of the dice, and that is all there is to it. Ever yours, T. R."

That letter is very characteristic of his usual attitude. Strain, yes; hard work, yes; but equally "I enjoy it to the full"! Equally also was he willing to abide by the "fall of the dice," having done what he fully believed to have been the right thing for the country.

That December, the day after Christmas, he writes again:

"Darling Sister: I so enjoyed seeing you here, but I have been so worried about you. I am now looking forward to Stewart's coming, and to seeing Helen and Ted. But I do wish you would take a rest.

"We had a delightful Christmas yesterday, just such a Christmas as thirty or forty years ago we used to have under Father's and Mother's supervision in 28 East 20th Street. At seven all the children came in to open the big, bulging stockings in our bed; Kermit's terrier, Allan, a most friendly little dog, adding to the children's delight by occupying the middle of the bed. From Alice to Quentin, each child was absorbed in his or her stocking, and Edith certainly managed to get the most wonderful stocking toys. . . . Then after breakfast we all went into the library, where the bigger toys were on separate tables for the children. I wonder whether there ever can come in life a thrill of greater exaltation and rapture than that which comes to one, say between the ages of six and fourteen, when the library doors are thrown open and one walks in to see all the gifts, like a materialized fairyland, arrayed on one's own special table.

"We had a most pleasant lunch at Bamie's [our sister, Mrs. Cowles]. She had given a delightful Christmas tree to the children the afternoon before, and then I stopped in to see Cabot and Nannie [Senator and Mrs. Lodge]. It was raining so hard that we could not walk or ride with any comfort, so Roly Fortescue, Ted and I played 'single stick' in the study later. All of our connections and all of the Lodge connections were at dinner with us, twenty-two in all. After the dinner we danced in the 'East Room,' closing with the Virginia Reel,—Edith looking as young and as pretty, and dancing as well as ever.

"It is a clear, cold morning, and Edith and I and all the children (save Quentin) and also Bob Ferguson and Cabot are about to start for a ride. Your loving brother."

Such were all Christmases at the White House; such was the spirit of the White House in those days.

During the early years of my brother's presidency, my husband and I always spent Thanksgiving at the White House, and joined in festivities very much like the Christmas ones, including the gay Virginia reel, which was also part, always, of the Thanksgiving ceremony. After they bought a little place in Virginia, they spent their Thanksgiving anniversary there.

During the following winter, I visited the White House more frequently than usual, and enjoyed the special ceremonies such as the diplomatic dinner, judicial reception, etc., and I used to station myself near the President when he was receiving the long line of eager fellow citizens, and watch his method of welcoming his guests. Almost always he would have some special word for each, and although the long line would not be held back, for he was so rapid in speech that the individual welcome would hardly take a moment, still almost every person who passed him would have had that extraordinary sense that he or she was personally recognized. It was either a reference to the splendid old veteran father of one, or some devoted sacrifice on the part of the mother of another, or a deed of valor of the person himself, or a merry reminiscence of hunting or Rough-Rider warfare; but with each and every person who passed in what seemed occasionally an interminable line, there was immediately established a personal sense of relationship. Perhaps that was, of all my brother's attributes, the most endearing, namely, that power of his of injecting himself into the life of the other person and of making that other person realize that he was not just an indifferent lump of humanity, but a living and breathing individual coming in contact with another individual even more vividly alive.

After my own visit of special festivity I apparently suggest certain people for him to ask to the White House, or at least I ask him to see them, for in a letter, also in his own handwriting, on February 21, 1904, he says: "Thank you for suggesting F. W. I am glad you told me; it was thoughtful of you. I will also try to see B——, but I don't know whether it will do any good. He is a kind, upright, typical bourgeois of the purely mercantile type; and however much we respect each other, we live in widely different and sundered worlds." So characteristic, this last sentence. Willing he always was to try to do what I wished or thought wise, but also he was always frank in giving me the reason why he felt my wish, in some cases, would bear but little fruit. The bourgeois, mercantile type did indeed live in a different and sundered world from that of the practical idealist, Theodore Roosevelt.

In the summer of 1904, when again I was far from well, he writes from the White House, August 14: "Darling Corinne: The news in your letter greatly worried me. I wish I could call to see you and try to amuse you. I think of you always. Let me know at once, or have Douglas let me know, how you are. Edith came back here for a week with me, and we had a real honeymoon time together. Then she went back to the children. . . . Every spare moment has been occupied with preparing my letter of acceptance. No one can tell how the election will turn out; but I am more than content, whatever comes, for I have been able to do much that was worth doing. With love to Douglas and very, very much love to you, I am, Your devoted Brother." In the midst of the pressing cares of the administration and the fatigue of his letter of acceptance he still has time for the usual unfailing interest in me and mine!

On October 18, again my brother writes:

"Of course, I am excited about the election, but there really isn't much I can do about it, and I confine myself chiefly to the regular presidential work. Nobody can tell anything about the outcome. At the present time, it looks rather favorable to me." And again to my husband on October 25: "As for the result, the Lord only knows what it will be. Appearances look favorable, but I have a mind steeled for any outcome!"

In spite of his "mind steeled for any outcome," the one great ambition of Theodore Roosevelt's life was to be chosen President on his own merits by the people of the United States. He longed for the seal of approval on the devoted service which he had rendered to his country, and one of my clearest memories is my conversation with him on Election day, 1904, when on his way back from voting at Oyster Bay, I met him at Newark, N. J., and went with him as far as Philadelphia. In his private drawing-room on the car, he opened his heart to me, and told me that he had never wanted anything in his life quite as much as the outward and visible sign of his country's approval of what he had done during the last three and a half years. I frankly do not feel that this wish was because of any overweening ambition on his part, but to the nature of Theodore Roosevelt it had always been especially difficult to have come into the great position which he held through a calamity to another rather than as the personal choice of the people of the United States. His temperament was such that he wished no favor which he had not himself won. Therefore, it seemed to him a crucial moment in his life when, on his own merit, he was to be judged as fit or unfit to be his own successor. Not only for those reasons did he wish to be elected in his own right, but because, as was the case in former days when he wished to be renominated governor of New York State, he had again initiated many reforms, and had made many appointments, and he wished to carry those reforms into effect and to back up those appointments with his own helpfulness and prestige.

When we parted in Philadelphia, I to return to my home in Orange and he to go on to meet this vital moment of his career, I remember feeling a poignant anxiety about the result of the election, and it can well be understood the joy I felt that evening when the returns proved him overwhelmingly successful at the polls. Late at night, we received a telegram from the White House directed to Mr. and Mrs. Douglas Robinson in answer to our wire sent earlier in the evening. It ran as follows: "Was glad to hear from you. Only wish you were with us this evening." The next morning I received a letter, only a few lines but infinitely characteristic. They were penned by my brother upon his arrival at the White House after we had parted in Philadelphia, some hours before he knew anything of the election returns. In this letter he describes his sudden reaction from the condition of nervous excitement from which he had suffered during the day. He says: "As I mounted the White House steps, Edith came to meet me at the door, and I suddenly realized that, after all, no matter what the outcome of the election should prove to be, my *happiness* was assured, even though my ambition to have the seal of approval put upon my administration might not be gratified,—for my life with Edith and my children constitutes my *happiness*." This little note posted to me on the eve of his great victory showed clearly his sense of proportion and his conception of true values.

On November 11, 1904, he writes again: "Darling Corinne: I received your letter. I have literally but one moment in which to respond, for I am swamped with letters and telegrams. We have received between eight and ten thousand. I look forward with keen eagerness to seeing you and Douglas."

And so the crucial moment was over, and by a greater majority than had ever before been known in this country, the man of destiny had come into his own, and Theodore Roosevelt, acclaimed by all the people whom he had served so faithfully, was, in his own right and through no sad misfortune, President of the United States of America.

Almost immediately after the excitement of the election, namely, on November 12, 1904, my brother writes to my husband: "If you and Corinne could come on with us to the St. Louis Fair, it would be the greatest possible delight. Now, for Heaven's sake, don't let anything interfere with both of your coming."

Needless to say, we accepted the invitation joyfully, and the trip to the St. Louis Fair was one of our most unique experiences. Coming as it did almost immediately after the great victory of his overwhelming election, wherever the train stopped he received a tremendous ovation, and my memory of him during the transit is equally one of cheering groups and swarming delegations.

In spite of the noise and general excitement, whenever he had a spare moment of quiet, I noticed that he always returned to his own special seat in a corner of the car, and became at once completely absorbed in two large volumes which were always ready on his chair for him. The rest of us would read irrelevantly, perhaps, talk equally irrelevantly, and the hours sped past; but my brother, when he was not actually receiving delegations or making an occasional impromptu speech at the rear end of the car to the patient, waiting groups who longed to show him their devotion, would return in the most detached and focussed manner to the books in which he absorbed himself.

Our two days at St. Louis were the type of days only led by a presidential party at a fair. Before experiencing them I had thought it would be rather "grand" to be a President's sister, with the aforesaid President when he opened a great fair. "Grand" it certainly was, but the exhaustion outbalanced the grandeur. I ran steadily for forty-eight hours without one moment's intermission. My brother never seemed to walk at all, and my whole memory of the St. Louis Fair is a perpetual jog-trot, only interrupted by interminable receptions, presentations of gifts, lengthy luncheons and lengthier evening banquets, and I literally remember *no night* at all! Whether we never went to bed during the time we were at the fair, or exactly what happened to the nights after twelve o'clock, is more than I can say. At the end of the time allotted for the fair, after the last long banquet, we returned to our private car, and I can still see the way in which my sister-in-law (she was not *born* a Roosevelt!) fell into her stateroom. I was about to follow her example (it was midnight) when my brother turned to me in the gayest possible manner and said: "Not going to bed, are you!" "Well," I replied, "I *had thought* of it." "But no," he said; "I told my stenographer this morning to rest all day, for I knew that I would need her services to-night, and now she is perfectly rested." I interrupted him: "But, Theodore, you never told *me* to rest all day. I have been following you all day—" He laughed, but firmly said: "Sit right down here. You will be sorry if you go to bed. I am going to do something that is very interesting. William Rhodes has asked me to review his second and third volumes of the 'History of the United States.' You may have noticed I was reading those volumes on the way from Washington. I feel just like doing it now. The stenographer is rested, and as for you, it will do you a great deal of good, because you don't know as much as you should about American history." Smilingly he put me in a chair and began his dictation. Lord Morley is reported to have said, after his visit to the United States, when asked what he thought most interesting in our country: "There are two *great* things in the United States: one is Niagara, the other is Theodore Roosevelt." As I think of my brother that night, Lord Morley's words come back to me, for it seemed as if, for once, the two great things were combined in one. Such a

Niagara as flowed from the lips of Theodore Roosevelt would have surprised even the brilliant English statesman. He never once referred to the books themselves, but he ran through the whole gamut of their story, suggesting here, interpolating there, courteously referring to some slight inaccuracy, taking up occasionally almost a page of the matter (referring to the individual page without ever glancing at the book), and finally, at 5 A. M., with a satisfied aspect, he turned to me and said: "That is all about 'Rhodes's History.'"

I rose feebly to my feet and said: "Good night, darling." But not at all—still gaily, as if he had just begun a day's work, instead of having reached the weary, littered end of twenty-four hours, he said once more: "Don't go to bed. I must do one other piece of work, and I think you would be especially interested in it. Peter Dunne—'Dooley,' you know—has sent me an article of his on the Irish Question, and wants a review on that from me. I am very fond of Dunne, and really feel I should like to give him my opinions, as they do not entirely agree with his in this particular article. I feel like doing this now. Sit down again." He never asked me to do anything with him that I ever refused, were it in my power to assent to his suggestion. How I rejoice to think that this was the case, and there was no exception made to my usual rule at 5 A. M. that November morning. I sat down again, and sure enough, in a few moments all fatigue seemed to vanish from me, as I listened with eager interest to his masterly review of Peter Dunne's opinions on the Irish situation at that moment. It was a little late, or perhaps one might say a little early, to begin so complicated a subject as the Irish Question, and my final memories of his dictation are confused with the fact that at about 7 A. M. one of the colored porters came in with coffee, and shortly after that I was assisted to my berth in a more or less asphyxiated condition, from which I never roused again until the train reached the station at Washington. That was the way in which Theodore Roosevelt did work. I have often thought that if some of us always had the book at hand that we wanted to read, instead of wasting time in looking for it, if we always had clearly in our minds the extra job we wanted to do, and the tools at hand with which to do it, we might accomplish in some small degree the vast numbers of things he accomplished because of *preparedness*.

As early as December 19, 1904, my sister-in-law wrote me: "Theodore says that he wants you and Douglas under his roof for the Inauguration." I always felt a deep appreciation of the fact that both my brother and his wife made us so welcome at the most thrilling moments of their life in the White House.

In January, 1905, he came to stay with me in New York to speak at several dinners, and a most absurd and yet trying incident occurred, an incident which he met with his usual sunny and unselfish good humor. We had had a large luncheon for him at my home, and when the time came for him to dress in the evening for the dinner at which he was to speak, I suddenly heard a call from the third story, a pitiful call: "I don't think I have my own dress coat." I ran up-stairs, and sure enough the coat laid out with his evening clothes, when he tried to put it on, proved to be so tight across his broad shoulders that whenever he moved his hands it rose unexpectedly almost to his ears. I called my butler, who insisted that he had taken the President's coat with the rest of his clothes to brush, and had brought it back again to his room. This, however, was untrue, for the awful fact was soon divulged that the extra waiter engaged for the luncheon, and who had already left the house, had apparently confused the President's coat, which was in the basement to be pressed, with his own, and had taken away the President's coat! No one knew at this man's house where he had gone. There seemed no method of tracing the coat. We dressed my brother in my husband's coat, but that was even worse, for my husband's coat fell about him in folds, and there seemed nothing for it but to send him to the large public dinner with a coat that, unless most cleverly manipulated, continued to rise unexpectedly above his head. No one but my brother would have taken this catastrophe with unruffled gaiety, but he started off apparently perfectly contented, rather than give me a more dejected feeling than I already had about the misadventure. I, myself, was to go later to the dinner to hear his speech from one of the boxes, and I shall never forget my trepidation when he began his address, as I saw the coat slowly rising higher and higher. At the most critical moment, when it seemed about to surmount his head, a messenger-boy, flurried and flushed with exertion, ran upon the stage with a package in his hand. The recalcitrant waiter had been found by my butler, and the President's coat had been torn from his back. Excusing himself for a moment, with a laughing gesture which brought the coat completely over his head he retired into the wings, changed the article in question, and a few moments later brought down the whole house by his humorous account of the reason for his retirement.

On March 3, 1905, as the guests of my cousin Emlen Roosevelt, who took a special car for the occasion, the members of my family, my husband, and myself started for the inauguration of Theodore Roosevelt as President. Memories crowd about me of those two or three days at the White House. The atmosphere was one of great family gaiety, combined with an underlying seriousness which showed the full realization felt by my brother of the great duties which he was again to assume this time as the choice of the people.

What a day it was, that inaugural day! As usual, the personal came so much into it. The night before, Mr. John Hay sent him a ring with a part of the lock of Abraham Lincoln's hair which John Hay himself had cut from the dead President's forehead almost immediately after his assassination. I have never known my brother to receive a gift for which he cared so deeply. To wear that ring on the day of his own inauguration as President of the United States, elected to the office by the free will of the great American people, was to him, perhaps, the highest fulfilment of his desires. The day dawned dark and threatening and with snow filtering through the clouds, but occasionally rifts of sunlight broke through the sombre bank of gray. The ceremonies were fraught, to those of us who loved him so deeply, with great solemnity. The Vice-President taking his oath in the senate-chamber, the arrival there of the judges of the Supreme Court, the glittering uniforms of the foreign ambassadors and their suites, the appearance of the President-elect, and our withdrawal to the porch of the Capitol, from which he was to make his inaugural address—all of this remains indelibly impressed upon my mind. His solemn, ardent words as he dedicated himself afresh to the service of the country, the great crowd straining to hear each sentence, the eager attitude of the guard of honor (his beloved Rough Riders)—all made a vivid picture never to be forgotten. An eye-witness wrote as follows: "Old Chief Justice Fuller with his beautiful white hair and his long, judicial gown administered the oath, and Roosevelt repeated it so loudly that he could be heard in spite of the wind. In fact the wind rather added to the impressiveness than otherwise, as it gave the President a chance to throw back his shoulders to resist it, and that gave you a wonderful feeling of strength that went splendidly with the speech itself. The speech was short, and was mainly a plea for the 'Peace of Justice' as compared with the 'Peace of the Coward.' It was very stirring. The applause was tremendous."

I would have my readers remember that when Theodore Roosevelt pleaded for such a peace it was in 1905, nine years before peace was broken by the armies of the Huns, and during those long years he never once failed to preach that doctrine, and to the last moment of his life abhorred and denounced the peace of the coward.

Following quickly on his inaugural speech came the luncheon at the White House, at which friends from New York were as cordially welcomed as were Bill Sewall's large family from the Maine woods and Will Merrifield, who, now a marshal, brought the greetings of the State of Montana. After luncheon we all went out on the reviewing-stand. The President stood at the front of the box, his hat always off in response to the salutes. The great procession lasted for hours—West Pointers and naval cadets followed by endless state organizations, governors on horseback, cowboys waving their lassos and shouting favorite slogans (they even lassoed a couple of men, *en passant*), Chief Joseph, the grand old man of the Nez Percé tribe, gorgeously caparisoned, his brilliant head-dress waving in the wind, followed by a body of Indians only a shade less superb in costume, and then a hundred and fifty Harvard fellows in black gowns and caps—and how they cheered for the President as they passed the stand! Surely there was never before such an inauguration of any President in Washington. Never was there such a feeling of personal devotion in so many hearts. Other Presidents have had equal admiration, equal loyalty perhaps, but none has had that loyalty and admiration given by so liberal and varied a number of his fellow countrymen.

It was dark before we left the stand, and soon inside of the White House there followed a reception to the Rough Riders. What a happy time the President had with them recalling bygone adventures, while the Roosevelt and Robinson children ran merrily about listening to the wonderful stories and feeding the voracious Rough Riders. Later the President went bareheaded to the steps under the porte-cochère and received the cowboys, who rode past one after another, joyfully shaking hands with their old chief, ready with some joke for his special benefit, to which there was always a repartee. It was a unique scene as they cheered the incoming magnate under the old porte-cochère, and one never to be repeated. And then the Harvard men filed past to shake hands. Needless to say, dinner was rather late, though very merry, and we were all soon off to the inaugural ball. It was a beautiful sight, the hall enormous, with two rows of arches and pillars, one above the other, along each side. The floor was absolutely crowded with moving people, all with their faces straining up at our box. Ten thousand people bought tickets. Mr. Matthew Hale, then tutor to my nephew Theodore Roosevelt, Jr., has described the scene as follows: "The whole room was beautifully decorated with lights and wreaths and flowers. As I stood looking down on the great pageant I felt as though I were in some other world,—as though these people below there and moving in and out were not real people, but were all part of some great mechanism built for our special benefit. And then my feeling would change to the other extreme when I thought of each one of those men and women as individuals, each one thinking, and feeling and acting according to his own will,—and that all, just for that one night, came together for a common purpose, to see the President. Soon an open place appeared in the throng before us, and the President and Mrs. Roosevelt, and behind them Vice-President and Mrs. Fairbanks, walked to the other end of the hall and back, while the people cheered and cheered." And soon it was time to go back to the White House, and then, best of all, came what we used to call a "back-hair" talk in Theodore and Edith's room. What fun we had as we talked the great day over in comfortable déshabille. A small round bottle of old wine was found somewhere by Mrs. Roosevelt, and the family drank the President's health, and we talked of old times and childhood days, and of the dear ones whose hearts would have glowed so warmly had they lived to see that day. We laughed immoderately over all kinds of humorous happenings, and we could hardly bear to say "good night," we still felt so gay, so full of life and fun, so invigorated and stimulated by the excitement and by the deeper thoughts and desires, which, however, only took the form that night of increasing hilarity!

Shortly after that March inauguration my daughter Corinne, just eighteen, was asked by her kind aunt to pay a visit at the White House, and I impressed upon her the wonderful opportunity she would have of listening to the great men of the world at the informal luncheon gatherings which were a feature of my brother's incumbency. "Do not miss a word," I said to my daughter. "Uncle Ted brings to luncheon all the great men in Washington—almost always several members of the cabinet, and any one of interest who is visiting there. Be sure and listen to everything. You will never hear such talk again." When she returned home from that visit I eagerly asked her about the wonderful luncheons at the White House, where I had so frequently sat spellbound. My somewhat irreverent young daughter said: "Mother, I laughed internally all through the first luncheon at the White House during my visit. Uncle Ted was perfectly lovely to me, and took me by the hand and said: 'Corinny, dear, you are to sit at my right hand to-day, and you must have the most delightful person in the room on your other side.' With that he glanced at the distinguished crowd of gentlemen who were surrounding him waiting to be assigned to their places, and picking out a very elderly gentleman with a long white beard, he said with glowing enthusiasm: 'You shall have John Burroughs, the great naturalist.' I confess I had hoped for some secretary in the cabinet, but, no, Uncle Ted did not think there was any one in the world that compared in thrilling excitement to his wonderful old friend and lover of birds. Even so, I thought, 'Mother would wish me to learn all about natural history, and I shall hear marvellous ornithological tales, even if politics must be put aside.' But even in that I was somewhat disappointed, for at the very beginning of luncheon Uncle Ted leaned across me to Mr. Burroughs and said: 'John, this morning I heard a chippy sparrow, and he sang twee, twee, right in my ear.' Mr. Burroughs, with a shade of disapproval on his face, said: 'Mr. President, you must be mistaken. It was not a *chippy* sparrow if it sang twee, twee. The note of the *chippy* sparrow is twee, twee, twee.' From that moment the great affairs of our continent, the international crises of all kinds were utterly forgotten, while the President of the United States and his esteemed guest, the great naturalist, discussed with a good deal of asperity whether that chippy sparrow had said 'twee, twee,' or 'twee, twee, twee.' We rose from the table with the question still unsettled." My brother always loved to hear my daughter tell this story, although his face would assume a somewhat sheepish expression as she dilated on the difference between her mother's prognostications of what a luncheon at the White House would mean from an intellectual standpoint, and what the realization actually became!

In spite of my daughter's experience, however, I can say with truth that there never were such luncheons as those luncheons at the White House during my brother's life there. The secretary of state, Mr. Elihu Root, with his unusual knowledge, his pregnant wit, and quiet, brilliant sarcasm; the secretary of war, Mr. Taft, with his gay smile and ready response; Mr. Moody, the attorney-general with his charming culture and universal kindliness, and Senator Henry Cabot Lodge, the brilliant scholar and statesman, my brother's most intimate friend and constant companion, were frequent members of the luncheon-parties, and always, the most distinguished visitor to Washington, from whatever country or from whatever State of our own country, would be brought in with the same informal hospitality and received for the time being by President and Mrs. Roosevelt into the intimacy of family life. The whole cabinet would occasionally adjourn from one of their most important meetings to the lunch-table, and then the President and Mr. Root would cap each other's stories of the way in which this or that question had been discussed during the cabinet meeting. I doubt also if ever there were quite such cabinet meetings as were held during those same years!

That spring Mr. Robinson and I took my daughter to Porto Rico to visit Governor and Mrs. Beekman Winthrop. My brother believed strongly in young men, and having admired the intelligence of young Beekman Winthrop (he came of a fine old New York family) as circuit judge in the Philippines, he decided to make him governor of Porto Rico. He was only twenty-nine, and his charming wife still younger, but they made a most ideal couple as administrators of the beautiful island.

After having been with them in the old palace for about a week, and having enjoyed beyond measure all that was so graciously arranged for us, I was approached one day by Governor Winthrop, who told me that he was much distressed at the behavior of a certain official and that he felt sure that the President would not wish the man to remain in office, for he was actually a disgrace to the United States. "Mrs. Robinson," he said, "will you not go to the President on your return, and tell him that I am quite sure he would not wish to retain this man in office? I know the President likes us to work with the tools which have been given us, and I dislike beyond measure to seem not to be able to do so, but I am convinced that this man should not represent the United States in this island." "Have you your proofs, Beekman?" I asked. "I should not be willing to approach my brother with any such criticism without accurate proofs." "I most assuredly have them," he answered, and sure enough he *did* have them, and I shortly afterward sailed with them back to New York. Immediately upon my arrival I telegraphed my brother as follows: "Would like to see you on Porto Rican business. When shall I come?" One of Theodore Roosevelt's most striking characteristics was the rapidity with which he answered letters or telegrams. One literally felt that one had not posted a letter or sent the telegram rushing along the wire before the rapid answer came winging back again, and *that* particular telegram was no exception to the rule. I had rather hoped for a week's quiet in which to get settled after my trip to Porto Rico, but that was not to be. The rapid-fire answer read as follows: "Come tomorrow." Of course there was nothing for me to do but go "tomorrow." It was late in April, and as I drove up to the White House from the station, I thought how lovely a city was Washington in the springtime. The yellow forsythias gave a golden glow to the squares, and the soft hanging petals of the fringe-trees waved in the scented air. I never drove under the White House porte-cochère without a romantic feeling of excitement at the realization that it was *my* brother, lover of

Lincoln, lover of America, who lived under the roof which symbolized all that America means to her children. As I went up the White House steps, he blew out of the door, dressed for his ride on horseback. His horse and that of a companion were waiting for him. He came smilingly toward me, welcomed me, and said: "Edie has had to go to Philadelphia for the night to visit Nellie Tyler, so we are all alone, and I have ordered dinner out on the back porch, for it is so warm and lovely, and there is a full moon, and I thought we could be so quiet there. I have so much to tell you. All sorts of political things have happened during your absence, and besides that I have learned several new poems of Kipling and Swinburne, and I feel like reciting them to you in the moonlight!" "How perfectly lovely," I replied, "and when shall I see you about Porto Rico?" A slight frown came on his brow, and he said, "Certainly not to-night," and then rather sternly: "You have your appointment at nine o'clock to-morrow morning in the office to discuss business matters." Then with a returning smile: "I will be back pretty soon. Good-by." And he jumped on his horse and clattered away toward Rock Creek.

It all came true, although it almost seemed like a fairy-tale. We *had* that dinner *à deux* on the lovely portico at the rear of the White House looking toward the Washington Monument—that portico was beautifully reproduced by Sargent's able brush for Mrs. Roosevelt later—and under the great, soft moon, with the scent of shrub and flower in the air, he recited Kipling and Swinburne, and then falling into more serious vein, gave me a vivid description of some difficulty he had had with Congress, which had refused to receive a certain message which he had written and during the interval between the sending of it and their final decision to receive it, he had shut himself up in his library, glad to have a moment of unexpected leisure, and had written an essay, which he had long desired to write, on the Irish sagas. The moon had waned and the stars were brighter and deeper before we left the portico. We

From the drawing by Jules Guérin.

We had that lovely dinner on the portico at the back of the White House looking toward the Washington Monument.

never could go to bed when we were together, and I am so glad that we never did!

The next morning I knocked at his door at eight o'clock, to go down to the early breakfast with the children, which was one of the features also, quite as much as were the brilliant lunches, of home life in the White House. He came out of his dressing-room radiant and smiling, ready for the day's work, looking as if he had had eight hours of sleep instead of five, and rippling all over with the laughter which he always infused into those family breakfasts. As we passed the table at the head of the staircase, at which later in the day my sister's secretary wrote her letters, the telephone-bell on the table rang, and with spontaneous simplicity—not even thinking of ringing a bell for a "menial" to answer the telephone-call—he picked up the receiver himself as he passed by. His face assumed a listening look, and then a broad smile broke over his features. "No," he said. "No, I am not Archie, I am Archie's father." A second passed and he laughed aloud, and then said: "All right, I will tell him; I won't forget." Hanging up the receiver, he turned to me half-sheepishly but very much amused. "That's a good joke on any President," he said. "You may have realized that there was a little boy on the other end of that wire, and he started the conversation by saying, 'Is that you, Archie?' and I replied, 'No, it is Archie's father.' Whereupon he answered, with evident disgust: 'Well, you'll *do*. Be sure and tell Archie to come to supper. Now, don't forget.' 'How the creatures order you about!'" he gaily quoted from our favorite book, "Alice in Wonderland," and proceeded to run at full speed down to the breakfast-room. There the children greeted us vociferously, and the usual merry breakfast ensued. For that half-hour he always belonged to the children. Questions and answers about their school life, their recreation when out of school, etc., etc., followed in rapid succession, interspersed with various fascinating tales told by him for their special edification.

After they had dispersed there was still a half-hour left before he went to the office at 9 o'clock, and whenever I visited the White House (my visits were rather rare, as my husband, being a busy real-estate broker in New York, could not often break away) that half-hour was always given to me, and we invariably walked around the great circle at the back of the White House. It was his most vigorous moment of the day, that hour from 8.30 to 9. He had not yet met the puzzling defeats and compromises necessitated by the conflicting interests of the many appointments in the office, and he was fresh and vivid, interested in the problems that were to be brought to him for solution that day, and observant of everything around him. I remember that morning as we walked around the circle he was discussing a very serious problem that had to be decided immediately, and he held his forefinger straight up, and said: "You know my temperament always wants to get there"—putting his other forefinger on the apex of the first. "I naturally wish to reach the goal of my desire, but would I not be very blind and stupid if, because I couldn't get *there*, I decided to stay here [changing his right forefinger to the base of the left] "rather than get here"—finishing his simile by placing the right finger to the third notch of the finger on his other hand.

Just as he was finishing this simile his eye caught sight of a tiny object on the pathway, so minute a little brown spot that I should never have noticed it; but he stooped, picked it up, and held it between his forefinger and thumb, looking at it eagerly, and then muttering somewhat below his breath: "Very early for a fox-sparrow." He threw the tiny piece of fluff again upon the path. "How do you know that that was a feather from a fox-sparrow, Theodore?" I said, in my usual astonishment at his observation and information. "I can understand how you might know it was a sparrow, but how know it belonged to the fox-sparrow rather than to any of the other innumerable little creatures of that species?" He was almost deprecatory in his manner as he said in reply: "Well, you see I have really made a great study of sparrows." And then we were back at the entrance to the White House, and in a moment I leaned out of the dining-room window and watched him walk across the short space between that window and the office, his head thrown back, his shoulders squared to meet the difficulties of the day, and every bit of him alert, alive, and glowing with health and strength and power and mentality.

I went up-stairs, put on my "best bib and tucker," and proceeded to go around the other way to the front door of the offices. As I rang the bell the dear old man who always opened the door greeted me warmly, and said: "Yes, Mrs. Douglas Robinson, your appointment is at 9. It is just time." I went into the outer hall, where a number of the appointees of 9.15, 9.30, etc., were already waiting, to be surely on hand for their appointments, and in a moment or two Mr. Loeb opened the door of the private office of the President, and came out into the hall and said in a rather impersonal way, "Mrs. Douglas Robinson's appointment," and I was shown into the room. My brother was seated at a large table, and on it was every imaginable paper marked "Porto Rico." As I entered he was still reading one of these papers. He looked up, and I almost felt a shock as I met what seemed to be a pair of perfectly opaque blue eyes. I could hardly believe they were the eyes of the brother with whom I had so lately parted, the eyes that had glistened as he recited the poems of Kipling and Swinburne, the eyes that had almost closed to see better the tiny breast-fluff of the fox-sparrow. These were rather cold eyes, the eyes of a just judge, eyes that were turned upon his sister as they would have been turned upon any other individual who came to him in connection with a question about which he must give his most careful and deliberate decision. He waved me to a chair, finished the paper he was reading, and then turning to me, his eyes still stern and opaque, he said: "I believe you have come to see me on business connected with Porto Rico. Kindly be as condensed as possible." I decided to meet him on his own ground, and made my eyes as much like his as possible, and was as condensed as possible. Having listened carefully to my short story, he said: "Have you proof of this?" still rather sternly. Again I decided to answer as he asked, and I replied: "I should not be here, wasting your time and mine, did I not have adequate proof." With that I handed him the notes made by the governor of Porto Rico, and proceeded to explain them. He became a little less severe after reading them, but no less serious, and turning to me more gently, said: "This is a very serious matter. I have got to be sure of the correctness of these statements. A man's whole future hangs upon my decision." For a moment I felt like an executioner, but realizing as I did the shocking and disgraceful behavior of the official in question, I knew that no sentimentality on my part should interfere with the important decision to be made, and I briefly backed up all that the governor had written. I can still hear the sound of the President's pen as he took out the paper on which the man's name was inscribed, and with one strong stroke effaced that name from official connection with Porto Rico forever. That was the way that Theodore Roosevelt did business with his sister.

During that same year, 1905, the old Provençal poet Frédéric Mistral sent him his volume called "Mireille," and the acknowledgment of the book seems to me to express more than almost any other letter ever written by my brother the spirit which permeated his whole life. It shows indisputably that though he had reached the apex of his desires, that though he was a great President of a great country, perhaps the most powerful ruler at the moment of any country, that his ideals for that country, just as his ideals for himself and for his own beloved home life, were what they had always been before the sceptre of power had been clasped by his outstretched hand.

White House, Washington,
December 15, 1905.

My dear M. Mistral:

Mrs. Roosevelt and I were equally pleased with the book and the medal, and none the less because for nearly twenty years we have possessed a copy of Mireille. That copy we shall keep for old association's sake, though this new copy with the personal inscription by you must hereafter occupy the place of honor.

All success to you and your associates! You are teaching the lesson that none need more to learn than we of the West, we of the eager, restless, wealth-seeking nation; the lesson that after a certain not very high level of material well-being has been reached, then the things that really count in life are the things of the spirit. Factories and railways are good up to a certain point, but courage and endurance, love of wife and child, love of home and country, love of lover for sweetheart, love of beauty in man's work and in nature, love and emulation of daring and of lofty endeavour, the homely work-a-day virtues and the heroic virtues—these are better still, and if they are lacking, no piled-up riches, no roaring, clanging industrialism, no feverish and many-sided activity shall avail either the individual or the nation. I do not undervalue these things of a nation's body; I only desire that they shall not make us forget that beside the nation's body there is also the nation's soul.

Again thanking you on behalf of both of us, believe me,

Faithfully yours,

(Signed) THEODORE ROOSEVELT.

To M. Frédéric Mistral.

No wonder that Mistral turned to a friend after reading that letter and said with emotion: "It is he who is the new hope of humanity."

XII

HOME LIFE IN THE WHITE HOUSE

(CONTINUED)

Men smile through falling tears,
Remembering the courage of his years
That stood each one for God, humanity,
And covenanted world-wide Liberty!

—Edith Daley.

ONE of the most extraordinary things about my brother was that in the midst of his full political life, a life "pressed down and overflowing," he still had time for the most loving interest in personal family matters. Just after the great moment of his inauguration, he sent me a number of photographs of my eldest son and his young wife, just married, who had gone around the world and were staying with General Wood in the Philippines, and adds in the letter: "It was such a pleasure to have Douglas and you down here for the inauguration, and to see the boy's and Corinne." In June of that same year, when my two younger boys had each won a boat-race at St. Paul's School, he takes a moment from his pressing duties to write another letter: "Darling Corinne: Good for Monroe and Stewart! Give them my hearty congratulations; I have only time for this line." Such unusual thoughtfulness could not fail to keep burning perpetually the steady fire of my love for him.

In July, 1905, he sent me one of the inauguration medals signed by Saint-Gaudens. In looking at the head upon that medal, one realized perfectly by the strong lines of temple and forehead that Theodore Roosevelt had come to the fulness of his intellectual powers.

About the same time there was a naval review at Oyster Bay, and Mrs. Roosevelt writes: "The review was a wonderful sight. I wish you could have been here. The morning was dark and stormy, with showers of driving rain, until Theodore's flag broke out from the *Mayflower*, when the clouds suddenly dispersed and the sun shone brightly." How often we used to feel that the sun always broke out when Theodore's flag flew!

One other little line from his pen, December 19, 1905, shows the same constant thoughtfulness. He says: "Will you send the enclosed note to Dora? I am not sure of her address. I hate to trouble you, but I want to have poor 'Dolly' get it by Christmas Day." Dora was his old, childhood nurse, one to whom we were very much devoted, and whom he never forgot.

At the beginning of the new year, 1906, he writes to my husband: "Dear Douglas,—By George! Stewart is doing well. [I think this referred to the fact that my youngest boy had been chosen as goal-keeper of the St. Paul's School hockey team!] That is awfully nice. I was mighty glad Wadsworth was elected. I shall have difficulties this year, and I cannot expect to get along as well as I did last year, but I shall do the best I can." Never blinded by past popularity, always ready for the difficulties to come, and yet never dwelling so strongly on these difficulties that by the very dwelling on them even greater difficulties were brought to bear upon him. It was quite true that it proved in many ways, a more difficult year than the one preceding, but a happy year all the same, a happiness which culminated in his satisfaction in the marriage of his daughter Alice to Nicholas Longworth, of Cincinnati, Ohio, an able member of the House of Representatives. His announcement to me of the engagement was made at the dinner-table one evening before it was known to the world, and not wishing to have it disclosed *to* the world through the table-servants, he decided to give me the news in French. His French was always fluent, but more or less of a literal translation from the English, which method he exaggerated humorously. "Je vais avoir un fils en loi," he said, smiling gaily at me across the table, delighted at my puzzled expression. With a little more explanation I realized what he was suggesting to my befuddled brain, and he then proceeded to describe a conversation he had had with the so-called "fils en loi," and how he had talked to him like "un oncle Hollandais," or "Dutch uncle"!

There was much excitement at the prospect of a wedding in the White House, and, needless to say, so many were the requests to be present that the line had to be drawn very carefully, and, in consequence, the whole affair assumed an intimate and personal aspect. Alice's Boston grandparents, Mr. and Mrs. George C. Lee, were especially welcomed by Mrs. Roosevelt, and my memory of the great morning of the wedding has a curiously "homey" quality. I much doubt if there was ever a function—for a wedding in the White House could hardly be anything but a function—so simple, so charming, and so informal as that marriage of the lovely daughter of the White House. Almost all the morning Mrs. Roosevelt knitted peacefully at the sunny window up-stairs near her secretary's desk, chatting quietly with Mrs. Lee. All preparations seemed to have been made in the most quiet and efficient manner, for there was no hurry, no excitement. My husband took Mr. Lee for a walk, as the dear old gentleman was very much excited at the prospect of his granddaughter's nuptials in the "East Room." Everything seemed to go on quite as usual until the actual moment came, and Alice Roosevelt, looking very beautiful in her long court train and graceful veil, came through the group of interested friends up to the white ribbon which formed, with flowers, a chancel at the end of the "East Room." My brother was at his best—gay, affectionate, full of life and fun, and later took his son-in-law (no longer "to-be") and all the ushers, members of Harvard's Porcellian Club like himself, into the state dining-room to drink the health of the bride and groom, and recall various incidents of his and of their college days.

In March of that year I wrote him that my youngest boy was to debate at St. Paul's School on the Santo Domingo question, and he answered at once, with that marvellous punctuality of his: "I wrote Stewart at once and sent him all the information I could on the Santo Domingo business. I wish you were down here. In great haste. Ever yours, T. R."

In great haste, yes, but not too busy to write to a schoolboy-nephew "at once," and give him the most accurate information that could be given on the question upon which he was to take part in school debate.

Again, when I suggested joining him in his car on his way that fall to vote at Oyster Bay, he writes: "Three cheers! Now you can join me. We will have lunch immediately after leaving. I am so anxious to see you. I shall just love the Longfellow." [Evidently some special edition that I am about to bring to him.]

On November 20, with his usual interest in my boys, he sends me a delightful letter from his ex-cowboy superintendent, Will Merrifield, with whom they had been hunting in August and September, 1906; and I am interested to see after reading his opinion of my boys how Mr. Merrifield, although many years had passed since the old days of the Elkhorn Ranch, still turns to him for advice, still, beyond all else, wishes to justify his various ventures in the eyes of his old "boss." Merrifield writes: "I have sold my ranch, and will be able to make good all my financial obligations, which was my great ambition, besides having something left, so that *I will not take office for the purpose of making money*. [That was one of Theodore Roosevelt's perpetual preachings, that no one should take office for the purpose of making money.] I can be independent as far as money goes, and *above all* will be able to make good my word to you years ago, as soon as my business is straightened out." He sends me the letter not because of that sentence, but because, as he says,

"This letter from Merrifield is so nice about Monroe and Stewart that I thought I would send it to you. How well they did." Always the same generous joy in the achievements of any of the younger generation.

Again, on December 26, comes a long letter describing another "White House Christmas." He deplores the fact that the children are growing a little older, and that "Ted" says in a melancholy way that he no longer feels the wild excitement of former years and the utter inability to sleep soundly during the night before Christmas. He adds, however: "Personally I think that 'Ted' also was thoroughly in the spirit of the thing when Christmas actually arrived, because by six o'clock every child of every size was running violently to and fro along the hall, in and out of all the other children's rooms, the theory being that Edith and I were still steeped in dreamless and undisturbed slumber!"

It is true that that winter *was* more difficult than the winter before, but he met the unusual difficulties with unabated courage, and writes in October, 1907, after giving me much family news: "Indeed times have been bad in New York, and as is always the case the atonement was largely vicarious, and innocent people suffered. I hope it does not extend through the rest of the country. If we check it, I think it will mean ultimate good, though it will also mean depression for a year at least."

In March, 1908, in the midst of harassing controversies and presidential difficulties of all kinds, he takes the time and interest to write concerning a young friend of mine into whose life had come an unfortunate trouble. The letter is so full of a certain quality—what perhaps I might call a righteous ruthlessness specially characteristic of Theodore Roosevelt—that I quote a few lines from it:

"I hate to think of her suffering; but the only thing for her to do now is to treat the past as past, the event as finished and out of her life; to dwell on it, and above all to keep talking of it with any one, would be both weak and morbid. She should try not to think of it; this she cannot wholly avoid, but she *can* avoid speaking of it. She should show a brave and cheerful front to the world, whatever she feels; and henceforth she should never speak one word of the matter to any one. In the long future, when the memory is too dead to throb, she may, if she wishes, speak of it once more, but if she is wise and brave, she will not speak of it now."

This note referring to a matter which did not come, except through the interests of affection, close to his own life shows with startling clearness the philosophy of his attitude toward sorrows wherein an original mistake had perhaps been the cause of sorrow. Of all the qualities in my brother, this one never failed him. It was not harshness; it was, as I said, a righteous ruthlessness. The thing that injured one's possibility for service in any way must be cut out or burnt out. When that great sorrow of his own life, the death of his splendid boy, came in July, 1918, although he never put aside the sympathy of others—indeed, he gladly welcomed it, and gladly even would talk with those in his innermost circle of the youngest he loved so well—still, as a rule, his attitude was similar to that taken in the above letter. Morbid craving could *not* bring back his child; morbid craving *could* hurt his own potential power for good. The grief must be met with high head and squared shoulders, and the work still to do *must* be done.

All through the spring of 1908 the question as to his successor in the White House was constantly in his mind. After serious thought he had come to the conclusion that of the men closest to him, William Howard Taft, who had done splendid work as governor in the Philippines and had been an able lieutenant in the work of the Roosevelt administration, would most conscientiously carry out the policies he thought vital for the country. This belief did not in any way mean that he wished Mr. Taft to be an automaton or dummy, possible of manipulation, but he felt that his then secretary of war was more thoroughly in sympathy with the policies which he believed to be the right policies for our country than any other man except the secretary of state, Mr. Elihu Root, whose possible election to the presidency he felt would be very doubtful. Many have criticised in later years, especially after the trouble in 1912, his choice of Mr. Taft to succeed him. There came out at one time an article in the periodical *Life* which, to my mind, explained well the confidence which my brother placed in almost every man who worked with him. The article said approximately: "The reason that Theodore Roosevelt occasionally made mistakes in feeling that some of his associates in the work of the government would continue to be what he believed them to be, is as follows: *While* any individual was working with Mr. Roosevelt, in fact, *under* Mr. Roosevelt, the latter had the power of inspiring the said individual with his own acuteness, his own energy, his own ability. The person, therefore, frequently shone with a reflex light, a light which seemed to Mr. Roosevelt to originate in him, but in fact, came from his own unfailing sources. The consequence is that when some official who had seemed to Mr. Roosevelt to be almost a *rara avis*, was left to his own devices, and without the magnetic personality of his chief to inspire in him qualities not really indigenous in him, the change in what that official could accomplish was very marked." Theodore Roosevelt was convinced that Mr. Taft was entirely in accord with the policies in which he so fully believed, and he had absolute confidence that in leaving in his hands the work which he had striven so hard to perfect. he was doing the best thing possible for the United States.

At that time the people wanted to renominate my brother as President. He, however, was convinced that a renomination would have defeated the spirit of the unwritten law that no man should succeed himself a third time in succession.

I was present at the convention in Chicago in 1908, and have fortunately retained a letter written to my children the very morning of that convention, which runs as follows:

"Oh, how I wish you could have been here this morning.

Such an ovation was never known as greeted Mr. Lodge's mention of your Uncle Ted. Mr. Lodge's speech was most scholarly and reserved, and in referring to the laws, he said, 'The President has invariably enforced the laws, and the President is the most abused and the most *popular* man in the country.' Then came a ripple and then a mighty shout of applause, growing louder and louder, increasing and increasing more and more every moment. They clapped, they shouted, they cheered. The whole great Convention sang the Star Spangled Banner, and then they clapped again, and carried 'Teddybears' around the hall. They took off their coats and swung them around their heads. You have never even imagined anything like it. Several times, Mr. Lodge raised his gavel, but with no result, and finally he started his speech again, and persevered until the deafening noise began to subside fifty minutes after it began. It really was a wonderful and thrilling scene. It was three o'clock before we could keep our luncheon engagement at George Porter's that first day."

The following day it required all Mr. Lodge's determination, and a ringing message over the telephone from the White House itself, to prevent the renomination of my brother. Not only did the people want him, but, what has been so often *not* the case, the *delegates* wanted him as well. It was one of those rare moments at a great convention when the people and the delegates were in accord, and yet, it was not to be. The will of Theodore Roosevelt was carried out, and William Howard Taft was chosen as the nominee of the Republican party for the next President of the United States.

On June 23, 1908, came a letter from the White House to me: "Darling Corinne—It was very good of you and Douglas to telegraph me. I am extremely pleased with the result of the Convention. I think Cabot's handling of it was masterly." And then, on June 26, an extremely interesting letter came, one, I think, which, written as it was four years before the great controversy of 1912, settles forever that question which was so much discussed as to what Theodore Roosevelt meant by his statement that he would not run for the presidency again. This letter, on White House paper, is dated Oyster Bay, June 26, 1908:

"Darling Corinne—My letter must have crossed yours. It was just exactly as you and Alice said. Now there is nothing to explain. I have been much amused at the fact that my English friends are wholly incapable of understanding my reasons for the view I take, and think it due to weakness or some fantastic scruple on my part. My theory has been that the presidency should be a powerful office, and the President a powerful man, who will take every advantage of it; but, as a corollary, a man who can be held accountable to the people, after a term of four years, and who will not in any event occupy it for more than a *stretch* of eight years. . . ." Nothing is more conclusive of my brother's attitude than that sentence "who will not in any event occupy it for more than a *stretch* of eight years." He did not believe in a third term *consecutively*, but in no way did he pledge himself at that time, or at any other time, not to consider again the possible gift of the highest place in the nation, should an interval come between his occupancy of the White House and the renewed desire of the people that he should fill that place in the nation once more. I have given some time to his attitude on this question, as it has been much misunderstood.

In amusing contrast to the seriousness of his decision not to accept a renomination comes a characteristic incident in the President's career. The account of this I quote from a letter to me of Mr. Gustavus Town Kirby, a participator himself in the event. The letter runs as follows:

"In 1908 the Olympic Games had been held at London, England, and when the athletes returned to this country, most of them went, with some heads of the American Olympic Committee, including the late James E. Sullivan and myself, to visit and receive the congratulations of the then President of the United States at his summer home in Oyster Bay. [What committee, on no matter *what* important business, did not receive the congratulations of that eclectic President at his summer home at Oyster Bay!] I shall never forget the enthusiasm of the gathering, nor how, no sooner had either Sullivan or I presented a member of the team to the President, than he would, by use of his wonderful memory and in his most inspiring manner, tell the special athlete all about his own performance,—how far he had put the shot to win his event, or how gamely he had run; by how much he had beaten his competitor; his new world-record time, and the like. At the time I marvelled, and I thought even one as great as he must have 'brushed up' for the occasion, but 'Billy' Loeb, his Secretary, told me afterwards that it was not so, and that all during the Games he was kept constantly informed of the result of the performances of our boys; and while he actually knew none of these boys by sight, he not only knew them by name, but their performances as well. Not only to me, but to all gathered at this reception was this feat of memory most astounding. Mr. Roosevelt's gracious cordiality, his fine speech of congratulation, and his magnetic personality had such an effect on all that it was with great difficulty that they could be literally *driven* from the grounds and onto the Long Island boat for their return to New York.

"Michael Murphy, the trainer, many years trainer at Yale, and thereafter at 'Pennsylvania,' and also for the New York Athletic Club, whose team in 1895 was triumphant over the great team of the London Athletic Club, was also a member of the party. On the way back in the boat I happened to pass through the cabin, which was entirely empty except for Michael Murphy, who, like the all but wizened-up old man he was, having but about a quarter of a lung, and deaf except to those things which he could not hear, sat huddled in a corner. I went up to Mike and said, 'What are you doing?' He answered, 'I am thinking!' I replied, 'Yes, that is evident; but what are you thinking about?' He then said: 'Well, Mr. Kirby, I suppose there is no doubt but that I am the greatest trainer of men in the world.' 'That certainly is true,' I said. He went on: 'Mr. Kirby, you are all wrong; until we went down to Oyster Bay I thought I might be, but now I know I am not.' 'But,' I said, 'Mike, that is nonsense. What do you mean?' Then Mike answered, 'Give me sixty men, every one of whom is a champion, and let that man at Oyster Bay have sixty other men, every one of whom is a dub, and his team would lick mine every time!' I said, 'Mike, this is impossible; it could not be,' and then Mike continued,—showing how that magnetic personality of Mr. Roosevelt's had taken hold of him, and how truly he, Mike Murphy, understood the psychology of inspiration,—'Yes, Mr. Kirby, you see it's this way; that man down there would tell a miler that he could reel off a mile in four minutes, (as you know, no one has run, or ever will run a mile in four minutes) and not only would that man *think* he could run a mile in four minutes, but, by Gad, he'd go out and *do* it.'"

Perhaps no one has ever more cleverly expressed the extraordinary power of that personality than that wizened old trainer, sunk into despondency because he realized that where men are concerned skill and science are as nothing compared to the genius of leadership.

That summer my brother showed to my husband and myself his never-failing love and consideration in a very special manner. My husband's mother had died a couple of years before, and her son and daughter and myself had decided that the most fitting memorial to one who was specially beloved and missed in the immediate vicinity of her old home would be the erection of a small free library to the memory of her and her husband. The building was completed, and my husband wished to have a dedication service, at which time he would hand over the keys to the library trustees in our village of Jordanville. My husband's old home, a grant in the time of Queen Anne to his great-great-great-grandfather, Doctor James Henderson, of Scotland, had always been a place for which my brother had a deep affection. Situated as it was on the high Mohawk hills overlooking the great sweep of typical American farm-land, we lived a somewhat Scotch life in the old gray-stone mansion copied from the manor-house of Mr. Robinson's Scotch ancestors. My brother delighted in our relationship with the neighbors in our environment, and accepted gladly my husband's earnest desire that he should make the speech of dedication when the library was given by us to the little village of Jordanville.

It was a great day for that tiny village when the President of the United States, his secretary of state, Mr. Elihu Root,. and the Vice-President-elect, James S. Sherman, a native of the next county, after being our guests at luncheon, proceeded on my husband's four-in-hand brake to the steps of the little colonial building three miles away, designed by our friend Mr. S. Breck P. Trowbridge.

What a day it was and what fun we had! After the library exercises we held a reception at our home, Henderson House, and hundreds of every sort and kind of vehicle were left or tethered along the high ridge near our house. My brother and I stood at the end of the quaint old drawing-room, and an endless file of country neighbors passed before him, and each and all were greeted with his personal enthusiasm and the marvellous knowledge of their interests with which the slightest word from me seemed to make him cognizant. The sunset lights faded over the Mohawk hills and lost their last gleam in the winding river below before the last "dead-wood coach" or broken-down buggy had disappeared from the grounds of Henderson House, and then in the old hall my own family servants—many of them had been twenty or thirty years upon the place—came in to greet him after supper, and sang the hymn which they often sang on Sunday evenings: "God be with you till we meet again." The stories of that day will be told in time to come by the children's children of my kind friends of Warren Township, Herkimer County. Theodore himself writes of the experience as follows:

"Oyster Bay, August 27, 1908. Dearest Corinne and Douglas: There is not a thing I would have missed throughout the whole day. It was a very touching little ceremony, and most of all it was delightful to see you two in your lovely home, living just the kind of life that I feel is typical of what American life should be at its best. I was so glad to see all your neighbors, and to see the terms they were on with you. Moreover, the view, the grounds, the house itself, and all there was therein, were delightful beyond measure; and most delightful of all was it to see the three generations ranging from you two to the babies of dear Helen and Teddy. Ever yours, Theodore Roosevelt." As usual, he never spared an effort to do the lovely thing, and then say the satisfying thing to those for whom he had done the service.

And now the time of Theodore Roosevelt's incumbency as President was drawing to a close. There is always a glamour as well as a shadow over "last times," and my last visit to the White House, in February, 1909, stands out very clearly. My brother, the year before, had sent the great American fleet around the world, an expedition discountenanced by many, and yet conceded later to have been one of his most brilliantly conceived strategic inspirations. "In time of peace, prepare for war," said Washington, and Theodore Roosevelt always followed that maxim. That trip around the world of the American fleet was more conducive to peace than any other action that could have been taken. The purpose was "friendly," of course, but those splendid battle-ships of ours, engineered by such able commanders, could not fail to be an object-lesson to any who felt that the United States was too isolated to care for her own defense.

But even in such a demonstration as this, he managed to include a touch of exquisite sentiment. When the great vessels neared the Hawaiian Islands, he ordered them to deflect their course to pass by and salute the tragic island of Molokai, home of the afflicted lepers, so that they too should know of the protection which America affords to its most unfortunate children.

During those days in February, 1909, he seemed as gay as a boy let out of school. He was making all the arrangements for his great African adventure. In fact, with his usual "preparedness," he had been preparing for that event for a whole year. Everything was accurately arranged, and he and his son Kermit were to start immediately after he was to leave the White House in March. The lectures which he was to deliver a year from the following spring were all written and corrected. One afternoon in the "Blue Bedroom," which I generally occupied on my visits, I heard a knock at my door, and he came in with several rolls of paper under his arm. "It is raining," he said; "and I think I won't take my ride. I want your opinion on the lectures I am to deliver at Oxford, in Berlin, and at the Sorbonne. I should like to read them to you," and we settled down for a long delightful, quiet time "à deux." As usual, he was more than willing to listen to any remark or criticism, and once or twice accepted my slight suggestions of what I thought could improve his articles.

Some people felt that my brother was often egotistical, and mistook his conviction that this or that thing was right for an egotistical inability to look at it any other way. When he was convinced that his own attitude was correct, and that for the good of this or that scheme no other attitude should be taken, then nothing could swerve him; but when, as was often the case, it was not a question of conviction, but of advisability, he was the most open-minded of men, and gladly accepted and pondered the point of view of any one in whom he had confidence. I was always touched and gratified beyond measure at the simple and sometimes almost humble way in which he would listen to a difference of opinion upon my part. Occasionally, after thinking it seriously over, he would concede that my point of view was right. In this particular case, however, they were the slightest of slight suggestions which I made, for each of those articles seemed to me in its own way a masterpiece.

During that visit also occurred the last diplomatic dinner, always followed when he was President by the delightful, informal supper at tables set in the upper hall of the White House.

That night he was particularly gay, and many witty repartees passed between him and our beautiful and gifted friend, Mrs. Cabot Lodge, the friend who had for us all, through her infinite charm and brilliant intellectuality, a fascination possessed by no other. She almost always sat at his table at the informal suppers, and, needless to say, those two were the centre of attraction. The table at which I myself sat that night had the distinguished presence of General Leonard Wood, General Young, and the French ambassador, Monsieur Jusserand, one of my brother's favorite companions on the famous White House walks, hero of the true story of the time when on one of those same famous walks they inadvertently came to the river, into which my brother plunged, followed immediately by the dauntless French ambassador, who refused to "take off his gloves for fear of meeting the ladies"!

I spent one whole morning in the office during that visit, having asked my brother if I might sit quietly in a corner and listen to his interviews, to which request he gladly acceded. One after another, people filed in to see him. I made a few notes of the conversations. One of his first answers to some importunate person who wished him to take a stand on some special subject (at that time he was anxious not to embarrass his successor, Mr. Taft, by taking any special stands) was: "As Napoleon said to his marshals, 'I don't want to make pictures of myself.'"

In receiving Mr. Hall, the president of the Gridiron Club, he remarked that he (Theodore Roosevelt) had been one of the few people who used these dinners as "a field of missionary endeavor." Doctor Schick, of the Dutch Reformed Church, in which he had been a regular attendant, came to arrange for a good-by meeting at the church. To a man who came in to see him on the subject of industrial peace, he replied: "The President believes in conciliation in industrial problems." Endless subjects were brought up for his consideration, and many times I heard him say: "Remember, a new man is in the saddle, and there can't be two Presidents after March 4th." These notes were taken at the time, February, 1909, and are not the result of memory conveniently adjusted toward later happenings.

Every time I talked with my brother on the subject of the future, he repeated the fact that he was glad to plunge into the wilderness, so that no one could possibly think that he wanted a "finger in the pie" of the new administration. Over and over again he would say: "If I am where they can't get at me, and where I cannot hear what is going on, I cannot be supposed to wish to interfere with the methods of my successor."

One quiet evening when we had had a specially lovely family dinner, I turned to him and said: "Theodore, I want to give you a *real* present before you go away. What do you think you would like?" His eyes sparkled like a child who was about to receive a specially nice toy, and he said: "Do you really want to make me a *real* present, Pussie? I think I should like a pigskin library." "A pigskin library," I said, in great astonishment. "What is a pigskin library?" He laughed, and said: "Of course, I must take a good many books; I couldn't go anywhere, not even into jungles in Africa without a good many books. But also, of course, they are not very likely to last in ordinary bindings, and so I want to have them all bound in pigskin, and I would rather have that present than any other." The next day he dictated a list of the books which he wished, and the following evening added in his own handwriting a few more. The list is as follows:

BOOKS IN THE PIGSKIN LIBRARY

Bible.
Apocrypha.
Borrow: Bible in Spain.
Zingali.
Lavengro.
Wild Wales.
The Romany Rye.
Shakespeare.
Spenser: Faerie Queene.

Marlowe.
Mahan: Sea Power.
Macaulay: History.
Essays.
Poems.
Homer: Iliad.
Odyssey.
La Chanson de Roland.
Nibelungenlied.
Carlyle: Frederick the Great.
Shelley: Poems.
Bacon: Essays.
Lowell: Literary Essays.
Biglow Papers.
Emerson: Poems.
Longfellow.
Tennyson.
Poe: Tales.
Poems.
Keats.
Milton: Paradise Lost (Books I and II).
Dante: Inferno (Carlyle's translation).
Holmes: Autocrat.
Over the Teacups.
Bret Harte: Poems.
Tales of the Argonauts.
Luck of Roaring Camp.
Browning: Selections.
Crothers: Gentle Reader.
Pardoner's Wallet.
Mark Twain: Huckleberry Finn.
Tom Sawyer.
The Federalist.
Bunyan's Pilgrim's Progress.
Froissart.
Gregorovius: Rome.
Percy's Reliques.
Euripides (Murray's translation):
Bacchæ.
Hippolytus.
Scott: Legend of Montrose.
Antiquary.

Guy Mannering.
Rob Roy.
Waverley.
Cooper: Two Admirals.
Pilot.
Dickens: Pickwick.
Mutual Friend.
Thackeray: Vanity Fair.
Pendennis.

The famous pigskin library, carried on the back of "burros," followed him into the jungles of Africa, and was his constant companion at the end of long days during which he had slain the mighty beasts of the tangled forests.

Immediately after that happy week at the White House, I was stricken by a great sorrow, the death of my youngest son by an accident. My brother came to me at once, and sustained me as no one else could have done, and his one idea during those next weeks was to make me realize his constant thought and love, even in the midst of those thrilling last days at the White House, when among other events he welcomed home the great fleet which had completed its circle of the world.

A few days before the death of my boy, and immediately after that enchanting last visit to the house we had learned to regard as Theodore's natural home, he wrote me the last letter I received from him dated from the White House. It was written February 19, 1909:

"Darling Corinne: Just a line to tell you what I have already told you, of how we shall always think of you and thank you when we draw on the 'Pigskin Library' in Africa. It was too dear of you to give it to me. That last night was the pleasantest function we had ever held at the White House, and I am so glad that you and Douglas were there. Tell Douglas he cannot imagine how I have enjoyed the rides with him." The above was typewritten, but inserted in his own handwriting at the end of the note were the characteristic lines: "You blessèd person. I have revelled in having you down here. T. R."

XIII

WALL STREET HOPES EVERY LION WILL DO ITS DUTY

THE LION THAT ROOSEVELT SHOT

Now in Elysian woods, at last foregathered,
Comrades, we range together, sire and sire,
We who on earth were kings, and nobly fathered,
And, regally, wore each his earth attire.
How proudly at his heel in dawn or gloaming,
With him, the lion-hearted, I am roaming!

—Isabel Fiske Conant.

A GREAT though quiet and personal demonstration came to Theodore Roosevelt just before he sailed for Africa. The heart of the people turned to him with overwhelming affection and he received, during the last week in his own country, between fifteen and twenty thousand farewell letters. Hundreds of mothers wrote him that they felt as if their own son were leaving them, and that their prayers would follow him in his wanderings; hundreds of others wrote that they would not feel that the country would be safe until he should return—but the "big business" men (not the "great" business men) of Wall Street, according to the "bon mot" of some wag, "hoped every lion would do its duty."

As my brother was leaving Oyster Bay to set sail on his great adventure, he wrote me that he would spend one whole day with me, except for necessary business engagements, to which engagements I took him in my motor. And so my last memories of the time before he sailed are, as usual, of his unfailing devotion. On March 26 he writes again from the steamer: "Your dear little note was handed me as I sailed, and I loved it. It was so good to see you as I did the day before. Darling sister, I think of you all the time. I suppose your children told you of the wild whirl of confusion in which I said 'Goodbye.' I was very much touched by the number of acquaintances who came down to see me off. Indeed hundreds of them were not even acquaintances. They came in the shape of clubs, societies, delegations, and even more, by scores of what might be called real friends."

All through his various sea trips—these sea trips rather bored him—he writes as follows: "There are plenty of people with whom it is really pleasant to talk in English or in those variants of volapuk which with me pass for French and German." He encloses me a photograph of Kermit and himself and Selous, the naturalist, which shows a merry moment on one of those same sea trips. In May of that year he writes from Juja Farm, Nairobi:

"Really, I have been so busy that I have had no time to myself, and even have not been regularly homesick; of course, down at bottom I am homesick the whole time, but it isn't able to come to the surface, so to speak, because when I am not actually hunting, I am lying still because I am tired out. . . . This house is as pretty and comfortable as possible, and my host and hostess are the very kindest of the kind. I am sitting on a cool verandah with vines growing over the trellises, having just returned from a morning hunt in which I killed a python and an impala antelope. Yesterday I killed two antelopes, and the day before, a rhino and a hippo, and the day before that, Kermit killed a leopard which charged him viciously after mauling one of the beaters. I have also killed six lions,—four of them big ones. I am sunburned and healthy, and look like a burly and rather unkempt ruffian.

"Kermit has really done very well. He is very handy, both cool and daring, in fact, rather too daring sometimes.

"Darling sister, I think of you continually, and would so love to see you. . . ."

Later, on his return to the same farm after an extended hunting trip, he says:

"I have worked very hard writing the articles about this trip, and have put my heart into them, for this trip has been to me one of absorbing interest; but of course, I haven't any idea whether I have written anything worth reading.

"I am happy to say that I know nothing whatever of politics at home, and I hope to keep in the same blessèd state of ignorance until I return next June. Then I shall take up political work again, but probably not in any direct partisan sense,—that is, I will go in with the *Outlook* people on such matters as the conservation of natural resources, the control of big corporations, and how to deal with socialism, and the like."

The above shows clearly how strong were his intentions not to interfere in any way with the administration then in power.

On June 21, in a letter headed "On Safari," he writes:

"I am so busy writing my *Scribner* articles that I have but little time to write family letters, except of course, the letters to Edith. I have had plenty to write about for *Scribner's*, but it is not always easy to write in the field, and I do not really know how I have done it. Sometimes when I come in early from a hunt, I just point blank refuse to write at all, and spend an hour or two reading a book from the 'Pigskin Library,' which has been the utmost possible comfort and pleasure. Fond though I am of hunting and of wilderness life, I could not thoroughly enjoy either if I were not able, from time to time, to turn to my books. I am anxiously looking for news of your Helen and the baby that is to be.

"Kermit is a great pleasure to me. My trouble with him is that he is altogether too bold,—pushing, daring, almost to recklessness."

Writing in October to my husband (there never was a more devoted friendship than existed between him and my husband), he says:

"You old trump, Douglas. I really do believe that you are

about the best fellow and the staunchest friend alive. Your letter was really delightful. I am so glad Bridges told you that they liked the *Scribner* articles. I only hope they guess right as far as the public is concerned.

"I hope the Robinson Minimus or Minima has arrived. [Referring to the expected baby in my eldest son's family.] Of course, to go back to Henderson was terribly hard for you both at first, but it would have been the worst possible mistake to have avoided it or left it. The nettle had to be grasped."

What a characteristic sentence! It *had* been very hard to go back to our old home, but, as he said, "the nettle had to be grasped." I don't think in his whole life he failed to grasp any nettle that had to be grasped. In a letter of the same date to me he says, referring again to our sorrow: "As our lives draw toward the end, we are sure to meet bitter sorrow, and we must meet it undauntedly. I have just been writing Cabot and Nannie [they had lost their talented son, the young poet George Cabot Lodge] and again, there was nothing for me to say. . . . It has been a horrible wrench for me to leave Edith during this trip, but I am sure I have done the wise thing from every standpoint."

On January 21, 1910, as he is nearing civilization once more, in a letter dated on the Upper Nile, he writes: "Certainly our trip has been a complete success. If we did not shoot another thing, it would still remain unique, for the great quantity of skins and other scientific specimens collected for the museum; and personally, I do not care if I do not fire off my rifle again. I have enjoyed the trip to the full and feel that it was well worth making. I am naturally overjoyed that I am to see Edith in less than eight weeks, and I shall never go away from her again if I can help it. The 'Pigskin Library' continues to be a wellspring of comfort. Darling sister, I love you very much. Your devoted brother."

On March 10, 1910, in another letter dated Upper White Nile, he says:

"Darling sister mine: At Gondokoro I found your welcome letter; and on the steamer, descending the 1100 miles to Khartoum, bumping into sand banks, and doing various odd things, I send you this line of answer.

"Joe Alsop [my only daughter had just become engaged to Joseph Wright Alsop, of Connecticut] represents to me what I like to think of as the ideal American citizen—pretty strong praise, and I mean every word of it. I should be overjoyed if Ethel married a man like him. He is the big, brave, strong, *good* man of sound common sense, who works hard *in the country*, who does his duty in politics, who would make a fine type of soldier in civil war. I have always put him in the same class with Bob Ferguson, and with Pinchot, Garfield, Cooley, and the rest of the 'Tennis Cabinet.'"

His "Tennis Cabinet" shared the same warm corner of his heart in which his "Rough Riders" were firmly ensconced!

His last letter from the White Nile, March 14, 1910, has in it the foreboding of what was to come. "Ugh!" he writes, "tell Douglas that I hate the prospect of being dragged into politics at home. I don't like the political outlook." Even then, although regretting the probability, he realized the imminence of being "dragged into politics at home."

His wonderful reception in Egypt and the admiring recognition shown him by kings and potentates when he emerged from his year of seclusion in the jungle are well known to the world. Emperors and monarchs and presidents vied with each other to do him honor, and never was there a more triumphant progress than that of Citizen Theodore Roosevelt through the great countries that had known him as President of the United States. His tales later of the various potentates were amusing to the last degree; everything he recounted was told in the most good-natured, although humorous, spirit, and in many cases he spoke with warm regard and even affection for the rulers who welcomed him so warmly to their homes and lives. He referred to the King of Italy as "a very intelligent and really good man." He had never felt that the Emperor of Germany was a *great* man, nor did he change his opinion, in spite of the many courtesies shown him by the Kaiser, although he enjoyed his experiences in Germany and was much interested when asked to review the great German army by the Emperor. Of all the reigning monarchs, he seemed to think with the most affection of the King of Norway, to whom he paid the characteristic compliment of saying that he "would enjoy having him settle down quietly near him at Oyster Bay," and he also spoke with regard of Alfonso of Spain. He gave an especially interesting account of the funeral ceremonies of King Edward VII, to which ceremonies he was appointed special envoy; but most of all he wrote with keen delight of his "bird walk" through the New Forest and over the adjacent lowlands and uplands with that fellow bird-lover, the secretary for foreign affairs, then Sir Edward, now Earl, Grey. Nothing could have been more characteristic of Theodore Roosevelt than the way in which that walk had been arranged.

Before he left America to plunge into the African jungle, he wrote to Lord Bryce in England to the effect that on his return, practically a year and a quarter from the date on which he wrote, he would like some one versed in the bird-songs of England to walk with him for a day at least to acquaint him with the notes of the British feathered singers. He knew, he said, the appearance and habits of every English bird, but had never had the chance to match the bird to the song, and he was very anxious to do so. Lord Bryce happened to meet Sir Edward Grey, the secretary for foreign affairs, and laughingly mentioned the desire on the part of President Roosevelt to make this somewhat premature engagement, and expressed uncertainty as to whom he could choose for the President's companion. Sir Edward immediately offered himself, saying that the knowledge of bird song and lore happened to be one of his assets, but even Sir Edward felt that the experiences with the mighty creatures of the jungle, the excitement of the political furor aroused by a certain speech of Theodore Roosevelt's in Cairo, and the triumphal procession through other parts of Europe might, perhaps, have effaced from his memory his desire for a walk in English woodlands. But not at all. Sir Edward Grey himself told me, not long ago, that on the 1st of May, 1910, several weeks before he was expected in England, there came a note reminding the British secretary for foreign affairs that the ex-President of the United States wished to be his companion for twenty-four hours at least of remote enchantment "far from the madding crowd," and so when the time came they started together and tramped through the New Forest, and later over lush meadows inundated by spring rains. Earl Grey told me that although he had often taken this particular walk, he had never encountered the slightest difficulty during the transit, but to be with Theodore Roosevelt was synonymous with adventure of some kind. While traversing a usually innocuous meadow, they suddenly came upon a piece of flooded lowland, in this particular case so flooded that unless they deflected or retraced their steps, it would mean walking breast-high in water for some distance. The secretary for foreign affairs referred the decision about the situation to the ex-President of the United States, and, needless to say, the man who was accustomed to swim the Potomac River in his stride, did *not* deflect his course because of the flooded English meadow. Later, as they stood under a tree drying themselves in the afternoon sunshine, a very sweet, delicate song was heard. My brother's keen ears caught the trickling notes, and turning with vivid interest to his companion, he said: "Of all the songs we have heard to-day, that is the only one which resembles in any degree an American-bird song," and he listened eagerly as the obliging bird repeated its dainty music. "That," said Earl Grey, "is the crested wren." "It is a wren also that sings like that in America," said my brother. Earl Grey was very much interested in this, and a few days afterward, meeting a great bird expert in the British Museum, he repeated the remark of my brother in connection with the fact that the crested wren's song was the only one of any English bird resembling the song of an

American bird, and the expert confirmed what my brother had said.

Mr. John Burroughs used to say, although he had given his whole life to ornithology, that Theodore Roosevelt, to whom in later years it became only a recreation, was almost as well informed on the subject as he was.

In June, 1910, he returned from Europe, and never in the annals of American history has such a reception been accorded to a private citizen. Frankly, I do not think that Theodore Roosevelt was ever regarded as a *private* citizen; he was always a public possession! What a day it was! We went to meet him in a special launch, and from the moment of his landing until he finally reached his beloved home at Oyster Bay there was nothing but one great call of delight from his fellow citizens to the man who still stood to them for the whole of America. His triumphs, the adulation which he had received from foreign countries, epitomized to them the regard and respect poured out to the United States by those other countries of the world. The great crowds of his waving, cheering fellow citizens lined the avenue of his triumphant progress, but when he finally joined us at the house at which the family were assembled as a vantage-point, he seemed just the same sweet, simple, joyous, and unostentatious comrade as of yore.

That very first day he gave us the most amusing accounts of some of his European experiences, humorously describing informal lunches in Buckingham Palace, when the children of King George and Queen Mary behaved very much as "young America" is accustomed to behave. He also gave us what our family has always been pleased to term a "personal charade" of certain events, especially one moment when the Kaiser behaved rather like an arrogant schoolboy to one of the other royalties. He laughingly referred to a message from the Kaiser during his stay in London, when the above potentate sent him word that he, William, would be glad to give him (ex-President Roosevelt) three-quarters of an hour the next day of his precious time!

And ex-President Roosevelt in return sent him a rapid message saying that *he* would be delighted to see William, but he regretted that he could only give him twenty-five minutes! He regaled us for a long while with many such amusing stories, and then went home to his beloved Sagamore Hill.

The following day an incident occurred which had a certain prophetic quality about it. A great dinner was to be given to him by Robert Collier, and as usual with his loving thought of me (I had just returned from a trip around the world and was in very ill health) he wished to come to my house to spend the night so as to see me. He arranged to be with me at five o'clock in the afternoon, thus to have a long, quiet talk before the dinner. I came in from the country and had afternoon tea waiting for him in my library. A half-hour passed, and then another half-hour, and I began to get distinctly nervous, because he was the most prompt of individuals. At a little after six he arrived looking jaded and worried, and as he took his cup of tea, he turned to me and said: "A very unpleasant thing happened which made me late. As you see, I am dressed perfectly inconspicuously, and I slipped into Scribners [his publishers] a little before five to say a word or two about my 'African Game Trails.' [Scribners at that time was situated at 22d Street and Fifth Avenue.] When I went in there was no crowd at all, but somebody must have seen me enter the bookstore, and when I came out a short while afterward, a huge crowd had assembled, and literally would not let me pass. They wanted to carry me on their shoulders; they wanted to do utterly impossible and objectionable things; and I realized at once that this was not the friendly reception of yesterday, but that it represented a certain hysterical quality which boded ill for my future. *That type* of crowd, feeling *that* kind of way, means that within a very short time they will be throwing rotten eggs at me. I may be on the crest of the wave now, but mark my words, the attitude of that crowd means that they will soon try to help me into the trough of the wave." He was so impressed by this incident that that night at the Collier dinner he repeated and enlarged upon the theme of the crest and the trough of the wave.

Yet, in looking back over my brother's life, I do not think it can be said that in the true sense of the word he ever experienced the trough of the wave. The great movement which resulted in the Progressive party, instigated by internal dissensions in the Republican party, brought Democratic rule into our country, but, although he was defeated for public office, it did not throw him into the trough of the wave, for in reality he emerged from that great movement the leader of the majority of the Republican party, as was shown on Election day in November, 1912, when the vote for Theodore Roosevelt was infinitely larger than that cast for the "regular" Republican candidate, William Howard Taft.

XIV

THE GREAT DENIAL

Who would not be
A baffled Moses with the eyes to see
The far fruition of the Promised Land!
—C. R. R.

How can we manage with our Brother gone,
We smaller folk who looked to him to voice our voicelessness?
. . . .
We do not call him to come back from that free plane where now he moves untrammeled—
Un-beset by littleness, by envy of his power to read our hearts,
And blazon forth the message that he found there,
So that those in highest place among us needs must hear
And heed the will of us—the silent ones—
Who work, and think, and feel,
And are America.
—Gene Stanton Baker.

THEODORE ROOSEVELT had been at home but a few short weeks when he realized fully that the policies so dear to his heart, and which he had left in what he considered absolutely safe-keeping, had not been carried out. Already, in Congress, a large number of the younger Republicans had combined together as what were then called "The Insurgents." In other words, the men who had fully believed in the policies of Theodore Roosevelt, who felt that no proper progress could be made toward better government of the United States unless those policies were followed, had met on all sides with great disappointment; and although the ex-President had hoped to keep as absolutely "out of politics" as he had done in the African jungle, these disheartened and disappointed men, representing largely the younger and more ardent spirits of his country, turned to him for leadership. These reminiscences of my brother are not a biography, nor are they a political analysis of his public life, and I must therefore pass over many occurrences, the most important of which was his effort in the autumn of 1910 to defeat the Barnes-Tammany combination in New York State by running Mr. Henry L. Stimson for governor, which finally resulted in the position he took in January, 1912.

During the eighteen months previous he had been contributing editor of *The Outlook*, and my letters from him in 1911 were few and far between, as we were frequently together. They were, as usual, full of deep interest in and affection for me and mine, and as at that time I began to publish verse, first anonymously and then under my own name, he gives me generous praise in a note dated August 21, 1911: "I saw B. the other day. He told me about the acceptance of your second poem, and spoke most strongly about it, and he, just like everyone else who has talked to me about the poem, dwelt upon its power and purpose. [The poem in question was "The Call of Brotherhood."] It is not merely pretty, pleasant, trivial, the kind of thing a boy or girl of twenty could have written; it is written about and for those who have toiled and suffered and worked, and who have known defeat and triumph; and it is written by one of them." In his busy life, called upon endlessly in every direction, he never failed to encourage any effort of mine worthy of encouragement, nor indeed to discourage any effort of mine of which he did not approve. "If convenient," he adds, "I will come in about five next Friday for an hour's talk with you and to see the other verses. I am sending you a zebra skin which I hope you will like."

On October 5, 1911, he writes, referring to a political situation in Herkimer County, where my son had run for state assemblyman, and where certain unsavory methods had been used to defeat him (later, through legal procedure, he was given his seat): "Teddy has been defrauded by as outrageous a piece of political scoundrelism as I have ever known. Of course, this scoundrelism could succeed, only because last year, the big business men, the great 'Conservatives,' and professional 'Intellectuals' and the like, joined in securing the victory of Tammany at the polls, and the consequent enthronement of the Barnes-Sherman crowd in our party. If only we could have elected Harry Stimson for governor, there would not have been an effort made to handle Teddy as he has been handled." Already his indignation was beginning to wax hot against certain methods much in vogue in the Republican party at that time.

He had had no intention of running for the presidential nomination in 1912, and, indeed, in the autumn of 1911 told many of his most faithful supporters that he was very much averse to doing so; but already a swelling tide of disapproval of the Taft administration had increased in volume to such an extent that it swept over a large part of the country. The Insurgents pleaded for a definite leadership, and to them, and to many who did not call themselves by that name, there was but one leader whom they were willing to follow, and that was Theodore Roosevelt.

The force of this great wave culminated in the letter of the seven governors in January, 1912, a letter in which those same seven governors begged him to take, openly, the leadership of Progressive Republicanism, and to allow his name to be used as a presidential nominee in the June convention of 1912. Just before that letter was published, he writes in his usual sweet way in connection with a visit which he and Mrs. Roosevelt had intended to pay me in New York (they were at Sagamore Hill). After speaking of an illness which prevented Mrs. Roosevelt from coming to me, he said, knowing that I had made certain engagements for them: "Do you wish to have me come alone? Do exactly what you think best. I will be in for Tuesday night in any case, and will be at your house as agreed. I don't know when I have ever enjoyed anything more than my lunch at Fannie's [our dear friend Mrs. James Russell Parsons],

—it was a real feast of Lucullus,—only far better." This letter is very boyish and content with friends and family, and most unlike a man absorbed in schemes of sinister usurpation, schemes of which he was so soon to be accused.

In the library at my own house in New York City, a fateful meeting took place shortly after this last letter came. I confess to having had serious doubts as to what his answer should be to that request of the seven governors. Personally, I felt the sacrifice asked of him was almost too great. I realized perfectly the great struggle before him and all that it probably would mean, and it seemed to me that he had already given all that was required of just such service to his beloved country. But, just as he felt in 1898 that, having preached war upon Spain, he must take active part in that war, so in 1912 he came to feel strongly that, having inaugurated certain policies as President which had not been carried out by his successor—having preached the necessity for industrial legislation which had not been backed by those in public authority—it was his duty to bare his breast to the "slings and arrows of outrageous fortune," and accept the position of leader of Progressive Republicanism in order to try to translate into practical reality the ideals which he had upheld before his countrymen. His answer to the seven governors pledged himself to such leadership, and the great upheaval of 1912 took place.

Never before in his varied career had Theodore Roosevelt felt such a sense of loneliness, for many of his nearest and dearest friends were not in sympathy with some of his beliefs in 1912. I shall never forget the great meeting at Carnegie Hall, when he proclaimed "the faith that was in him." He was like an inspired crusader that night when he cast away the notes from which he had occasionally been reading and made the magnificent peroration in which he proclaimed the fact that his doctrine was "Spend and Be Spent," and that no man worthy the name of man would not be willing to be an instrument for the success of his ideals—a broken instrument if need be. He returned after that thrilling speech to my house, and we sat a long while talking over the serious step he had taken and the possibilities the future held for him, and I felt that there was a sense of dedication about him such as I believe the martyrs of old must have felt.

In spite of the storm that broke around him after this declaration, in spite of the manifold activities into which he immediately cast himself, he takes the time to write to me, March 5, 1912, when my infant grandchild, born the month before, had died of whooping-cough: "My darling Sister: You have indeed been through the waters of bitterness. The little baby! I love little babies so, and I think of my own little granddaughter, and I mourn with you and Douglas. Now, I think only with a pang of our lovely day last Sunday. [We had spent that Sunday with him at Oyster Bay.] If I could have come up to Albany I would have done so. Ever your devoted brother."

The great convention of 1912 took place, and through the ruling of the chairman certain delegates pledged to Theodore Roosevelt were deprived of their seats, a ruling which meant his defeat as Republican candidate. I was ill at the time and could not be present on that epoch-making occasion. I only know that its result after the above ruling was considered by my brother absolutely inevitable, and that he never regarded that result, as did so many people, as the most unfortunate circumstance of his life. Writing a year and a half later for the *Century Magazine*, in October, 1913, he says: "Fundamentally the reason for the existence of the Progressive Party was found in two facts: first, the absence of real distinctions between the old parties which correspond *to* those parties; and, second, the determined refusal of the men in control of both parties to use the party organizations and their control of the Government, for the purpose of dealing with the problems really vital to our people. . . . A party which alternately nominated Mr. Bryan and Mr. Parker for President, and a party wherein Messrs. Penrose, LaFollette, and Smoot, stand as the three brothers of leadership, can by no possibility supply the need of this country for efficient and coherent governmental action as regards the really vital questions of the day." In the same article he proceeds to analyze the reasons for the formation of the Progressive Party, and continues:

"The problems connected with the trusts, the problems connected with child labor, and all similar matters can be solved only by affirmative national action. No party is progressive which does not set the authority of the National Government as supreme in these matters. No party is progressive which does not give to the people the right to determine for themselves, after due opportunity for deliberation, but without endless difficulty and delay, what the standards of social and industrial justice shall be; and, furthermore, the right to insist upon the servants of the people, legislative and judicial alike, paying heed to the wishes of the people as to what the law of the land shall be. The Progressive party believes with Thomas Jefferson, with Andrew Jackson, with Abraham Lincoln, that this is a government of the people, to be used for the people, so as to better the condition of the average man and average woman of the nation in the intimate and homely concerns of their daily lives; and thus to use the government means that it must be used after the manner of Hamilton and Lincoln to serve the purposes of Jefferson and Lincoln.

"We are for the people's rights. Where these rights can best be obtained by exercise of the powers of the State, there we are for *States'* rights. Where they can best be obtained by the exercise of the powers of the *National* Government, there we are for *National* rights. We are not interested in this as an abstract doctrine; we are interested in it concretely. . . . We believe in the principle of a living wage. We hold that it is ruinous for *all* our people, if *some* of our people are forced to subsist on a wage such that body and soul alike are stunted."

Referring to the Industrial and Social Justice plank of the platform of the Progressive party, he continues:

"The propositions are definite and concrete. They represent for the first time in our political history the specific and reasoned purpose of a great party to use the resources of the government in sane fashion for industrial betterment. . . .

"To sum up, then, our position is, after all, simple. We believe that the government should concern itself chiefly with the matters that are of most importance to the average man and average woman, and that it should be its special province to aid in making the conditions of life easier for these ordinary men and ordinary women, who compose the great bulk of our people. To this end we believe that the people should have direct control over their own governmental agencies, and that when this control has been secured, it should be used with resolution, but with sanity and self-restraint, in the effort to make conditions fairer and better for the men and women of the nation."

I have inserted this quotation from his own writings in 1913, for it gives clearly the objects and aims of that party, born at Chicago amid scenes of almost religious enthusiasm in June, 1912, nor did that enthusiasm wane for one single moment during the following months; on the contrary, it rose to the heighths of dedication.

There were some who lost their sense of proportion, but by far the greater number of those who followed Theodore Roosevelt in that extraordinary campaign were imbued with a high sense of a "Great Cause," a cause which had never before been translated into the common sense of possible achievement. The New York State Progressive Convention met at Syracuse, and at that assemblage I was able to be present, and whatever doubts might have been in my breast before were swept away by a deep conviction of the fact that the Progressive Party was the true interpretation of the highest ideal of democracy.

Just about the time of the Progressive Convention at Syracuse, an article appeared, written by a citizen of Unadilla, N. Y., C. C. Penny by name, in which the above citizen gives the reasons which induced him to vote for "Teddy," as he affectionately calls the colonel.

"*To the Editor of the Utica Daily Press:—*

"Having had the question put up to me as to what Roosevelt has ever done politically to better conditions, I would submit the following: First,—What did Mr. Roosevelt do as President that he should not have done in the public interest, or that was dangerous or hurtful to business? Mr. Roosevelt's intervention in the coal strike benefited all consumers; Mr. Roosevelt is responsible for the Pure Food and Drugs Act; the open door to American commerce with China; the settlement of the Russo-Japan War; Panama Canal project; conservation of natural resources; reduction of interest-bearing debt by more than ninety million dollars; settlement of the Alaska boundary dispute; an act calling for the extension of forest reserves; national irrigation act; employers' liability act; safety appliances and regulation of railroad employees' hours of labor.—Was Mr. Roosevelt's work in bringing about the settlement of the Russo-Japan War dangerous and hurtful to business? Was Roosevelt's Panama Canal project dangerous and hurtful to business? Was his movement for the conservation of our natural resources dangerous and hurtful to business? These are a few of the things which he suggested and carried through with the help of his followers. Besides, he recommended many other reforms such as Postal Savings Bank, Parcels Post, and Inheritance Tax and Income Tax which he had not time to carry through during his last term.

"All these, it seems to me, are reforms to better the conditions of the great mass of people. The Progressive platform has been growing for the last sixteen years all through the Northwest, and West and South, only waiting for a man to come out, bold enough to take the lead. Mr. Roosevelt, it seems, has dared to take this step, and whether we win or lose, it is a step forward to the betterment of the conditions of all who toil and consume.

I have always voted the Republican ticket, but I consider that true Republican principles at this time rest with the Progressive Party, and I shall vote for that party this Fall, and for Teddy, win or lose."

In October that year my volume of poems called by the title of its first poem, "The Call of Brotherhood," was published, and my brother writes me at once, though in the midst of pressing duties: "I love 'The Call of Brotherhood'; somehow it seems to express just what we are now battling for in the political arena. Well, the feeling, the longing, the desire, the determination you have made throb in these poems, also make it impossible for us to sit in fat content and not strive for better things in *actual life*. When we felt rather inarticulately just what you have written, we simply couldn't refrain from the effort [he refers to the Progressive Party] as a practical means to realize high ideals. That is what we must do with high ideals,—apply them and try to live up to them, and to make them work.—Joe and Teddy have done wonderful work; and so has Douglas. . . . I seem to have cost my friends much in all kinds of ways in this campaign; that was one of the reasons why I so hated to go into it." Many people misjudged his motives and thought that he went into it for selfish purposes; never was there a more mistaken conception of the actions of a patriot.

In a letter written September 1, he says: "I am just leaving for the West. It has been a very interesting fight, and never was there a fight better worth making, but the exertion is tremendous, and I look forward to Election Day as the end of a battle."

During that Western trip, he had one of his greatest personal ovations. One of the Western newspapers says:

"In Portland, Oregon, the city practically stopped business and turned out to receive its guest. In each city, the personal element of the greeting was remarkable. No one was thinking of Colonel Roosevelt in connection with his past office as President. He was 'Roosevelt.' It was 'Hello Teddy' and 'Hurrah for Teddy' everywhere along the densely packed streets where he appeared. His speeches to these multitudes were neither original nor new, but the people understood them. The enthusiasm of these western cities for the ex-President seems almost fabulous. At Portland, hundreds of school children escorted the automobile. Women brought their children, cripples were wheeled to horse blocks, men climbed on cornices and pediments, mothers of twins pressed to the side of the car, people literally blackened sidewalks, residence verandas, windows of houses, even the trees. At Tacoma a woman was heard to remark, 'If this ex-President has lost his popularity, I would hate to be in a crowd that had gathered to see an ex-President who had *not* lost his popularity,'—and everywhere he preached the common-sense doctrine:—

"Now friends, what I have said to you is pretty elementary,—so elementary that it comes mighty near being commonplace, but I will tell you that the truths that really count are the elementary truths. The individual whom we respect is not merely the brilliant individual. The man whom we wish our sons to resemble is the man who has the ordinary virtues developed to more than the ordinary degree."

He himself believed that he was not a man of genius but only a man with average talents, talents which by sheer determination and will-power he had developed to a more than ordinary degree.

Shortly after the ovation in Oregon, he writes on September 15 from San Francisco: "Of course this trip is inconceivably wearing, but what a fine fight it is, anyhow!" To him it was a great crusade for the right, and his soul was at white heat in the cause of righteousness.

Later came the dramatic moment in Milwaukee when he received in his breast the bullet of a would-be assassin. He protected the man, believing him to be insane, from the angry crowd who would have gladly torn him limb from limb; and then proceeded, though bleeding from an open wound, to make what he fully believed would probably be the last speech that he would ever make in this world. The doctors could not influence him to give up the speech, for he said that should it prove to be his last, it was all the more important that he should make it. But, thank Heaven, it was not his last!

During his convalescence in the hospital in Chicago, he sent me one of his sympathetic letters about another recently published poem, and also replied to a letter from Sir George Trevelyan as follows: "I must say I have never understood public men who got nervous about assassination. For the last eleven years I have, of course, thoroughly understood that I might at any time be shot, and probably *would* be shot sometime. I think I have come off uncommonly well. What I cannot understand is any serious-minded public man not being so absorbed in the great, vital questions with which he has to deal, as to exclude thoughts of assassination. I don't think this is a matter of courage at all. I think it a question of the major interest driving out the minor interest. Exactly as with the army,—a private may have qualms,—not so a General. He is responsible for more than his personal safety. It is not a question of courage, it is a question of perspective, of proper proportion." Nothing has ever been more in keeping with the actions of Theodore Roosevelt than the above sentence: "it is a question of the major interest driving out the minor interest." With him, all through his life, the sense of proportion was a prominent part of his make-up. The "major interest" always drove out the "minor interest," and so strong was his sense of responsibility, so absorbed was he in the great affairs of his country, that the thought of possible assassination never entered his valiant breast.

The greatest moment of all that inspiring period of his life came late in October, at the end of the campaign, when Theodore Roosevelt, the bullet still in his breast, but miraculously restored to health and strength, came to the city of his birth to make the final speech of the Progressive campaign at Madison Square Garden. Not only was the spirit of the Crusade higher than ever, but the danger so lately experienced by their leader had given to his followers an exaltation never surpassed at any time in our political history. I have always been glad that for some unexplained reason the pass which had been given to me that night for my motor was not accepted by the policeman in charge, and I, my husband, my son Monroe, and our friend Mrs. Parsons were obliged to take our places in the cheering, laughing, singing crowd which formed in line many blocks below the Garden to walk up to the entrance-door. How it swayed and swung! how it throbbed with life and elation! how imbued it was with an earnest party ambition, and yet, with a deep and genuine religious fervor. Had I lived my whole life only for those fifteen minutes during which I marched toward the Garden already full to overflowing with my brother's adoring followers, I should have been content to do so. We could hardly get into the building, and indeed had to climb up the fire-escape, which we were only allowed to do after making it well known that I was the sister of the "Colonel." (There never was but one "Colonel" in American history!) The whole meeting was one of an ineffable and intense emotional quality. We could hear the singing and the cheers of the thousands outside on the street, as inside my brother came forward to the platform, and the vast audience rose to its feet to acclaim its hero. Such moments do not often occur in a lifetime, and when they do, they leave in their wake a wonderful sense of what the highest type of religion should mean—a religion selfless as the Christlike faith upon which all true religion is founded.

A few days later, Woodrow Wilson, the Democratic though minority candidate, was elected President of the United States.

XV

WHISPERINGS OF WAR

SAGAMORE HILL

He is a moose,
Scarred, battered from the hunters, thickets, stones:
Some finest tips of antlers broken off,
And eyes where images of ancient things
Flit back and forth across them, keeping still
A certain slumberous indifference,
Or wisdom, it may be.

—Edgar Lee Masters.

Rightly to be great
Is not to stir, without great argument,
But greatly to find quarrel in a straw
When Honour's at the stake.

—Hamlet.

NO man in America ever received the backing of so large a personal following as did Theodore Roosevelt in the election of 1912, but owing to the fact that opinion was divided, the Democratic party, although a minority party, was put in power. It has been the habit of some to speak of my brother as having split the Republican party. This has always seemed to me an unfair criticism. It was proved by the actual vote at the polls that the larger half of what up to that time had been the Republican party was in favor of Theodore Roosevelt for President. His majority over Mr. Taft was unquestioned. A minority, not a majority, disrupts a party. Nothing is truer, however, than that a really great man cannot be defeated. He can lose official position, he can see the office which he craved because of its potential power for right doing pass into the hands of another; but in the higher sense of the word he cannot be defeated if his object has been righteousness, if his inner vision has been the true betterment of his country.

And so during the years that followed 1912, Theodore Roosevelt, although holding no official position, became more than ever the leader of a great portion of the people of America. Loyal as he was, he felt that having (as he phrased it) "led a vast army into the wilderness," he must stand by them through thick and thin.

In 1913, having been asked to make certain addresses in South America, he decided to accept the invitation. But before sailing he went to Rochester, N. Y., to make a speech, and arranged that my husband and I should meet him and have an evening quietly with him. Immediately after that there was a great farewell dinner to him in New York, at the Hotel Astor. The crowd was suffocating. It seemed as if the enthusiasm for him and for Progressive principles was even more poignant than the year before—perhaps the realization that their leader was to leave them, even for a comparatively short time, increased the ardor of the convictions of his followers—and the spirit of that evening was so vital, so dedicated in quality, that it will never fade from my mind. The next day he and Mrs. Roosevelt sailed for the Argentine Republic, and within a few months she returned home, and he again lost himself in a new adventure. The little boy of six in the nursery at 20th Street had read with fervent interest of the adventures of the great explorer Livingston. He had achieved his ambition to follow those adventures as a mighty hunter in Africa; he had achieved many another ambition, but none was more intense with him than the desire to put a so-called "River of Doubt" on the map of the world.

Again Kermit was his companion, and the latter has given, as no one else could give, the most vivid description of that trip in his book called "The Happy Hunting Grounds." In that book he describes his father's desperate illness, and his heroic and unflinching courage when, with a temperature of one hundred and five, he struggled on through the mazes of the jungle, weak and weary, unselfishly begging his companions to leave him to die, for he felt that his condition endangered the possibility of their escape alive from their difficulties. As in Africa, so in South America his tireless energy, even when weakened by illness, never failed to accomplish his purpose, and not only did he put the "River of Doubt" on the map—a river which from that time forth was called Rio Teodoro, after Theodore Roosevelt, the explorer—but during those suffering, exhausting weeks he never once failed to keep his promise to his publishers, and to write, on the spot, the incidents of each day's adventures. Robert Bridges, of Scribners, has shown me the water-soaked manuscript, written in my brother's own handwriting, of that extraordinary expedition. In several places on the blotched sheets he makes a deprecatory note—"This is not written very clearly; my temperature is 105." Such perseverance, such persistence are really superhuman; but perhaps it is also true that the *human* being must eventually pay the price of what the superman achieves.

Theodore Roosevelt returned from that Brazilian trip a man in whom a secret poison still lurked, and although his wonderful vitality, his magnificent strength of character, mind, and body, seemed at times to restore him to the perfect health of former days, he was never wholly free from recurrent attacks of the terrible jungle fever, which resulted in ill health of various kinds, and finally in his death.

True to his loyal convictions, he was determined to give all the aid possible to the candidates on the Progressive ticket for the election of 1914. His wife writes, August, 1914: "Theodore seems really better, although I scarcely think he will have voice for the three speeches he has planned for the last of the month. I asked him if I could say anything from him about the War, and he simply threw up his hands in despair." This letter was written nine days after the cataclysm of the Great War had broken upon the world. From the beginning he said to his family what he did not feel he could state publicly, owing to the fact that he did not wish to embarrass President Wilson. Having been President himself, he knew it was possible for one in high authority to have information which he could not immediately share with all the people, and he hoped this might be the reason of President Wilson's failure to make any protest when the enemy troops invaded Belgium.

To his family, however, he spoke frankly and always with deep regret that the President enjoined a neutral attitude in the beginning. He felt, from the very first, that the Allies were fighting our battles; that the British fleet was the protector of the United States as much as it was the protector of Great Britain; that a protest should have immediately been made by the United States when the Germans marched through Belgium. All these views he stated to his family and to his friends, but for the first few months after August 1, 1914, he felt that, as an influential citizen, he might hurt the fulfilment of whatever plan the President might have in view in connection with the Allies were he openly to criticise the President's course of action. Later in the war he told me how much he regretted that, from a high sense of duty toward the Executive, he had controlled himself during those first few months when we were asked by President Wilson to be neutral even in thought.

In my sister-in-law's letter, quoted above, she speaks of her doubt as to whether my brother would be strong enough to make the speeches which he had agreed to make. The Philadelphia *North American* published, about that time, an editorial called "The Amazing Roosevelt," a few paragraphs of which run as follows:

"On April 30th, there came out of the seething jungles of Brazil to a river port 1000 miles up the Amazon, a man who was heralded by cable dispatches as broken in body and permanently impaired in mind. . . . On his arrival at home, there were grave dicta from former critics that never again would this man be a force in public life. The solemnity of these pronouncements scarcely concealed the gratification which they gave to some who promulgated them. Unbiassed stories of the hardships suffered in the tropical forests appeared to be cumulative evidence to support the belief that Theodore Roosevelt was 'done for' as a factor in public life.

"A sick man had virtually dragged himself through the most obdurate jungle still unmapped. . . . It had looked as if the entire party might be sacrificed and he had begged his followers to go on and leave him to take care of himself. On his return, he was warned by an eminent specialist that he must eschew speech-making if he hoped to avoid permanent injury to his throat. Another specialist warned him that impaired vital organs necessitated his withdrawing altogether from public activities. This was the Roosevelt who went to Pittsburgh to speak to the Progressives of Pennsylvania this week. What was it the Progressives gathered there to hear? Was it a swan song, —was it the plea of a broken man,—what was the character of the gathering? Was it a congregation of saddened and disheartened people, come to pay a kindly tribute to a passing leader? It was none of these things. The demonstration for Roosevelt and Progressive principles surpassed anything in the 1912 campaign, and the Roosevelt who greeted this great demonstration was the vigorous, fighting Roosevelt who so long had led the people's battles. He was never received with more enthusiasm. The New York *Times*, not a paper in favor of Colonel Roosevelt, said: 'The Pennsylvania Progressives gave Colonel Roosevelt a welcome tonight which must have reminded him of 1912. The demonstration was a remarkable one.' And *The World* said: 'The Colonel enjoyed every minute. Malaria was forgotten and all physical weakness along with it as he stood at the vortex of the night's enthusiasm.'

"No one can read the speech which Roosevelt made that night without being convinced that the dismal forebodings that came out of that Amazon port last April, have already been discredited, and that the man who in 1912 stood with an assassin's bullet near his heart, and insisted upon delivering a message which might be his last, is not to be broken or even impaired in 1914 by the hardships of a South American jungle. It is but another example of the amazing Roosevelt."

That same autumn of 1914 he came to our old home in Herkimer County once more, but this time he was the guest of my son Theodore Douglas Robinson, and stayed at his house, which adjoins the old home. From there Mrs. Parsons and he and I joined the candidate for governor on the Progressive ticket, State Senator Frederick A. Davenport, and former State Senator Newcomb, for a short speaking tour to uphold the candidacy of Senator Davenport. We knew there was very little hope of success, but my brother had recuperated apparently from the Brazilian trip, and we spent two merry days dashing through Herkimer and Otsego counties. In spite of anxiety and a deep sense of distress about Old World conditions, for a brief moment we threw off all care, and in the glorious autumn sunshine, followed by cheering crowds, we enjoyed one of the triumphal processions which were almost always a *sine qua non* wherever he appeared. One specially merry afternoon and evening was spent at the home of James Fenimore Cooper. My brother was to speak at Cooperstown in the afternoon, and Mr. Cooper invited us to dinner, but I told him that the party must reach Oneonta for dinner, so that we could only take afternoon tea at his house. I had not confided this refusal to Theodore, simply taking it for granted that it would be impossible for us to accept the Cooper invitation and reach Oneonta in time for his evening speech. The Cooper home, full of treasures that had descended from Mr. Cooper's grandfather, the author of "The Last of the Mohicans," etc., and equally full of charming people, gave us so warm a welcome, and we had such an agreeable time there, that my brother was very loath to leave, but at 6.30 I insisted that we must start for Oneonta. We were already in the motors when Mr. Cooper, leaning over to say good-by, assured Colonel Roosevelt of his regret that he could not stay to dinner. "Dinner?" said my brother. "I didn't know I was asked to dinner."

"Yes, you were, of course," said Mr. Cooper; "but your sister, Mrs. Robinson, refused to let you stay for dinner, saying that you would have to reach Oneonta at 8 o'clock." "May I ask," said my brother in a high falsetto, "what business my sister, Mrs. Robinson, had to refuse a dinner invitation for me?" And, with a bound, he leaped from the automobile, shaking, laughingly, his fist at me, and said, "Dinner with the Coopers! Well, of course, I am going to stay to dinner," and returned rapidly to the house, followed meekly by his party. The hospitable and resourceful Coopers, who naturally, after my refusal, had not expected seven extra people to dinner, turned in, assisted by Theodore himself, and proceeded to scramble eggs and broil bacon, much to the amusement and delight of the cook, who had never had an ex-President in her kitchen before, and of all the merry dinner-parties that I have ever attended, that one, forced upon the delightful Fenimore Coopers, was about the merriest.

Senator Davenport had been in poor health at the time, and my brother called him entirely "Little Eva," after the angel child of Harriet Beecher Stowe's "Uncle Tom's Cabin," both because of his rather transparent appearance and his high-minded principles (upon which the Colonel dilated in his speeches). He called himself "Uncle Tom," and Senator Newcomb "Simon Legree," and those cognomens and no others were used throughout the entire trip, which proved a veritable holiday.

But neither that trip nor any other trip could have changed the fate of the Progressive candidates in 1914, and New York State showed at election time, as did various other states in the country, that America was not prepared for a third party, even though that party stood, more than did any other party, for the practical common sense and high idealism of Theodore Roosevelt.

Just before Election day I accompanied him to Princeton, where Doctor John Grier Hibben, president of the university, received him with distinction, and asked him to speak to the body of students there not only on political faiths but on "Preparedness." Unless I am very much mistaken, the first speech on that subject in the United States during the Great War was that very address made in the auditorium of Princeton in November, 1914, by my brother. His young and eager listeners among the student body applauded him to the echo. The cause of preparedness and true Americanism had no stancher upholder at that time, nor in the difficult years to come, than President Hibben of Princeton University. Theodore Roosevelt, Henry Cabot Lodge, Leonard Wood, John Grier Hibben, Augustus P. Gardner, and other far-seeing patriots, stood from the beginning for the Allies against the Huns, and for "Preparedness" of a thorough kind. Had their advice been followed, Germany would very soon have sensed how formidable an influence in the war America could be. I am convinced there would have been no sinking of the *Lusitania*, and hundreds of thousands of gallant young men would not have lost their lives on Flanders Fields.

On November 12, 1914, after Election day, my brother writes me: "Darling Corinne:—That is a very dear letter of yours! I shall make no further statement. Did you see my quotation from Timothy II, Chapter 4, verses 3 and 4? It covers the whole situation. Ever yours, Theodore Roosevelt."

The verses referred to are as follows:

(3) For the time will come when they will not endure sound doctrine; but after their own lusts shall they heap to themselves teachers, having itching ears;

(4) And they shall turn away their ears from the truth, and shall be turned unto fables.

He was very apt to sum up a situation in some pregnant verse from the Bible.

The winter of 1915 was trying to him in certain ways, especially on account of the Barnes libel suit. He had made the statement that Mr. Barnes had, politically, a bipartisan attitude, and indeed more than attitude, and Mr. Barnes decided to bring a suit for libel against him. In spite of this annoyance, however, he writes me various letters, some merry, and all dealing with subjects where he or I could be of help to others less fortunate. In one case, in connection with a certain French pastor, to whom I could not be of assistance in the way in which he had hoped, he writes: "I understand perfectly. I felt like a swine when I wrote you, but the poor, dear pastor was such a pathetic figure that from sheer mushy weakness I yielded, and strove to do something for him." And later, in connection with a penniless poet: "Can you give me any advice? I wish I knew some wealthy creature who was interested in poor struggling poets and could help them, and also help their poor wives and children after their deaths. Lord! how hard life is!" That time I was able to help him, and raised quite a sum for the struggling individual in question, whom I thought truly deserved help.

Just then Mrs. William Astor Chanler arranged a charming play for the benefit of a war charity, a play in which there were scenes depicting Washington at Valley Forge. My little grandson took the part of his many times great-grandfather, Captain Isaac Roosevelt, and my brother, with sympathetic pleasure, came as an honored guest to the performance, and was later photographed with the small actors. He writes from Syracuse, where he had gone to take the defense for himself in the libel suit: "Was little Captain Isaac Roosevelt one of the bewildering number of small Revolutionary leaders who had their photographs taken with me? I have felt a pang that I did not particularly seek him out, but the confusion was so great that I could not identify any one of the constantly revolving small boys and girls behind the scenes; and until we were actually in place I had supposed that they were all to have their photographs taken with me." In this same letter he says, speaking of the fact that his wife had been ill when he left New York: "I have been so worried about Edith that this libel suit has bothered me very little. Of course I was rather tired by my nine days on the witness stand, but I felt I made my case pretty clear. How the suit will go I have no idea, but in any event I do not feel that my friends have any cause to be ashamed of me." On May 24, at the end of the suit, in which he scored a great triumph, he writes: "Dearest Corinne and Douglas: It was fine to get your telegrams and letters. You two were among those who I knew would stand by me absolutely, win or lose; but I am awfully glad it is a case of winning and not losing. Just as soon as you get back from Virginia I must see you both and tell you everything." He did tell us everything, and many were the things that he told!

Twice in his life Theodore Roosevelt took part in libel suits. In the first case *he* brought the suit against a newspaper which had openly accused him of intoxication. In the second place he was the defendant, as I have already mentioned. Nothing was ever more unfounded than the strange and persistent rumor that Theodore Roosevelt indulged in intoxicating liquors. It has been my great good fortune to have been associated with men of great self-control as regards drink, but of all my intimate contemporaries, no one ever drank as little as my brother. I do not think he ever in his life tasted a cocktail, and he hated whiskey, and it rarely could be found at Sagamore Hill. He occasionally took a glass of sherry or port or champagne, but those, even, only occasionally; and how the report started that he overindulged in drink no one has ever been able to discover; but like many another sinister thing it swelled with its own volume, and after serious thought he chose an occasion when he could make a definite charge, and demanded a trial when the newspaper in question *printed* the heretofore only whispered untruth. I do not believe that so many distinguished men ever before travelled to a remote Western town, as travelled to give testimony about the sobriety of Theodore Roosevelt. Foreign ambassadors, famous generals, scientists, literary men, artists, all journeyed in an endless trail to give, with ardent loyalty, their personal knowledge of the impeccable habits of my brother.

The result was an award of damages which my brother refused to take and the most abject apologies on the part of the editor. The other suit, the Barnes suit, was entirely different, for in that transaction he was the man to make the accusation, and his opponent was a most brilliant and acute individual, and even although my brother's followers were confident of the accuracy of the statement he had made, for his statements were consistently accurate, still we felt that some apparent lack of proof, even though only apparent, might bring about an unfortunate result. Mr. John Bowers, one of the most able of his profession, was my brother's lawyer, and he later gave me many an amusing description of that extraordinary case. The counsel for the plaintiff were always averse to allowing my brother to testify, for the effect he produced upon the jury was immediate and startling. The opposing side would object to nearly *everything* he said, simply because *anything* he said induced a rapid and favorable response from the jury. In one part of the testimony Mr. Bowers told me that my brother had repeated a conversation between Mr. Barnes and himself, and had gone into accurate detail, which was listened to by the jury with intense and sympathetic excitement, whereupon the lawyer for the plaintiff objected to Mr. Roosevelt's statement as an "irrelevant monologue." Quick as a flash my brother turned upon the objector and said that "of course the gentleman in question might *call* it a monologue, but as Mr. Barnes had had as much to do with the conversation as himself, he, personally, would call it a *dialogue*." This retort brought down not only the house but the jury, and the unfortunate opposing lawyer withdrew his objection. That story and many others my brother recounted to us with humorous and sarcastic delight, shortly after the end of the trial, around a family teatable one Sunday evening at Sagamore Hill.

In September of that year, 1915, we suffered the loss of our beloved friend Mrs. Henry Cabot Lodge. Since the early days of 1884, she had shared the joys and sorrows of our lives. Beautiful, brilliant, sympathetic, exquisite in her delicate individuality, in her intellectual inspiration, in her fine humor and sense of values—her beautiful head like a rare cameo, her wonderful gray-blue eyes looking out under dark, level brows, she remains one of the pictures most treasured in the memories of the Roosevelt family. My brother was always at his best with her, and I have rarely heard him talk in a broader and more comprehensive way of politics and literature than in the homelike library at 1765 Massachusetts Avenue, the house where Senator and Mrs. Lodge were always surrounded by an intimate circle of friends. By her tea-table, in the rocking-chair bought especially for him, Theodore Roosevelt would sit and rock when he snatched a happy half-hour after his ride with the senator in those old days when he was the President of the United States. Mrs. Lodge had the power of stimulating the conversation of others, as well as the gift of leading in conversation herself, and the best "talk" that I have ever heard was around her tea-table in Washington. Her sudden death was a great blow to my brother as it was to us all.

All through that year and through the year to come, although severely censured for his criticisms of the President's policies, my brother worked with arduous determination, shoulder to shoulder with General Leonard Wood and Augustus P. Gardner, to arouse the American people to the danger of non-preparedness, and to the shame of allowing the exhausted Allies to bear without America's help the brunt of the battle. Those men of vision realized, fully, that in a world aflame, no nation could possibly escape the danger of conflagration. Not only from that standpoint did the apostles of preparedness press forward, but from the love of democracy also. These courageous patriots wished to have their country share spontaneously from the beginning the effort for righteousness for which France, England, and Italy were giving the lives of the flower of their youth.

By pen, and even more by word of mouth, always at the expense of his energy, Theodore Roosevelt went up and down the country, preaching the doctrine of brotherhood and preparedness for self-defense. As early as January, 1915, General Wood had asked me to have a meeting to interest some of the men of New York in his plans for the training-camps, which later developed into the "Plattsburg idea." Many of the men who in later days were patriotically ardent in their support of that Plattsburg idea spoke to me with amused indifference at the end of that meeting in January, 1915, and asked me why I had made such a point of their coming to it! At the same time, Augustus P. Gardner, in the House of Representatives, struggled to arouse the country from its lethargy. Gradually, however, the force of the truth of the doctrine which was being preached by the few percolated through the minds and hearts of many of the American people, and at the beginning of the year 1916 one could feel a certain response to a higher ideal. In May, 1915, after the dastardly sinking of the *Lusitania*, the country could have been easily led in the path of duty and high ideals. The psychological moment was at hand when over a hundred women and children, non-combatants, and over whom flew the British flag, were hurled into the sea by the dastardly tactics of Germany,—but this is a digression. In January, 1916, I was chosen a delegate by the National Security League (an organization started during the first year of the war to uphold the policy of "Preparedness") to its first conference at Washington, and there I was asked to read a letter from my brother, as he could not be present at the conference. He writes me on January 22, 1916: "I was very much surprised and much pleased when I saw in the papers that you had read my letter to the Security League." And again, two days later, came one of his characteristic little notes (no one ever took such pains to do and say loving and lovely things): "Darling Pussie," he says this time: "Judge Nortoni and Bob Bacon have been out here to Sagamore Hill separately, and both feel that your speech was the feature of the Washington meeting. I will tell you all that they say next Sunday when you come to us. I was really touched by their enthusiastic admiration of you and the speech. *My* letter was apparently regarded only as the peg on which the speech was hung. Ever yours, T. R." Needless to say, my speech was only an insignificant addendum to his letter, but he truly believed that his sister's speech was the more important of the two things!

In February he gladly lent me his name for the New York advisory committee of "The Fatherless Children of France," a society started by two magnificent Englishwomen, Miss Schofield and Miss Fell, for which I was privileged to form the New York City committee. "Of course use my name," he says. I do not remember ever asking him for it that he did not lend it to me—that name which counted more than almost any other name of his time.

In March, 1916, he sailed with Mrs. Roosevelt for Trinidad, and during his absence there began again the rumblings of desire on the part of the people of the United States to have him named as presidential candidate on the Republican ticket in the forthcoming convention. A certain faction of the Progressive party still clung to the hope that it could achieve its heart's desire and name him on their ticket, but he had come more and more to the conclusion that the Republican and the Progressive parties must amalgamate in their choice of a nominee, for he firmly believed that Mr. Wilson's policies had been of sinister influence in the country, and he was convinced that nothing was so important as to remove this, from his standpoint, unfortunate influence. More and more he believed that our country should bear a gallant part in the terrible adventure across the sea; more and more he preached the doctrine that we should go to the aid of the war-worn countries who sorely needed America's help.

I cannot refrain from inserting here a letter written by Colonel Roosevelt to his dear friend and classmate Charles G. Washburn, who had just published his able book called "Theodore Roosevelt—The Logic of His Career." That book had special interest because, although Mr. Washburn never wavered in his personal, loyal, and devoted attachment to Colonel Roosevelt, his political convictions were such that he had not found it possible to follow the Colonel into the Progressive party. The book in question, having been written during the period between 1912 and 1916, the period when many people felt that my brother was politically dead, was published, strange to say, just as the pendulum swung back again, when the people realized the need of strong leadership in the crisis of the Great War, and Theodore Roosevelt seemed to many to be the man of the hour.

"Dear Charlie:" writes Colonel Roosevelt, "We leave on the 10th of this month [for Trinidad]. I am much amused to think that there is a momentary revival of my popularity or notoriety or whatever you choose to call it, at the very time your book is to appear, for when you started to write it, indeed, while you were writing it, I was down at the very nadir; and only a very devoted friendship—others would call it a very blind friendship—would have made you write it. I, myself, thought that it was not wise for you to publish it, that nobody would take any interest in me, and that they would only laugh at you for your loyalty and affection."

The following day he writes again: "Just after I had written you, the book came. I am immensely pleased with it, and I am very proud that my children and grandchildren are to have it. . . . Of course, old friend, you have said of me far more than I deserve, but I am glad you said it." The book to which he refers shows, perhaps, more than any other book written about my brother, the accurate realization by the author that my brother's attitude in January, 1912, when he took the step which directly or indirectly brought about the formation of the Progressive party, was in no sense an erratic swerving from the path upon which he had always walked, but, on the contrary, a direct and logical justification of beliefs—and the actions with which he always squared beliefs—held in his early manhood and retained in his later years.

On March 27, after his return from Trinidad, he writes:

"Well, here we are, back from our little trip along 'the path to Nowhere.' [He refers here to some verses I had just published under that title.] We did not get entirely out of the path to Somewhere—thanks to the 'hurrying, struggling, and striving' of very kind people who insisted on entertaining us—but we had, at intervals, a number of hours on the path to Nowhere, although, in that latitude, there were no adders' tongues, and the lilies were less in evidence than palms, bougainvillea, scarlet hibiscus and poinsettia in hedges, and rocks and flowering trees, and little green cities of St. Mary's (I wish I had seen Masefield)—and the trade wind tossing the fronds of the palms on the white beaches.

"I loved your letter, and read and re-read every word of it. I think as highly of 'Ordeal by Battle' as you do; did I show you the letter Oliver sent me with a copy of the first edition? He has just sent me a copy of the second edition. I am very glad you are taking a rest cure. You sorely needed it, but when you leave Nonkanawha, can't you bring Cortissoz and the Corbins out here for lunch. I am very glad you like my book. My soul was in it. [He had just published "Fear God, and Take Your Own Part."] . . . Well, I don't see much chance of our doing what is right in politics. The trouble is that we have complacently sagged back for fifty years while Germany has surged forward and has forced her nearest competitors to some kind of forward movement in order to avoid death at her hands."

Shortly afterward, when in answer to his suggestion I wrote him that I would bring some of the friends he mentioned to luncheon, he writes: "Three cheers—I shall expect you with the Cortissoz, Corbins, and O'Hara."

That letter was written on April 2, 1916, and shortly afterward I motored those friends to Oyster Bay, and we had a peculiarly delightful luncheon and afternoon, at which I was, as usual, struck with the manner in which he adapted himself to the interest of the individual. Mr. John Myers O'Hara, an American poet of classic and lyric quality, was shown a special poem in which my brother felt that there was similarity between his work and that of the author of the lines in question; Mr. Cortissoz, whose delicious humor was a special delight to my brother, found the Colonel not only sympathetic in those ways, but also in the quality of his artistic thought; he adapted himself to each in turn, and we all motored away from that full and rich environment each more stimulated than before along the line of the special achievement to which he aspired.

On his return from Trinidad, he had been beset by questions as to whether he would consent again to be the presidential nominee. The Progressive party, after its severe defeat in various States in 1914, still showed a grim desire to be at least a strong factor in the nomination for a presidential candidate in the coming election, and various combinations of individuals were already in process of coalition in the happy thought that Theodore Roosevelt might be the combined nominee of both Progressive and Republican forces. A certain number of such citizens formed what they called The Roosevelt Non-partisan League, and the secretary of that league, Guy Emerson by name, wrote, in part, as follows to Colonel Roosevelt:

"Dear Colonel Roosevelt:—The Roosevelt Non-partisan League is a movement inaugurated by citizens of all parties who believe that Americanism is the great issue before the country today, and that you are the strongest available man as leader under that issue. You stated the platform in your Chicago speech, which, in our opinion, is vital for the safety of the country during the four momentous years which lie ahead."

In answer to the above letter, my brother wrote:

"Because of your attitude, I earnestly approve your work. The safety of this country depends upon our immediate, serious, and vigorous efforts to square our words with our deeds, and to secure our own national rehabilitation. The slumbering patriotism of our people must be waked and translated into concrete and efficient action. The awakening must be to a sense of national and international duty and responsibility." After going into greater length as to his personal principles and opinions, Mr. Roosevelt continues: "Our citizens must act as Americans, not as Americans with a prefix and qualifications. . . . Cowardice in a race, as in an individual, is the unpardonable sin. The timid man who cannot fight, and the selfish, short-sighted or foolish man who will not take the steps that will enable him to fight, stand on almost the same plane. Preparedness deters the foe and maintains right by the show of ready might without the use of violence. Peace, like Freedom, is not a gift that tarries long in the hands of cowards, or of those too feeble or too short-sighted to deserve it, and we ask to be given the means to insure that honorable peace which alone is worth having."

In answering from other sources the same suggestion—namely, that he should take anew the leadership and be himself the nominee against President Wilson—he boldly replied that he doubted if it would be wise to name him, for if he should be named, his followers would have to be in a "heroic mood."

On May 31 he announced: "I speak for universal service based on universal training. Universal training and universal service represent the only service and training a democracy should accept. . . . Performance of international duty to others means that in international affairs, in the commonwealth of nations, we shall not only refrain from wronging the weak, but, according to our capacity and as opportunity offers, we should stand up for the weak when the weak are wronged by the strong."

Every speech by Colonel Roosevelt had again become the subject of national discussion, and as the Democratic policy began to shape itself, each position taken by the Republican party, as well as by the Progressive party, followed the lines laid down in some speech made by Colonel Roosevelt. By this time he had fully come to realize that, if it were possible to defeat the policies which, from his standpoint, were lulling the country into ignoble avoidance of its national and international duty, such defeat could only be brought about by the amalgamation of the Progressive and Republican parties, a result extremely difficult to accomplish.

On April 14 he said: "*The Tribune* says of the approaching convention, 'We are choosing which way the country shall go in the era that is now opening, just as our fathers chose the nation's path in the days of 1860.' This sentence should be in the mind of every man who at Chicago next June takes part in formulating the platform and naming the candidate. The men at Chicago should act in the spirit of the men who stood behind Abraham Lincoln. . . . There is one great issue on which the fight is to be made if the highest service is to be rendered the American people. That issue is that the American people must find its own soul. National honor is a spiritual thing that cannot be haggled over in terms of dollars. [He refers to the issue of the tariff which had been prominently brought forward.] We must stand not only for America First but for America first, last, and all the time and without any second. . . . We can be true to mankind at large only if we are true to ourselves. If we are false to ourselves, we shall be false to everything else. We have a lofty ideal to serve and a great mission to accomplish for the cause of Freedom and genuine democracy, and of justice and fair dealing throughout the world. If we are weak and slothful and absorbed in mere money getting or vapid excitement, we can neither serve these causes nor any others. We must stand for national issues, for national discipline and for preparedness—military, social and industrial—in order to keep the soul of this nation. We stand for Peace, but only for the Peace that comes as a right to the just man armed, and not for the Peace which the coward purchases by abject submission to wrong. The Peace of cowardice leads in the end to war after a record of shame."

Even the Democratic newspaper, the New York *Times*, spoke about that time of Colonel Roosevelt's capacity to rouse a true patriotism. It said: "The passion of his Americanism, his unerring instinct for the jugular vein, make him, in a good cause, an unrivalled compeller of men. He has had his fill of glories, his name is blown about the world;—by preparing America against war, to unite America in patriotism, there are no nobler laurels." And almost coincident with this unexpected appreciation of a newspaper frequently the enemy of Colonel Roosevelt came a letter from his former attorney-general, William H. Moody, written to their mutual friend Mr. Washburn, the author of the book which I have already mentioned. In the heat of the controversy which was once more beginning to rage around the figure of Theodore Roosevelt, it was interesting to read the calm and quiet words penned by the able man who had served as attorney-general in my brother's cabinet, but, alas, laid low by the painful illness which later proved the cause of his premature death. "For five years," writes Mr. Moody, "I was in almost daily association with him in the details of work for a common purpose and in his relation to all sorts and conditions of men. There are some parts of his work as President which I think no one knew better than I did, and there are results of it which ought to receive thorough study and be brought clearly to light. I have here specially in mind, the effect of his acts and preachments upon economic thought, and the development of the constitutional theory of our government. If one contrasts the state of opinion as to the proper relation between capital and labor, and the proper attitude of government toward both as that opinion existed just before the war with Spain, and as it exists today, one cannot fail to see that there has been an extraordinary change. In this change, I believe he was the one great leader in this country. . . . What was needed was a man with a great genius for leadership, great courage, great intelligence, and the highest purpose. That man came in Theodore Roosevelt. Perhaps, many would scout the idea that he had been a guide in constitutional interpretation. I remember the state of legal thought and the attitude of the Supreme Court in the nineties toward what we called the new internationalism. I believe no one appreciates more clearly than I the great change that has come to both since then. By the legislation which he, Theodore Roosevelt, promoted against great odds, there have been drawn from the Supreme Court decisions which have declared that nationalism which is necessary to our future national life."

This deliberate decision on the part of a man essentially legal in mind throws interesting light upon my brother's actions and attitudes, assailed as he was at the time for lack of the very devotion to the Constitution for which Mr. Moody praises him. About the same time, from Kansas City, on May 30, 1916, my brother writes to me: "I hope you will like the speech I am about to make here. I have scrupulously employed the 'we' in describing our governmental short-comings!"

Unless I am mistaken, it was about that time that my brother made a speech in Arkansas which—while the quotation which I am about to give has little to do with the issue of the moment—is so characteristic of his own fearlessness that I cannot pass it over.

The strongest theory which I have evolved from the study of the ups and downs of political life consists in the belief that of all factors in permanent success (and permanent success means a place in history), there is none so important as that of moral as well as physical courage. More men have lost their heart's desire because at the most crucial moment they lacked the courage to barter that very desire for an honest conviction than from any other cause. Theodore Roosevelt believed that he could help not only his country but the countries of the world were he nominated and elected in 1916, just as he firmly believed that should Mr. Wilson be renominated and re-elected to that position, America and the countries of the world would be worse off rather than better off, and yet, no matter before what audience he spoke, were it East, West, North, or South, he spoke with the ardor of conviction, never for one moment withholding one belief, no matter how unpalatable it might be to the section of the country to which he was giving his message, did he feel that that belief should be clearly demonstrated to that portion of the people.

At Little Rock, Ark., the Governor of the State (I was told of this incident by a Methodist minister who was present on the occasion), during a speech in which he introduced Colonel Roosevelt to his stupendous audience, said: "We have an unwritten law in the Southland that when a vile black wretch commits the unmentionable crime, we hang him without judge or jury." As Theodore Roosevelt rose to make his address, he turned to the governor and said: "Before I make my address to the people, Governor, I want to say to you that when any man or set of men take the law into their own hands, and inflict summary punishment on the 'vile black wretch' of whom you speak they place themselves upon the same base level as that same 'vile black wretch.'" The stunned audience, silent for a moment, burst into vociferous applause. But the governor made no response to Colonel Roosevelt's interpellation.

It was about this same time that in response to a letter from Mr. Guy Emerson, Mr. Thomas A. Edison wrote of Colonel Roosevelt as follows: "My dear Sir:—Answering your question as to my views of Colonel Roosevelt for our next President, I would say that I believe he is absolutely the only man that should be considered at this crucial period. He has more real statesmanship, a better grasp of the most important needs of this country and greater executive ability to handle the big, international problems that will arise at the close of the war than all the other proposed candidates put together. His energy, capacity, and vast experience in large affairs of state and nation for many years, together with his great patriotism, and his intense Americanism, and his great knowledge in all lines of human endeavor, make him decidedly the most striking figure in American life."

Mr. Edison voiced the sentiment of hundreds of thousands

of his fellow citizens, and as the time approached for the Republican Convention of 1916, feelings of all kinds waxed almost as hot as in those thrilling days of 1912. In fact, in many ways, there was even a greater excitement in the hearts of the more valiant Americans, who believed that the time was already ripe to make the world safe for democracy. These more valiant Americans also believed that the man most fitted to aid in making the world thus safe was Theodore Roosevelt. On the other hand, the stand-pat Republicans were still smarting from what they considered, I think unjustly, his betrayal of them, and they were not ready to enroll themselves under his banner. The Progressives, on the other hand, were equally opposed to any compromise, and when the great convention met in Chicago, peace between the contending factions seemed an illusive and unattainable ideal, and so it proved. Those were days of tragic excitement in the great auditorium, where sat, tied hand and foot, what seemed to be a mercenary army, so little did true patriotism appear to actuate the delegates to that important congregation of individuals. On the other hand, near by, in a smaller hall, the almost fanatic enthusiasm for the much higher ideal was also to make itself a party to the defeat of its own object, although at that moment of honest and high-minded enthusiasm it could hardly be blamed for any attitude born of that enthusiasm.

Again the battle raged, and again the personality of Theodore Roosevelt became the deciding factor. Conferees were chosen by both the Republican Convention and the Progressive Convention, but they could not find a common ground upon which to agree, and that fateful week in early June ended with the nomination of Charles E. Hughes by the Republican Convention, and, against his wish, with the nomination of my brother on the Progressive ticket. Perhaps there was never a more dramatic moment, a moment of more heartfelt disappointment, than when the convention of the Progressive party received the statement brought to it by John McGrath, secretary of Colonel Roosevelt, which ran as follows (I quote from a contemporary newspaper in Chicago):

"Announcement was made here this afternoon at 4:50 o'clock that Roosevelt has refused to accept the Progressive nomination for President.

"Colonel Roosevelt's statement was brought to the convention by John McGrath, his secretary. It follows:

"'To the Progressive Convention: I am very grateful for the honor you confer upon me by nominating me as President. I cannot accept it at this time. I do not know the attitude of the candidate of the Republican party toward the vital questions of the day. Therefore, if you desire an immediate decision, I must decline the nomination. But if you prefer it, I suggest that my conditional refusal to run be placed in the hands of the Progressive National Committee.

"'If Mr. Hughes' statements, when he makes them, shall satisfy the committee that it is for the interest of the country that he be elected, they can act accordingly and treat my refusal as definitely accepted. If they are not satisfied they can so notify the Progressive party, and at the same time, they can confer with me and then determine on whatever action we may severally deem appropriate to meet the needs of the country.'

"'I move,' said James R. Garfield, 'that the letter of Colonel Roosevelt be received in the spirit in which it is meant, and that it be referred to the National Committee, with power to act thereon.'

"The motion was carried, and at 5 P. M. the Progressive Convention, the liveliest in the history of politics, came to an end with the playing of the national air."

The closing scenes of the Republican Convention were as cold and as unemotional as was the reverse in the body sitting in the other hall, so close at hand. I, myself, went from one spot to the other, torn with conflicting emotions. In the Republican Convention there had been no enthusiasm whatsoever for any candidate up to the moment when Senator Fall, of New

Mexico, put the name of Theodore Roosevelt in nomination. Then, and then only, did the thousands of people in that great auditorium rise to their feet with one prolonged shout of approval. The delegates—and, alas! it is the delegates to a convention, not the people, who apparently choose the men who are to govern the people—were cold and unresponsive no matter what name was put before them, and, were it possible, they were even colder, even more unresponsive, when Theodore Roosevelt's name was mentioned than they were at any other time; but the masses—they were neither cold nor unresponsive! How they cheered as that beloved name was heard for the first time in that Republican Convention! Over and over again the chairman tried to bring the convention to order. No blaring bands, no stimulated marchings, were the cause of the great ovation. It was actually and vividly the cry of those who wanted a leader and wanted *their* leader that was heard in that great hall, but there was no echo in the hearts of those who held the balance of power in their hands. That evening there was printed in one of the Chicago newspapers so exquisite a rhapsody, so loving a swan song, that I can but reproduce it.

AH! TEDDY DEAR

Ah, Teddy dear, and did ye hear the news that's goin' round?

They say you're gone from off the stage, that strange cold men, whom we respect but love not, must be our meat for all the campaign days to come.

Gray is the prospect; dull is the outlook.

We felt all the while that over in the Auditorium and the Coliseum they were breaking to us the news of a death in the family. They were merciful; they held it back; they did not let us have the shock of it all at once. They meant kindly.

But now that the news has come the kindness of friends can help but little. Our hearts are broke! We need you and we want you every minute.

Ah the fun of you and the glory of you!

Where lies the American whose passion or whose imagination you have not set a-tingling? Who else has meant the savor of life for us? Who but you has taken us and set our feet upon the high places?

Before you came, all in politics was set and regular. Those who were ordained to rule over us did so with that gravity with which stupid grown-ups so oft repress the child. No one ever talked to us as you did. They called us "voters" or "constituents" or such big names as these. They never took us by the hand and laughed and played with us as you did.

They never understood us. They could preach Sunday school and arithmetic. But the good Lord never gave it to them to speak to the heart.

And then you came!

Dancing down the road you came with life and love and courage and fun stickin' out all over you. How we loved you at the first sight! And how you loved us!

Friends we were, tho' you were in the White House and we were making mud pies. Friends we were together with nothing to come between us.

Your love would let no harm come near us and we knew it. With your courage you fought for us. With your life and your fun you took us out of the drab grind.

You told us of the birds in the air and of the fishes in the sea. The great tales of the old heroes, the sagas of the past, you spread before our 'stonished eyes. You gave us new words—delightful words—to play with; and jokes—delightful jokes—to make us laugh.

How we wanted you back when you went away! But they stole our right from us and they wouldn't let you come back. So we followed you. Four million of us, in a fight the like of which we never knew. Joy and religion were in it in equal measure. Hymns and cleanness and color and battle all were jumbled in it. The good of it is set forever into the life of the nation.

But the schoolmaster beat you, and the Great War came to crowd you from our thoughts. We thought only of ourselves because you were no longer there to make us think of our country. At last we turned to you—when it was too late.

So now we are not to have you. We must go stumbling on alone, hoping that the man they've given us may show something of that fire and strength upon which you taught us to rely.

It's our fault, not theirs. It's our fault, not yours. You warned us that we must be ready to go thru to the end. We weren't. Fear had come upon us, fear of ourselves. We were split up. We eyed each other with distrust. The spirit of your old sagas had gone from us.

Now we must face it alone, unless you help us. Do not forsake us to sulk in your tent. Make the sacrifice they demand, not for their sake but for ours. Help them win with the cold, good man they've chosen. Help that man to hold his courage and fight worthily for the things which you have taught us—tho the real right to fight for them was yours, not his. Don't let our councils be divided. Don't let hotheaded friends force their personal claims upon you.

But whatever you do or whatever you don't do, be sure of one thing—we shall never hold it against you. For all that is gone, you can do no wrong in our sight. The memory of you shall never fade from our hearts.

Ah, Teddy dear—we love you now and always.*

* From the Chicago *Evening Post*, June, 1916. The article was written by Julian Mason, the gifted son of one who had been a hospitable host of Theodore Roosevelt when, as a young man, he wrote "The Winning of the West."

XVI

"DO IT NOW"

> Sad America
> Dreamed in the distance as a charmed thing
> Till Roosevelt, like Roland, blew his horn.
> —John Jay Chapman.

> One who rang true when traitor thoughts were rife,
> One who led straight through all the years of strife.
> —From *Horace Mann School Record.*

I WENT to Sagamore Hill the very moment that I returned from Chicago after that exciting convention. In fact, I took the first train possible to Oyster Bay. My heart was aflame, for it seemed to me then, as it has seemed to me frequently in such contests (nor does this refer solely to contests in which my brother took part), that the will of the people had been frustrated.

My brother was seated in the library when I arrived at Sagamore Hill, and when I burst out, "Theodore—the people wanted you. It seems terrible to me that they could not have you," he answered, with a smile that had a subtle meaning in it: "Do not say that; if they had wanted me *hard* enough, they could have had me." By which he meant that after all, if enough citizens in our great country would take seriously the duties of citizenship, the delegates to our conventions would have to do their will. From that moment, putting himself entirely aside, his whole thought, his whole effort were given to the achievement of what he considered the vital need for his country; namely, the election of the Republican candidate. Waiting until Mr. Hughes had definitely stated his policy, Colonel Roosevelt, upon that statement, immediately sent to the Progressive

Convention, which met within a few weeks, a letter stating his position as follows:

"*Gentlemen:* In accordance with the message I sent to the National Progressive Convention as soon as I had received the notification that it had nominated me for President, I now communicate to you my reasons for declining the honor which I so deeply appreciate. . . . Before speaking of anything else, I wish to express my heartiest and most unstinted admiration for the character and services of the men and women who made up the National Progressive Convention in 1916. . . . They represent the spirit which moved Abraham Lincoln and his political associates during the decade preceding the close of the Civil War. The platform put forth in 1912 was much the most important public document promulgated in this country since the death of Abraham Lincoln. It represented the first effort, on a large scale, to translate abstract formulas of economic and social justice into concrete American nationalism. . . .

"Events have shown us that the Progressive party in 1912 offered the only alternative to the triumph of the Democratic party. . . . The results of the terrible world war of the past two years have now made it evident to all who are willing to see, that in this country there must be spiritual and industrial preparedness, along the lines of efficient and loyal service to the nation, and of practical application of the precept that 'each man must be his brother's keeper.' Furthermore, it is no less evident that this preparedness for the days of peace forms the only sound basis for that indispensable military preparedness based on military universal training, and which finds expression in universal obligatory service in time of war. Such universal obligatory training and service are necessary complements of universal suffrage and represent the realization of the true American, the democratic ideal in both peace and war.

"Sooner or later, the national principles championed by the Progressives of 1912 must, in their general effect, be embodied in the structure of our national existence. With all my heart, I shall continue to work for these great ideals, shoulder to shoulder with the men and women, who, in 1912, championed them. . . . The method however by which we are to show our loyalty must be determined in each case by the actual event. Our loyalty is to the fact, to the principle, to the ideal, and not merely to the name, and least of all, to the party name. The Progressive movement has been given an incalculable impetus by what the Progressive party has done. Our strongest party organizations have accepted and enacted into law, or embodied in their party platforms many of our most important principles. Yet it has become entirely evident that the people under existing conditions are not prepared to accept a new party. . . . Under such circumstances, our duty is to do the best we can and not to sulk because our leadership is rejected.—It is unpatriotic to refuse to do the best possible, merely because the people have not put us in a position to do what we regard as the very best. . . . In my judgment, the nomination of Mr. Hughes meets the conditions set forth in the statement of the Progressive National Committee, issued last January and in my own statements. Under existing conditions, the nomination of a third ticket would, in my judgment, be merely a move in the interest of the election of Mr. Wilson. I regard Mr. Hughes as a man whose public record is a guarantee that he will not merely stand for a program of clean-cut, straight principles before election but will resolutely and in good faith put them through if elected. It would be a grave detriment to the country to re-elect Mr. Wilson. I shall, therefore, strongly support Mr. Hughes. Such being the case, it is unnecessary to say that I cannot accept the nomination on a third ticket. I do not believe that there should be a third ticket. I believe that when my fellow Progressives actually consider the question, they will, for the most part, take this position.

"They and I have but one purpose,—the purpose to serve our common country. It is my deep conviction that at this moment we can serve it only by supporting Mr. Hughes."

From that moment, "squaring," as he always did, "conviction with action," Theodore Roosevelt set his strong shoulder to the political wheel which he hoped with all his heart would put Charles E. Hughes into the White House.

In my brother's own "Autobiography" he says: "I have always had a horror of words that are not translated into deeds, of speech that does not result in action; in other words, I believe in realizable ideals and in realizing them; in preaching what would be practicable and then practising it."

He put the same idea in somewhat different words in a speech in that very campaign of 1916: "Of course, the vital thing for the nation to remember is that while dreaming and talking both have their uses, these uses must chiefly exist in seeing the dream realized and the talking turned into action. . . . Ideals that are so lofty as always to be unrealizable have a place,—sometimes an exceedingly important place in the history of mankind—*if* the attempt, at least partially to realize them is made; but, in the long run, what most helps forward the common run of humanity in this work-a-day world, is the possession of realizable ideals and the sincere attempt to realize them."

Never did my brother more earnestly fulfil the convictions expressed in the above sentence than in his campaign for the election of Mr. Hughes. Never did he give himself more selflessly, and with more tireless zeal, than when he tried to put one so lately a rival for the presidental nomination into the White House, because of his strong belief that to do so would be for the good of his beloved country.

On June 23, just before the meeting of the Progressive Convention, he writes to me: "I should like to show you my letter to the National Committee which will appear on Monday afternoon. I will then, I trust, finish my active connections with Politics." And again, in another letter on July 21, he says: "For six years I have been, I believe, emphatically right, emphatically the servant of the best interests of the American people; but just as emphatically,—the American people have steadily grown to think less and less of me, and more definitely determined not to use me in any public position, and it is their affair after all. Your Teddy [my son at the time was running for the nomination for New York State Senator] may experience the same fate and may find that through no fault of his,—in my case the fault may have been mine,—his talents may be passed by."

It is interesting to note that although so frequently a justified prophet in national affairs, my brother's prophecies concerning himself rarely came true. The above prophecy was no exception to this rule, for during the years to come, the Republican party was to turn once more to Theodore Roosevelt as its greatest leader, and to pledge its support to him both inferentially and actually in their great effort to make him the nominee for governor of New York State. In the campaign of 1918 the leaders of the Republican party turned to him as almost one man, feeling as they did that his election again to that position would positively secure him the election to the presidency in 1920.

Perhaps the hardest thing for him to bear connected with the political situation in 1916 was the keen disappointment of those Progressives for whom he had such devoted affection when he refused to run on the Progressive ticket as the candidate for President. He felt that in the hearts of many there was, in spite of their personal devotion to him, a sense of disillusion, and he tried with earnest effort to make them see the point of view which he was convinced was the right point of view, which made him support the candidate of the Republican party.

A Mrs. Nicholson, of Oregon, for whom he had a sincere regard, having written to him on the subject, he answers on July 18, 1916:

"My dear Mrs. Nicholson: . . . You say you do not understand 'Why we men make such a fetich of parties.' I cannot understand how you include me with the men who do so.

Four years ago I declined to make a fetich of the Republican party, when to do so meant dishonor to the nation, and this year I declined to make a fetich of the Progressive party when to do so meant dishonor to honor. I agree with you that issues and men are the things that count. A party is good only as a means to an end. Nevertheless, we have to face the fact that has been made strikingly evident during the past four years that with ninety per cent of our country-men the party name of itself has a certain fetichistic power, and we would be very foolish if we did not take this into account in endeavoring to work for good results. Moreover, it is unfortunately true that the dead hand of a party sometimes paralyzes its living members. The ancestral principles of the Democratic party are so bad it seems to be entirely impossible for it to be useful to the country except in spasms.

"I believe Mr. Hughes to be honest and to have the good of his country at heart."

He was not able to visit us in our country home on the Mohawk Hills, as we had hoped he might possibly do, during that summer, but on October 5 he writes to me: "I fear I shall be West on the 25th, otherwise I should jump at the chance to lunch with you and Fanny at the Colony Club. Can I accept for the first subsequent day when I find that you and she are available? I am now being worked to the limit by the Hughes people who are the very people who four months ago were explaining that I had 'no strength.' . . . I most earnestly desire to win; I, above all things, do not wish to sulk, and therefore, from now on my time is to be at the disposal of the National Committee. Of course, Teddy's nomination meant far more to me personally than anything else in this campaign. I look forward eagerly to seeing you. Do look at my *Metropolitan Magazine* article which is just out. I think you will like the literary style!" The "literary style" was combined with a certain amount of plain talk in this particular instance!

On October 12 Colonel Roosevelt, taking the exploits of

the German submarine U-boat 53 off the shores of America as a text, launched an urgent protest. Colonel Roosevelt declared that the conduct of the war had led to a "complete breakdown of the code of international rights." The man who as long ago as in his inauguration speech in March, 1905, inveighed against the "peace of the coward," was stirred to red-blooded indignation at the Democratic slogan of that campaign of 1916, which laid all the stress on "He kept us out of war," a sentence which Colonel Roosevelt described as "utterly misleading."

He said:

"Now that the war has been carried to our very shores, there is not an American who does not realize the awful tragedy of our indifference and our inaction. Nine-tenths of wisdom is being wise in time. By taking the right step at the right time, America's influence and leadership might have been made a stabilizing force.

"In actual reality, war has been creeping nearer and nearer until it stares at us from just beyond our three-mile limit, and we face it without policy, plan, purpose, or preparation. No sane man can to-day be so blind as to believe President Wilson's original statement that the war was no concern of ours. Every thinking man must realize the utter futility of a statesmanship without plan or policy until such facts as these now stare us in the face."

Such were the virile statements used many times during the following campaign. One of the most interesting human documents connected with Theodore Roosevelt during this period was written by a young reporter, Edwin N. Lewis, in private letters to his own family, from the special train upon which Theodore Roosevelt travelled for one of the most active ten days of his active life, during which he urged the American people to accept the Republican candidate. With Mr. Lewis's permission, I am quoting from these interesting letters, written by the kind of young American for whom my brother had the warmest and most friendly feeling, the kind of young American whose family life had been such that he wished to share with his family whatever was of interest in his life.

The first letter, dated October 17, 1916, begins:

"Just getting into Rochester—7 P. M.—Dear Ma:—The big tour is on. I was presented to Colonel Roosevelt by his secretary before the train pulled out. Since there are only three correspondents in the party, he insists that we eat in his private car with him. The trip is going to be a little family party with the Colonel a sort of jovial master of ceremonies. He permits me, a stranger, to take part in the conversation with the group. In fact, I feel, now, after my experiences at luncheon, that I have known him a long while. He is just as remarkable, energetic, mentally alert and forcible as his chroniclers picture him. I could entertain you and pa for an evening with the stories he told this noon, and dinner is coming in a half hour! Wonderful meals too,—with the New York Central chefs straining every effort to give Theodore Roosevelt something fine to eat. Cronin of *The Sun* and Yoder of the United Press are the only other newspaper men along. . . . Tomorrow we face a busy day. From Cincinnati, we turn down through a mountain section of Kentucky which has never seen a President, an ex-President or a Presidential candidate. Mountaineers will drive from miles around to see the man they have worshipped for years. The Colonel makes thirteen stops between Falmouth and Louisville. I realize how you are thinking of me on this trip. It helps me to make good."

Leaving Louisville, Ky., October 18, 11 P. M.:

"This has been a long day with hundreds of miles travelled by our special train through the valleys of Kentucky in a steady run. I wrote about 2000 words but do not imagine that all of it will get in the first edition which you will see in New England. Tonight, "T. R." pulled one of his familiar stunts with his changing the whole introduction to his speech at one-half hour's notice. He spoke for half an hour on the Adamson law and what he would have done to prevent the threatened railroad strikes. I had to shoot in 500 words additional just as we pulled out. It was written in long hand while the Colonel delivered the tail end of his talk. Louisville went wild over him. As we climbed down in the mud and rain, red fire burned, rockets glared in the mist, and the factory whistles screeched their welcome. As the New York correspondents travelling with the Colonel, we are members of his personal body-guard. You can imagine how seriously we take the job, when you remember that Mr. Roosevelt was shot and severely wounded when speaking at Milwaukee a few years ago; a man of such intense affections and such stirring convictions always has venomous enemies. For this reason, when we take the Colonel through a crowd as we did tonight, we completely surround him and use our elbows and fists if need be to protect him. If any harm should come to him, we would all be crushed. Tonight, however, he was only liable to be hurt by the overwhelming love of Louisville citizens. . . . Our relations with him could not be more cordial and democratic. This noon Colonel Roosevelt was terribly excited because Cronin and I did not get luncheon with him owing to the prevalence of Kentucky politicians who swarmed on the train like rats caught in a flood. He swore that he would eat nothing tonight until we had been fed. Tonight at 7 P. M. the porter came into my compartment and announced that Mr. Roosevelt was waiting dinner for Mr. Lewis and Mr. Cronin. He still apologized although we protested that the chef had filled our most prominent cavity successfully with sandwiches and coffee at 3 P. M. This gives you just one little glimpse of this remarkable man. I could write all night along this line. Mind you, he is taking all these precautions not for old friends but for two newspaper men whom he has never seen before and whose articles he has never read.

"Tonight as he left the hall, I jumped around to his right side, grabbed him by the arm and offered to act as a bumper against his admirers who fought like bears to shake his hand. He still remains the great idol of the American people. He smiled at me, drew his arm through mine and we swayed, pushed, and shoved our way out.

"The Colonel is a little older than he used to be. I think he will be fifty-eight the day we return to New York. At times, in the thick of the excitement, an expression of fatigue flashes across his features. There is a touch of sadness too, I believe, in his face, as he looks out over these crowds of people who have come for miles just to see him. He is not a candidate for President, thanks to the Chicago Convention,—but in spite of all these things which would discourage an ordinary man, he is travelling four thousand miles to win the election. . . . If the Colonel likes a person, he loves them with gigantic affection. His favorite character in literature is Great Heart from 'Pilgrim's Progress.'

"We fought our way into the hall tonight after passing through miles of streets lined with black and white people, standing patiently in the rain just to see the Colonel go by. We had a difficult time getting him out by the rear entrance for the larger crowd which could not get inside insisted on a brief speech from a bandstand outside. Then, we hustled back through the rain to the railroad station, climbed on the train and now we are approaching the Indiana border en route to Arizona through Missouri and Kansas. We are to take our meals with the Colonel three times a day. He promises that this rule will be lived up to. He relies on us to read the daily newspapers, giving him material. He never reads the papers as near as I can make out. We look forward to these next days with great pleasure. We are to tour the plains and run almost to the rim of the Grand Canyon. The Colonel expects to present us to some of the old horse thieves and other respectable men with whom he associated in his cow-punching days!"

October 21, 1916, near Phœnix:

"The trip has been a wonderful experience for me in every way. Think of chatting with the Colonel three times a day at meals,—Mr. Roosevelt personally explaining the significance of every adobe, cactus, pinyon tree, or prairie dog! When we go by a piece of desert, scorching in the white heat of sun-baked alcali, T. R. recalls an experience thirty years ago, when he lost some cattle that had sunk in quicksand in a dry river channel. He has taken us into his absolute confidence. He tells us stories and gives us opinions which if put on the telegraph would convulse the country. We are all convinced that not only is he the greatest American citizen, but also the greatest American humorist. His sense of humor is as marvelous as his physical and mental energy. To show you how thoughtful the Colonel is, . . . listen to this:—two of his friends climbed aboard at Prescott early this morning when I was shaving. That made two extra for breakfast, so Cronin and I insisted upon waiting for a second table. As we munched our toast and looked out at the giant cacti swiftly flowing by our window, who should come back to the table but T. R. 'Are you boys getting enough to eat?' he asked, sitting down. 'I am so sorry that this inconvenience occurred. If my visitors had not been old friends who had not breakfasted, I should never have permitted it.' How can a fellow help admiring a fellow like that, especially when he is an ex-President and one of the most famous characters in the world today?"

October 24, near Albuquerque:

". . . It was nearly 100 sitting in the afternoon sun in front of the speaking stand today. My cloth touring hat was too hot for the occasion, but without it I imagine I would have keeled over from prostration or gradually melted away under the press-stand. When the Colonel got through, his face was dripping. He delivered a corking talk. There was no heckling because he had been tipped off to answer at the beginning, the question as to what he would have done in Mexico had he been President. After he got into his proper speech, and he read every word of it, there were no interruptions except cheers of approval. My confidential opinion is, however, that he realizes that while these western crowds are for him personally, and cheer whenever he shows his familiar face, they do not understand,—they are not in down-right serious accord with, the doctrine he preaches. The Republicans are up against a hopeless situation. . . . The Roosevelt plan for compulsory military service, and preparedness are not practical *this year* because they have not wide-spread public support. The crowds come to hear *Roosevelt*. . . . The crowds in this country are too busy making money and planning how to make that money make some more, to realize the deep-rooted appeal of Theodore Roosevelt to their Americanism. Perhaps, through this hasty review of my impressions in Arizona, you dear folks at home can enter into this opportunity with me. I will have an interesting yarn to spin when I return to vote."

October 25, leaving Denver for Chicago:

"We are swinging down from the lofty Denver plateau surrounded with white-topped mountain peaks, through the sugar-beet and cattle farms to Nebraska. We shall wake up in Chicago tomorrow morning on the last leg of our tour. Colonel Roosevelt makes two or three speeches in Chicago and then pulls out for New York. Everything was rush—rush—rush in Denver. . . . We came by Colorado Springs and Pike's Peak at night but were all up, dressed and shaved when the enthusiastic Denverites descended on the Colonel with bands, bombs, bandannas, and general noise. Here was an old-fashioned, wild demonstration for the ex-President. He had not been in Denver for nearly six years. At one big meeting of 8000 women he showed them the fallacy of Mr. Wilson's argument, 'I have kept you out of war.' He told them why he was for suffrage. He had them with him from the start. All of this stuff was extemporaneous and I had to write 1000 words on it. The night meeting was a near-riot. We had a stiff fight to get the Colonel out of the auditorium which is one of the largest halls in the country. They have an excellent arrangement for getting the speakers in—wide doors open like a circus and the automobile with the Colonel and ourselves was driven close to the speaker's platform. Such a bedlam of noise I never heard. On the platform were the women speakers from the women's special train. When they tried to speak, however, the crowd hooted them down with cries of 'We want Teddy—Give us Teddy and Sit down,' etc. Then as soon as he began to speak, the Wilson hecklers started shouting, 'Hurrah for Wilson'—it was all very exciting. . . . 'Let me shake hands with the greatest President since Lincoln,' one old chap bawled, while I kept my fist under his chin as we formed a ring around the Colonel, and half-shoved and half-carried him to his automobile. The Colonel reached his hand around back of his neck and grasped the old man's finger-tips, whereupon he subsided and fell back to tell his children that this had been the greatest moment in his life.

"There is no antagonism to the Colonel out here. Even the Wilson supporters love Roosevelt. We have to protect him against his friends, however. . . . There is a chap on the train now, an old friend of the Colonel who has been collecting pictures along the Mexican border. Some of the atrocities, particularly the burning of bodies and the execution of soldiers are the most gruesome sights I have ever seen. The Colonel mentions them when he ridicules the cry that 'Wilson has kept peace in Mexico.' He told me today that some day next week he will entertain the four of us fellows at Oyster Bay at luncheon in his home. He wants to show us the trophies room, filled with relics from his African explorations and his early western life. That will be a compliment to us as newspaper men on this trip."

Friday, October 27, Pullman private car leaving Buffalo.

"We have just turned our watches ahead an hour, making it 10:15, and signifying that we are back in the home zone of eastern time. The trip is almost over. The rush and hustle of the trip, and the speed with which we have had to write and file our stories, make it seem a moving picture hodge-podge, now that it is over. Take yesterday, for instance,—we pulled into Chicago at 2 P. M. and were greeted by one of the wildest street demonstrations I have ever seen. The Colonel never sat down in his seat from the time he left the station until we arrived at the Congress Hotel. He was up waving his wide-brimmed black hat and bowing to the cheering mob. Every minute there was a flash, 'some miscreant photographer,' as T. R. calls them, had taken a bang at the Colonel. We had less than an hour to check our baggage in our rooms, wash up, arrange with the Western Union for filing stories, and get ready to accompany the Colonel to the Auditorium Theatre across the street.

"Thanks to the excellent police arrangements, we were able to walk unmolested through a human line of admirers who had been pushed into place by the mounted police. At 8 P. M. we called to interview the Colonel just before he left for the stock-yards. After the Women's meeting Cronin and I had to run for the Western Union to get a start on our story. We taxi-cabbed back to the Congress Hotel, omitted dinner, and joined the Roosevelt auto procession to the stock-yards pavilion which is six miles out of Chicago. How those cars did shoot through the wide Chicago streets, preceded by a motor squad police patrol with the mufflers on the machines wide open. It seemed more like going to a fire than riding to a political meeting.

"In the mêlée of getting the Colonel into the hall, I got separated from the party and found myself confronted with six wooden-headed Chicago cops who refused to recognize the official ticket of admission, distributed to members of the Roosevelt party. I got by one of them by telling him that I had been all the way to Arizona with the Colonel. 'Well, I'll be damned' he ejaculated. 'If you've been in Arizona, there is no reason in h— why you can't get in here.' After I got inside, however, there were more difficulties. The cops and ushers refused to let me up on the platform with the Colonel and the other correspondents. While I was fighting, pushing, and kicking around in the crowd, I heard someone shout down from above, 'We want Mr. Lewis up here right away. Make way for Mr. Lewis.' I looked up and saw that James R. Garfield, son of President

Garfield, himself former Secretary of the Interior, had come to my rescue. Mr. Garfield had been travelling with us for two days, and with his assistance the rest was easy. I was almost carried reverently to the platform and placed on a perfectly good chair where I could see everything.

"By the way,—Mr. Garfield, next to the Colonel, is the most likeable, lovable man I met on this trip. He has a face that you like to watch silently, and contemplate, because you know how fine and corking he must be. I never heard such a long demonstration as the one which greeted the Colonel as he stepped out before 18,000 men and women, each of whom seemed to have a small flag. It began at three minutes before eight and it stopped at thirty-two minutes past eight. In that long interim you could hear nothing but one continuous roar of cheering shouts and stamping feet. There was nothing articulate, no special cries distinguishable from others, just one blast as though some Titan engineer had tied down the heavy chain which released the whistle of 100,000 voice power. All efforts to stop it were futile. There was nothing to do but to let it run down. The band played 'Gary Owen' and the 'Star Spangled Banner' and other selections,—T. R. beating time with a large replica of a 'Big Stick' which had been handed to him. Meanwhile, in this bedlam, Cronin and I were writing new 'leads' to our story on pads in our laps. A Western Union man was sneaking up to the platform every ten minutes to get copy which was placed on wires on the pavilion. By writing this way, we got the story into New York before eleven o'clock, that is, when the meeting was over, by ten o'clock in Chicago; then there was the rapid shooting ride back to the hotel, a little grub and bath, and to bed. I *was* tired.

"We left Chicago at 6.25 A. M., the Colonel's car being hitched behind a regular train on the New York Central. The Colonel is fifty-eight years old today, as you will know, doubtless, before this letter reaches New Britain. I discovered the fact in reading his autobiography. He has been so fine to all of us; he has gone out of his way to make sure that we were treated like members of his own family; he has entertained us, as correspondents never were entertained; because what can excel the most interesting American, if not the greatest, telling anecdotes by the dozen of one of the most interesting, democratic, dynamic, forcible careers in American History? A thought that we ought to give him something to remember us by sprang simultaneously into the minds of Yoder and myself. . . . Our suggestions included a fountain-pen, pocket knife, or silver pencil—something that he could use. We elected Yoder to scout through the Colonel's pocket. He went out on the observation platform and casually asked the Colonel if he could borrow his knife. 'Yes—Yoder,' T. R. said, digging into his pocket, 'but I am ashamed of it. The blades are rusty, the handle is cracked. By George, I must get a new one.' We decided after hearing Yoder's report, that a knife was the thing. A handsome, little, flat, gold knife was picked out and the presentation came at luncheon today. Odell, in his solemn way, said that I had found out that he was born on October 27th. 'Now, Colonel, you have been telling us of many desperate characters you met in the Southwest. . . . We decided, therefore, that you should have a weapon. We have taken counsel and have determined to give you a little reminder of our pleasure on this trip. . . .' The Colonel took the little box, pulled forth the knife, and smiling a more than Roosevelt smile, 'By George, isn't that fine!' he exclaimed. 'I have never had a good pocket knife in all my life, and I was going to buy one tomorrow. I shall always cherish this gift,—I shall always carry it with me,' whereupon he attached it to the chain with his Phi Beta Kappa key and his little pencil;—'and I want to say that I have enjoyed immensely having you with me, and the trip has been a pleasure to me mainly because you young men have been such good company. I am too old at the political game to enjoy making speeches. I do not like it, but we have had a bully good time on this tour, and we have met a lot of my old friends,—and now, gentlemen, remember this, if Mr. Hughes is elected on November 7th, I shall never be seen in politics again. I am through.' I felt rather sorry to hear the Colonel say this. He is so energetic and courageous, so full of the fighting spirit that we need to tone up the national affairs, that it seems a pity to contemplate his retirement before he attains 60. Of course, he will write his views for the benefit of the reading public, but if he follows his inclination, he will become a quiet figure in the background, leaving younger men to carry through the ideas he created. We do not believe that the American people, however, will ever permit him to retire. Just as sure as Wilson is re-elected, there will be a demand for Theodore Roosevelt in 1920. He knows it and he is trying to start the talk now through us to show that it is the last thing on earth he cares to do. He would, I think, have liked to run *this year;* he would have liked to grapple with the problems which will arise after the war is over, but he took his licking at the hands of the old-line Republicans, and he really wants to see their candidate elected."

On my brother's return from this trip, so graphically described by the young and able correspondent whose prophecy that America would not let Theodore Roosevelt retire into obscurity was so soon to come true, he continued, up to the evening of the election, to hammer his opinions in strong, virile sentences into the minds of the audiences before whom he spoke. I was present in the Brooklyn Theatre, where the crowd was so great that one of the newspapers reported the next day:

"Say what you will,—there is no other one man in this country that can draw as large a crowd as Theodore Roosevelt. He is always an interesting talker as well as an interesting personality. He is not running for *any* office this Fall, though to hear some of the other speakers and to read some of the other newspapers, one might be pardoned for thinking that he was running for *all* of them."

It was at that great meeting in Brooklyn that he referred to a speech made a few days before by President Wilson in Cincinnati. In the Cincinnati speech Mr. Wilson had made the remark "that it would never be right for America to remain out of *another* war."

Colonel Roosevelt, after ringing the changes on the fact that what would be necessary in the future was in this case just as necessary in the present, ended with a stirring exhortation and the emphatic words: "Do it now, Mr. President."

In spite of Colonel Roosevelt's strong plea that we should take our stand shoulder to shoulder on the side of the Allies in the great cause for which they were fighting, it must not be thought for one moment that Theodore Roosevelt put internationalism above nationalism. All through the exciting campaign of 1916, he laid the greatest emphasis upon true Americanism. At Lewiston, Maine, in August, 1916, he said: "I demand as a matter of right that every citizen voting this year shall consider the question at issue, from the standpoint of America and not from the standpoint of any other nation. . . . The policy of the United States must be shaped to a view of two conditions only. First—with a view of the honor and interest of the United States, and second—with a view to the interest of the world as a whole. It is, therefore, our high and solemn duty, both to prepare our own strength so as to guarantee our own safety, and also to treat every foreign nation in every given crisis as its conduct in that crisis demands. . . . Americanism is a matter of the spirit, of the soul, of the mind; not of birthplace or creed. We care nothing as to where any man was born or as to the land from which his forefathers came, so long as he is whole-heartedly and in good faith an American and nothing else. . . . The policies of Americanism and preparedness taken together mean applied patriotism. Our first duty as citizens of the nation is owed to the United States, but if we are true to our principles, we must also think of serving the interests of mankind at large. In addition to serving our own country, we must shape the policy of our country so as to secure the cause of international right, righteousness, fair play and humanity.

Our first duty is to protect our own rights; our second, to stand up for the rights of others."

The above quotation seems to me to answer indisputably the mistaken affirmation that "America First" could ever be a selfish slogan.

On October 24, 1916, a letter had been sent, directed to "The Honorable Theodore Roosevelt, en route, Denver, Colorado." This missive was received on the special train from which young Edwin Lewis had just written to his family the stirring letters which I have quoted above. It is an interesting fact that the letter which I am about to give was signed by men the majority of whom had not followed Theodore Roosevelt on his great crusade for a more progressive spirit in American politics. Some of them had agreed with him in 1912, but the majority had felt it their duty to remain inside of the political party to which they had given their earlier faith. Now, in the moment of the great crisis of our nation, these very men turned for leadership to the man whom they realized was in truth the "noblest Roman of them all." The communication ran as follows:

"It is our conviction that no other Presidential campaign in the history of the nation ever presented graver issues or more far-reaching problems than does this. Not only is the domestic welfare of the nation profoundly to be affected by the result, but the honor and the very safety of the Republic are at stake. . . . In this momentous hour, the vital need is for such a presentation of the issues as will arrest the widest attention and carry the clearest message to the public mind, and this task we commend to your hands. No living American has a greater audience. You have done memorable service to your country in awakening it to a sense of its perils and obligations and you have revealed an unselfish patriotism that makes your voice singularly potent in councils and inspiration. Will you not lend it to the cause once more by addressing the people of the nation from a vantage ground of a great mass meeting in the metropolis? Under these circumstances, a message from Theodore

Roosevelt on America's crisis would ring from coast to coast. . . . The undersigned suggest Cooper Union as the place. . . ."

The signatures included many of the most distinguished citizens of the various States of America. My brother accepted this call to duty, although he had hoped to speak but little after his exhausting campaign in the West. I regret to say that I was not present at that meeting, at which, from what I have heard, he spoke with a conviction and a spiritual intensity rare even in him. The speech was called "The Soul of the Nation."

With burning words Theodore Roosevelt tried to arouse the nation's soul; with phrases hot from a heart on fire he portrayed the place we should take by the side of the countries who were fighting for the hope of the world, but the ears of the people were closed to all but the words that we had been kept "out of war." The day of the Lord was not yet at hand.

XVII

WAR

Thou gavest to party strife the epic note,
And to debate the thunder of the Lord;
To meanest issues fire of the Most High.
Hence eyes that ne'er beheld thee now are dim,
And alien men on alien shores lament.

—Stephen Phillips on Gladstone.

ELECTION DAY, 1916, dawned with the apparent success of the Republican party at the polls, but it eventually proved that the slogan, "He kept us out of war," had had its way, and that the Democrats were returned to power.

Needless to say, the disappointment both to the followers of Charles E. Hughes and of Theodore Roosevelt was keen beyond words. My brother, however, following his usual philosophy, set himself to work harder than ever to arouse his countrymen to the true appreciation of the fact that, with Europe aflame, America could hardly long remain out of the conflagration.

During the following winter, however, in spite of the great cloud that hung over the whole world, in spite of the intimate knowledge that we all shared that neither would we nor could we avoid the horror that was to come, occasionally there would be brief moments of old-time gaiety in our family life, little intervals of happy companionship, oases in the desert of an apprehension that was in itself prophetic. I remember saying to my brother one day: "Theodore, you know that I belong to the Poetry Society of America, and a great many of its members wish to meet you. I have really been very considerate of you, and although this wish has been frequently expressed for some years in the society, I have spared you heretofore, but the moment has come!" "Must I meet the poets, Pussie?" he said laughingly and rather deprecatingly. "Yes," I replied firmly. "The poets have their rights quite as much as the politicians, and the time for the poets is at hand." "All right—name your day," he answered, and so a day was named, and I invited a number of my friends amongst the poets to take tea with me on a certain afternoon to meet Colonel Roosevelt. I remember I asked him to try to come from his office early enough for me to jog his memory about some of the work of my various poet friends, but a large number of verse writers had already gathered in my sitting-room before he arrived. I placed him by my side and asked a friend to bring up my various guests so that I might introduce them to him. I remember the care with which I tried to connect the name of the person whom I introduced with some one of his or her writings, and I also remember the surprise with which I realized how unnecessary was all such effort on my part, for, as I would say, "Theodore, this is Mr. So-and-So, who wrote such and such," he would rapidly respond, "But you need not tell me that. I remember that poem very well, indeed," and turning with that delightful smile of his to the flattered author, he would say, "I like the fifth line of the third verse of that poem of yours. It goes this way," and with that, in a strong, ringing voice, he would repeat the line referred to. As each person turned away from the word or two with him, which evidently gave him almost as much pleasure as it gave them, I could hear them say to each other, "How did he know that poem of mine?" When I myself questioned him about his knowledge of modern American poetry, he answered quite simply: "But you know I like poetry and I try to keep up on that line of literature too." He was very fond of some of Arthur Guiterman's clever verse, and quoted with special pleasure a sarcastic squib which the latter had just published on the navy, apropos of Mr. Daniels's attitude: "We are sitting with our knitting on the twelve-inch guns!"

Robert Frost, who was with us that afternoon, had shortly

before published a remarkable poem called "Servant to Servants," which had attracted my brother's attention, and of which he spoke with keen interest to the author. Nothing distressed him more than the realization of the hard work performed by the farmer's wife almost everywhere in our country, and in this poem of Mr. Frost's that situation was painted with his forceful pen.

This remarkable memory of my brother's was shown not only that afternoon amongst the poets, but shortly afterward by an incident in connection with an afternoon at the Three Arts Club, where he also generously consented to spend an hour amongst the young girls who had come from various places in our broad country to study one of the three arts—drama, music, or painting—in our great metroplis. My friend Mrs. John Henry Hammond, the able president of the Three Arts Club, was anxious that he should meet her protégées and mine, for I was a manager of the club. I remember we lined the girls up in a row and had them pass in front of him in single file—several hundred young girls. Each was to have a shake of the hand and a special word from the ex-President, but none was supposed to pause more than a moment, as his time was limited. About fifty or sixty girls had already passed in front of him and received a cordial greeting, when a very pretty student, having received her greeting, paused a little longer and, looking straight at him, said: "Colonel Roosevelt, don't you remember me?" This half-laughingly—evidently having been dared to ask the question. Holding her hand and gazing earnestly at her, he paused a moment or two and then, with a brilliant flashing smile, said: "Of course I do. You were the little girl, seven years ago, on a white bucking pony at El Paso, Texas, where I went down to a reunion of my Rough Riders. I remember your little pony almost fell backward into the carriage when it reared at the noise of the band." There never was a more surprised girl than the one in question, for seven years had made a big difference in the child of twelve, the rider of the bucking white pony, and it had really not occurred to her that he could possibly remember the incident, but remember it he did, and one very happy heart was carried away that day from the Three Arts Club.

As the winter of 1917 slipped by, there was evidence on all sides that the slogan on which the Democratic party had based its campaign efforts must soon be falsified; nothing could keep the American people longer from their paramount duty, and on April 2, 1917, President Wilson appeared before the united bodies of the House and the Senate in Washington, and asked that Congress should declare a state of war between Germany and ourselves. Colonel Roosevelt, always anxious to back up the President in any action in which he thought he was right, went to Washington, or rather stopped in Washington, for he was in the South at the time, to congratulate him on his decision and to offer his services to assist the President in any way that might be possible.

Within a few weeks of the actual declaration of war, Mr. Roosevelt was already begging that he might be allowed to raise a volunteer division, and urging that the administration Army Bill should be supplemented with legislation authorizing the raising of from one hundred to five hundred thousand volunteers to be sent to the firing-line in Europe at the earliest possible moment. In a letter to Senator George E. Chamberlain, of Oregon, Colonel Roosevelt writes as follows:

"I most earnestly and heartily support the administration bill for providing an army raised on the principle of universal obligatory military training and service, but meanwhile, let us use volunteer forces in connection with a portion of the Regular army, in order, at the earliest possible moment,—within a few months,—to put our flag on the firing line. We owe this to humanity; we owe it to the small nations who have suffered such dreadful wrong from Germany. Most of all, we owe it to ourselves; to our national honor and self-respect. For the sake of our own souls, for the sake of the memories of the great Americans of the past, we must show that we do not intend to make this merely a dollar war. Let us pay with our bodies for our souls' desire. Let us, without one hour's unnecessary delay, put the American flag at the battle-front in this great world war for Democracy and civilization, and for the reign of Justice and fair-dealing among the nations of mankind.

"My proposal is to use the volunteer system not in the smallest degree as a substitute for, but as the, at present, necessary supplement to the obligatory system. Certain of the volunteer organizations could be used very soon; they could be put into the fighting in four months. . . . I therefore propose that there should be added to the proposed law, a section based on Section 12 of the Army Act of March 2nd, 1899. . . ."

At the same time Representative Caldwell made an open statement as follows: "The Army Bill suggested by Secretary Baker will, in all probability, be introduced in the House on Wednesday. There have been suggestions made that a clause be placed in the proposed bill which would give Colonel Roosevelt the power to take an army division to Europe. Colonel Roosevelt outlined his plans to me. . . . I am a Democrat and intend to abide by the wishes of President Wilson and told Colonel Roosevelt so. We agreed that there was no politics in this matter, and from my talk with Mr. Roosevelt, I believe him to be sincere in his purpose. He gave me the names of men throughout the country who signified their intention of joining his division. They include a number of men who served as officers with him in the Spanish War, many college students, former officers and members of the National Guard, all of whom are in the best of physical condition and ready to go at a moment's notice. Colonel Roosevelt said that a large majority of the men whom he hoped to take with him are from the south and west."

Already, at the first intimation that Colonel Roosevelt might lead a division into France, there had flocked to his standard thousands of men, just as had been the case in the old days of the Rough Riders. As immediate as was the rallying to his standard were also the attacks made upon him for having wished to dedicate himself to this patriotic enterprise, and one of the most acrimonious debates that ever occurred in the Senate of the United States was on the subject of the amendment to that Army Bill. The Democrats, led by Senator Stone, had much to say about the unfitness of the Colonel. They did not seem to realize how strong was the desire of France to have America's best-known citizen go to her shores at the moment when her morale was at the ebb; nor did they realize, apparently, the promise for the future that there would be in the rapid arrival of a large body of ardent American soldiers, well equipped to tide over the period of waiting before a still larger force could come to the assistance of the Allies.

Senator Hiram Johnson, orator and patriot, made a glowing defense of Colonel Roosevelt in answering Senator Stone. It is interesting to realize at this moment, when former Senator Harding is the President of the United States, that it was he who offered the amendment to the Army Bill, making it possible for Colonel Roosevelt to lead that division into France. Senator Johnson said:

". . . I listened with surprise—indeed, as a senator of the United States, with humiliation—to the remarks of the senior senator from Missouri as he excoriated Theodore Roosevelt and as he held up to scorn and contumely what he termed contemptuously 'The Roosevelt Division.' What is it that is asked for The Roosevelt Division? It is asked only by a man who is now really in the twilight of life that he may finally lay down his life for the country that is his. It is only that he asks that he may serve that country, may go forth to battle for his country's rights, and may do all that may be done by a human being on behalf of his nation. My God! When was it that a nation denied to its sons the right to fight in its behalf? We have stood shoulder to shoulder both sides of this Chamber in this war. To say that Roosevelt desires, for personal ambition and political favor hereafter, to go to war is to deny the entire life of this patriot. . . . Our distinguished senator has said that Roosevelt has toured the land in the endeavor to do that which he desires. Aye, he has toured the land; he toured the land for preparedness two and a half years ago, and he was laughed at as hysterical. He toured the land two and a half years ago and continuously since for undiluted Americanism, and you said he was filled with jingoism. To-day *you* have adopted *his* preparedness plan; to-day *his* undiluted Americanism that he preached to many, to which but few listened, has become the slogan of the whole nation. He toured the land for patriotism! . . . After all, my friends, Roosevelt fought in the past and he fought for the United States of America; after all, he asks only that he be permitted to fight to-day for the United States of America. He is accused of a lack of experience. . . . There is one thing this man has—one thing that he has proven in the life he has lived in the open in this nation—he has red blood in his veins and he has the ability to fight and he has the tenacity to win when he fights, and that is the sort of an American that is needed and required in this war. I say to you, gentlemen of this particular assemblage, that if a man can raise a division, if he wishes to fight, die, if need be, for his country, it is a sad and an awful thing that his motive shall be questioned and his opinions assailed in the very act that is indeed the closing act of his career.

"Oh! for more Roosevelts in this nation; oh! for more men who will stand upon the hustings and go about the country preaching the undiluted Americanism that all of us claim to have! Oh! for more Roosevelts and more divisions of men who will follow Roosevelt! With more Roosevelts and more Roosevelt divisions, the flag of the United States will go forth in this great world conflict to the victory that every real American should desire and demand."

Part of the afternoon just before the final vote on the above amendment to that Army Bill was spent by Theodore Roosevelt in my library in New York. Those were the days when

Mr. Balfour, M. Viviani, and General Joffre were receiving the acclamation and the plaudits of the American people. At several of the great ovations given to them, Theodore Roosevelt was also on the platform, and it was frequently brought to my notice by others that the tribute to him when he entered or left the assemblage was equal in its enthusiasm to that for the distinguished guests. On the afternoon to which I have referred, the French ambassador came for a quiet cup of tea with me and my brother, and to his old friend and his sister the Colonel was willing to unbosom his heart. He spoke poignantly of his desire to lead his division into France. Over and over again he repeated: "The President need not fear me politically. No one need fear me politically. If I am allowed to go, I could not last; I am too old to last long under such circumstances. I should *crack* [he repeated frequently: "I should *crack*"] but [with a vivid gleam of his white teeth] I *could* arouse the belief that America was coming. I could show the Allies what was on the way, and then if I did crack, the President could use me to come back and arouse more enthusiasm here and take some more men over. That is what I am good for now, and what difference would it make if I cracked or not!"

The amendment *was* passed that made it possible for volunteers to go to France, but the beloved wish of his heart was denied by those in authority to that most eager of volunteers, Colonel Theodore Roosevelt.

In July my brother wrote an open letter of farewell, disbanding the division for which there had been tentatively so many volunteers. After a correspondence with the secretary of war, a correspondence which Theodore Roosevelt himself has given to the world, the definite decision was made that he would not be allowed to "give his body for his soul's desire," and shortly after that decision I sent him the following poem, which had been shown to me by one of his devoted admirers, the poet Marion Couthouy Smith. It ran as follows:

FAREWELLS

"In old Fraunces Tavern,
    Once I was told
Of Washington's farewell to his generals,
    Generals crowned with victory,
And tears filled my eyes.—

"But when I read
    Roosevelt's letter disbanding his volunteers,—
Volunteers despised and rejected,—
    Tears filled my heart!"

In acknowledging the poem on July 3, 1917, from Sagamore Hill, my brother writes:

"I loved your letter; and as for the little poem, I prize it more than anything that has been written about me; I shall keep it as the epitaph of the division and of me. We have just heard that Ted and Archie have landed in France. Lord Northcliffe wired me this morning that Lord Derby offered Kermit a position on the staff of the British army in Mesopotamia. [After hard fighting in Mesopotamia, Kermit was later transferred to the American forces in France.] I do not know when he will sail. Quentin has passed his examinations for the flying corps. He hopes to sail this month. Dick [Richard Derby, his son-in-law] is so anxious to go down to Camp Oglethorpe that Ethel is almost as anxious to have him go. Eleanor [young Theodore's wife] sails for France on Saturday to do Y. M. C. A. work. *I* remain, as a slacker 'malgré lui!' Give my love to Corinne and Joe and Helen and Teddy. I am immensely pleased about Dorothy's baby. [Dorothy, my son Monroe's wife.] Edith asked Fanny to come out on Friday with our delightful friend, Beebe the naturalist. I thoroughly enjoyed it. Beebe is a great friend of mine."

The "slacker malgré lui" accepted the gravest disappointment of his life as he did any other disappointment—eyes forward, shoulders squared, and head thrown back. It was hard for him, however, to busy himself, as he said, with what he considered "utterly pointless and fussy activities," when his whole soul was in the great conflict on the far side of the water, from which one of his boys was not to return, and where two of the others were to be seriously wounded.

Writing on October 5, 1917, he says: "Of course I stood by Mitchel." This refers to a hot campaign which was waging around the figure of the young mayor of New York City, John Purroy Mitchel, who had given New York City the best administration for many a long year and was up for re-election but, unfortunately, due to many surprising circumstances, was later defeated. My brother had the greatest admiration for the fearlessness and ability of the young mayor, and later, when that same gallant American entered the flying service and was killed in a trial flight, no one mourned him more sincerely than did the man who always recognized courage and determination and patriotism in Democrat or Republican alike.

About the same time, in speaking of General Franklin Bell, who was in charge of Camp Upton, he says: "The latter is keenly eager to go abroad. He says that if he is not sent, he will retire and go abroad as a volunteer." By a strange chance, a snapshot was taken of the first division of drafted men sent to Camp Upton just as they were passing the reviewing-stand, on which stood together Franklin Bell, John Purroy Mitchel, and Theodore Roosevelt. The expression on my brother's face was one so spiritual, so exalted in aspect, that I am reproducing the picture.

All through that autumn he gave himself unstintedly to war work of all kinds, and amongst other things came, at my request, to a "Fatherless Children of France" booth at the great Allied Bazaar. The excitement in front of the booth as he stood there was intense, and as usual the admirers who struggled to shake his hand were of the most varied character. We decided to charge fifty cents for a hand-shake, and we laughed

From a photograph, copyright by Underwood and Underwood.

A review of New York's drafted men before going into training in September, 1917.

Neither Colonel Roosevelt nor his companions to the left and right, General Bell and Mayor Mitchel, lived to see the final review.

immoderately at the numbers of repeaters. One man, however, having apparently approached the booth from curiosity, said "it wasn't worth it." The indignation of the crowd was so great that immediately there were volunteers to pay for three and four extra hand-shakes to shame the delinquent!

Shortly before that, a friend of Colonel John W. Vrooman's wrote to him about a certain meeting at the Union League Club called to witness a send-off to some of the soldiers. The writer says:

"The moment Colonel Roosevelt appeared on the reviewing stand he was recognized and the vicinity of the Club was in an uproar. Later on when visiting a party in the private dining room, he had only been in the room about three minutes when he was recognized by the girls and boys who were looking at the review from a building on the opposite side of the street. Just to show you how he reaches the heart of the people, they cheered and waved at him until his attention was attracted and he had to go to the window and salute them. Although he was an hour and a half in conversation in the club, he did not forget his little friends across the way but on leaving, went to the window and waved goodbye to them. Every youngster present will relate this incident, I am sure, for a long time to come. In leaving the Club house, he was set upon, it seemed to me, by the youngsters of the East Side so that he had to beg his way through the crowd that had been waiting in the rain three hours just to see him, and in getting into the automobile, they appeared to an on-looker to be clambering all over him, and I would not be surprised if he carried a few of them away in his pockets as he carried most of their little hearts with him."

In the midst of all the excitement, we occasionally snatched a moment for a quiet luncheon. "Fine!" he writes me on November 5. "Yes,—Thursday,—the Langdon at 1:30. It will be fine to see Patty Selmes." How he did enjoy seeing our mutual friend Patty Selmes that day! As "Patty Flandrau" of Kentucky she had married Tilden Selmes just about the time that Theodore Roosevelt had taken up his residence in the Bad Lands of Dakota, where the young married couple had also migrated. Nothing was ever more entertaining than to start the "don't you remember" conversations between my brother and his old friend Mrs. Selmes. Each would cap some wild Western story of the other with one equally wild and amusing, and the tales of their adventures with the Marquis de Morés would have shamed Dumas himself!

Another little note came to me shortly after the above, suggesting that he should spend the night and have one of the old-time breakfasts that he loved. "Breakfast is really the meal for long and intimate conversation." He writes the postscript which he adds he knew would please my heart, for one of my sons, owing to a slight defect in one eye, had had difficulty in being accepted in the army, but through strong determination had finally achieved a captaincy in the ammunition train of the 77th Division. My brother says in the postscript: "I genuinely admire and respect Monroe." About New Year's eve a letter came to my husband from him in answer to a congratulatory letter on the fine actions of my brother's boys. "Of course, we are very proud of Archie, and General Duncan has just written us about Ted in terms that make our hearts glow. Well, there is no telling what the New Year has in store. The hand of Fate may be heavy upon us, but we can all be sure that it will not take away our pride in our boys. [My son Monroe was expecting to be sent soon to France in the 77th Division, and my eldest son, who had broken his leg, was hoping to get into a camp when the leg had recovered its power.] I cannot tell you, my dear Douglas, how much you and Corinne have done for us and have meant to us during the last six months. Ever yours, T. R."

In the "Life and Letters of George Eliot" she dwells upon the fact that so many people lose the great opportunity of giving to others the outward expression of their love and appreciation, and as I re-read my brother's treasured letters, I realize fully what the authoress meant, and how much the giver of such honest and loving expression wins in return from those to whom the happiness of appreciation has been rendered.

The year 1917 was over; the American people once more could look with level eyes in the faces of their allies in the great world effort for righteousness. In the midst of thoughts of war, in the midst of clamor of all sorts, in the midst of grave anxiety for the sons of his heart, wearing a service pin with five stars upon it—for he regarded his gallant son-in-law Doctor Richard Derby as one of his own flesh and blood—Theodore Roosevelt still had time to speak and write on certain subjects close in another way than war to the hearts and minds of the people. Writing for the *Ladies' Home Journal* an article called "Shall We Do Away with the Church?" he says certain things of permanent import to the nation.

"In the pioneer days of the West, we found it an unfailing rule that after a community had existed for a certain length of time, either a church was built or else the community began to go downhill. In these old communities of the Eastern States which have gone backward, it is noticeable that the retrogression has been both marked and accentuated by a rapid decline in church membership and work, the two facts being so interrelated that each stands to the other partly as a cause and partly as an effect." After reviewing the self-indulgent Sunday in contradistinction to the church-going Sunday, he says:

"I doubt whether the frank protest of nothing but amusement has really brought as much happiness as if it had been alloyed with and supplemented by some minimum meeting of obligation toward others. Therefore, on Sunday go to church. Yes,—I know all the excuses; I know that one can worship the Creator and dedicate oneself to good living in a grove of trees or by a running brook or in one's own house just as well as in a church, but I also know that as a matter of cold fact, the average man *does not* thus worship or thus dedicate himself. If he stays away from church he does not spend his time in good works or in lofty meditation. . . . He may not hear a good sermon at church but unless he is very unfortunate he will hear a sermon by a good man who, with his good wife, is engaged all the week long in a series of wearing and hum-drum and important tasks for making hard lives a little easier; and both this man and this wife are, in the vast majority of cases, showing much self-denial, and doing much for humble folks of whom few others think, and they are keeping up a brave show on narrow means. Surely, the average man ought to sympathize with the work done by such a couple and ought to help them, and he cannot help them unless he is a reasonably regular church attendant. Besides, even if he does not hear a good sermon, the probabilities are that he will listen to and take part in reading some beautiful passages from the Bible, and if he is not familiar with the Bible, he has suffered a loss which he had better make all possible haste to correct. He will meet and nod to or speak to good, quiet neighbors. If he doesn't think about himself too much, he will benefit himself very much, especially as he begins to think chiefly of others. . . .

"I advocate a man's joining in church work for the sake of showing his faith by his works; I leave to professional theologians the settlement of the question, whether he is to achieve his salvation by his works or by faith which is only genuine if it expresses itself in works. Micah's insistence upon love and mercy, and doing justice and walking humbly with the Lord's will, should suffice if lived up to. . . . Let the man not think overmuch of saving his own soul. That will come of itself, if he tries in good earnest to look after his neighbor both in soul and in body—remembering always that he had better leave his neighbor alone rather than show arrogance and lack of tactfulness in the effort to help him. The church on the other hand must fit itself for the practical betterment of mankind if it is to attract and retain the fealty of the men best worth holding and using."

Space forbids my quoting further from this, to me, exceptionally interesting article which closes with this sentence: "The man who does not in some way, active or not, connect himself with some active working church, misses many opportunities for helping his neighbors and therefore, incidentally, for helping himself."

And again, in an address at the old historic church of Johnstown in Pennsylvania, he makes a great plea for the church of the new democracy, and lays stress upon the fact that unless individuals can honestly believe in their hearts that their country would be better off without any churches, these same individuals must acknowledge the fact that it is their duty to uphold, by their presence in them, the churches which they know to be indispensable to the vigor and stability of the nation.

In the first week of February, 1918, he had arranged to come to me for a cup of tea to meet one or two literary friends, and the message came that he was not well and was going to the hospital instead. The malignant Brazilian fever, always lurking, ready to spring at his vitality, had shown itself in a peculiarly painful way, and an operation was considered necessary. As his own sons were far away, my son Monroe, who was soon to sail for France, was able to assist in taking him to Roosevelt Hospital, and there the operation was successfully performed; but within twenty-four hours, an unexpected danger connected with the ears had arisen, and for one terrible night the doctors feared for his life, as the trouble threatened the base of the brain. The rumor spread that he was dying, and on February 8th the New York *Tribune* printed at the head of its editorial page this short and touching sentence: "Theodore Roosevelt—listen! You must be up and well again; we cannot have it otherwise; we could not run this world without you." At the time these words were printed, I was told by my sister-in-law and by the doctor that he wanted to speak to me (I had been in the hospital waiting anxiously near his room) and that they felt that it would trouble him if he did not have his wish; they cautioned me to put my ear close down to his lips, for even a slight movement of the head might bring about a fatal result. My readers must remember what was happening on the other side of the ocean as Theodore Roosevelt lay sick unto death in the city of his birth. The most critical period of the Great War was at hand. Very soon the terrible "March offensive" was to begin. Very soon we were to hear that solemn call from General Haig that his "back was against the wall." We were all keyed up to the highest extent; all of my brother's sons were at the front, my own son was about to sail, and at this most critical moment the man to whom the youth of America looked for leadership was stricken and laid low.

As I entered the sick-room, all this was in my mind. Controlling myself to all outward appearance, I put my ear close to his lips, and these were the words which Theodore Roosevelt said to his sister, words which he fully believed would be the last he could ever say to her. Thank God he did speak to me many times again, and we had eleven months more of close and intimate communion, but at that moment he was facing the valley of the shadow. As I leaned over him, in a hoarse whisper he said: "I am so glad that it is not one of my boys who is dying here, for *they* can die for their country."

As he gradually convalesced from that serious illness, many were our intimate hours of conversation. The hospital was besieged by adoring multitudes of inquirers. I remember taking a taxicab myself one day to go there, and when I said to the Italian driver, "Go to the Roosevelt Hospital," the quick response came: "You go see Roosevelt—they all go see Roosevelt—they all go ask how Roosevelt is—he my friend, too—you tell him get well for me." Every sort of individual, as he grew stronger, waited in the corridor for a chance to consult him on this or that subject. Of course few were allowed to do so, but it was more than ever evident by the throng of men, distinguished in the public affairs of the country, who begged admittance even for a few moments that the "Colonel" was still the Mecca toward which the trend of political hope was turning!

After a brief rest at Oyster Bay he insisted upon keeping the appointments to speak in various states, appointments the breaking of which his illness had necessitated. His great ovation in Maine showed beyond dispute how the heart of the Republican party was turning to its old-time leader, and every war work, needless to say, clamored for a speech from him. One of his most characteristic notes was in connection with my plea that he should speak at Carnegie Hall for the Red Cross on a certain May afternoon. Josef Hofmann had promised to come all the way from Aiken to play for the benefit if Theodore Roosevelt were to be the speaker of the occasion, and in writing him on the subject, I laid stress on the sacrifice of time and energy of the great pianist, and in my zeal apparently gave the impression that my brother was to do a great favor to Josef Hofmann rather than the Red Cross, and he answers me humorously: "Darling Corinne:—All right!—A ten-minute speech for the *pianist.* That goes!" He always considered it a great joke that it was necessary for Josef Hofmann to have him speak.

That same May one lovely afternoon stands out most clearly. John Masefield, the great English poet, had been several times in the country. My brother knew his work well but had not met him, and I had had that privilege. I wished to take him to Oyster Bay, and the invitation was gladly forthcoming. It proved fair and beautiful, and Mr. Masefield and I motored out to luncheon. On the veranda at Sagamore Hill were my brother and Mrs. Roosevelt, their daughter Mrs. Derby and her lovely children, and later John Masefield took little Richard on his lap and wove for him a tale to which we grown people listened, my brother resting his eyes gladly on the little boy's head as he leaned against the poet. After the story was told, we wandered off to a distant summer-house overlooking both sides of the bay, and there Theodore Roosevelt and John Masefield spoke intimately together of many things. It was a day of sunlight in early spring, and the air was full "of a summer to be," but under the outward calm and beauty of the sun and sea lay a poignant sadness for our sons who were in a distant land, for the moment had come when the American troops were to show their valor in a great cause.

The day after the Carnegie Hall speech for the Red Cross, one of his most flaming addresses, in which he pictured the young men of America as Galahads of modern days, I wrote to him of my gratitude and emotion, and he answers at once (how did he ever find the time to answer so immediately so many letters which came to him):

"Darling Corinne:—That is a very dear letter of yours; your sons and my sons were before my eyes as I spoke. I am leaving tomorrow for the West until May 31st. I leave again on June 6th, returning on the 13th, and on Saturday, the 15th, must go to a Trinity College function and stay with Bye. [Referring to my sister, Mrs. Cowles.] Will you take me out in your motor to Oyster Bay for dinner when I return?" Already he had plunged into what he considered his active duty and was overtaxing his strength—that strength only so lately restored, and not entirely restored—in the service of his country.

It was at Indiana University in June of that year that he made one of his most significant pronouncements, a pronouncement especially significant in the light of the so-called Sinn Fein activities during the last two years in this country. He was very fond of the Irish, and fond of many of the Irish-born citizens of America, and always loved to refer to his own Irish blood, but he had no sympathy whatsoever with certain attitudes taken by certain Irish-born or naturalized Americans under the name, falsely used, of patriotism, and he speaks his mind courageously and clearly at Indiana University.

"Friends, it is unpatriotic and un-American to damage America because you love another country, but there is one thing worse and that is to damage America because you hate another country. The Sinn Feiner who acts against America because he hates England is a worse creature than the member of the German-American Alliance who has acted against

America because he loves Germany. I want to point out this bit of etymological information: Sinn Fein means 'Us, Ourselves.' It means that those who adopt that name are fighting for themselves, for a certain division of people across the sea. What right have they to come to America? Their very name shows that they are not American; that they are for themselves against America."

In July, when I had been threatened with rather serious trouble in my eyes, he again writes with his usual unfailing sympathy: "I think of you all the time. I so hate to have you threatened by trouble with your eyes or any other trouble. Edgar Lee Masters spent a couple of hours here yesterday. Ethel and her two blessed bunnies have gone. I miss Pitty Pat and Tippy Toe frightfully." Little "Edie," his youngest granddaughter, was a special pet, and rarely did one visit Sagamore at that time without finding the lovely rosy baby in his arms. He could hardly pass her baby-carriage when she slept without stopping to look at her, for which nefarious action he was sometimes severely chastised by the stern young mother. But the burning heart of Theodore Roosevelt could hardly ever be assuaged even by the sweet unconsciousness of the little children who knew not of the dangers faced so gallantly by their father and their mother's brothers.

America had been over fourteen months in the Great War when an editorial appeared in one of the important newspapers called "The Impatience of Theodore Roosevelt." It ran as follows:

"There is a certain disposition to criticise Theodore Roosevelt for what is termed his ultra views regarding the war. It is not all captious criticism. Some people honestly feel that he has been impatient and fault-finding. Much of the picture is true. He *has* been impatient; he *has* taken what may be called an ultra position; he *has* found fault, but we should like to point out one very distinct fact. Theodore Roosevelt from the first day we entered the war has stood unswervingly and whole-heartedly for throwing the complete strength of the nation into the war. For that matter, he held this position, preached this doctrine long before we entered the war. He preached the draft, he preached preparation, he preached the sending of the largest possible army to France,—*from the beginning*. Now the fact we wish to point out is that the country is not growing *away* from Theodore Roosevelt's position,—it is growing toward it. It has been actually moving toward it of late very rapidly. This is true not merely of the great mass of people, but of their representatives at Washington, . . . and perhaps even some members of the Cabinet and the President himself. Practically the whole nation *now* is unreservedly for throwing the whole strength of the nation to the side of the allies. This was not true a year ago today, although we had then been offically at war with Germany for more than two months. Today the whole nation stands where Theodore Roosevelt stood one year ago, and two years ago, and three years ago.—In point of fact, ever since the day when by the sinking of the *Lusitania*, Germany declared itself an outlaw to the name of civilization. We do not mean to say that Theodore Roosevelt was the nation's sole leader, but we do wish to say that he was very distinctly a leader, and later, in the highest and best sense,—a man who saw, far ahead of many others, what ought to be and what must be, and then threw his whole heart and soul into bringing the nation and many reluctant minds to his point of view. We write: He may have been impatient; he may have found fault, but we think that most Americans of whatever party color, if they now have any regrets, have these regrets because we could not earlier have come nearer to the ideal set up a year, or two years, or three years ago by Theodore Roosevelt. If this is not one of the highest standards of leadership, we do not understand the meaning of the term."

Events were moving rapidly. Our American soldiers were already playing a gallant part in the terrible drama enacted on the fields and forests of France and in the fastnesses of the

Italian hills. News had come of "Archie's" wounds and of "Ted's" wounds, and Quentin had already made his trial flights, while Kermit had been transferred from the British army to his own flag.

Political events in America were also marching rapidly forward. Already, wherever one lent a listening ear, the growing murmur rose louder and louder that Theodore Roosevelt was the only candidate to be nominated by the Republican party in 1920. The men who had parted from him in 1912, the men who had not rallied around him in 1916, were all eagerly ranging themselves on the side of this importunate rumor. A culminating moment was approaching. It was the middle of July, and the informal convention of the Republican party in New York State was about to take place at Saratoga. My eldest son, State Senator Theodore Douglas Robinson, led a number of men in the opposition of the then incumbent of the gubernatorial chair, Charles S. Whitman. The hearts of many were strong with desire that my brother himself should be the Republican nominee for the next governor of New York State. No one knew his attitude on the subject, but he had promised to make the address of the occasion, my son having been appointed to make the request that he should do so. My husband and I had arranged to meet him in Saratoga, my son having preceded us to Albany to make all the formal arrangements. The day before the convention was to take place the terrible news came that Quentin was killed. Of course there was a forlorn hope that this information might not be true, that the gallant boy might perhaps have reached the earth alive and might already be a prisoner in a German camp, but there seemed but little doubt of the truth of the terrible fact. My son telephoned me the news from Albany before the morning paper could arrive at my country home, and at the same time said to me that he did not feel justified in asking his Uncle Theodore whether he still would come to Saratoga, but that he wanted me to get this information for him if possible.

My country home in the Mohawk Hills of New York State is many miles from Sagamore Hill on Long Island, and it was difficult to get telephone connection. My heart was unspeakably sore and heavy at the thought of the terrible sorrow that had come to my sister-in-law and my brother, and I shrank from asking any question concerning any matter except the sad news of the death of Quentin, or imminent danger to him. My brother himself came to the telephone; the sound of his voice was as if steel had entered into the tone. As years before he had written me from South Africa in my own great sorrow, he had "grasped the nettle." I asked him whether he would like me to come down at once to Oyster Bay, and his answer was almost harsh in its rapidity: "Of course not—I will meet you in Saratoga as arranged. It is more than ever my duty to be there. You can come down to New York after the convention." The very tone of his voice made me realize the agony in his heart, but duty was paramount. The affairs of his State, the affairs of the nation, needed his counsel, needed his self-control. His boy had paid the final price of duty; was he, the father who had taught that boy the ideal of service and sacrifice, to shrink in cowardly fashion at the crucial moment?

The next day I met him in Albany and motored him to Saratoga. His face was set and grave, but he welcomed my sympathy generously. Meanwhile, the night before there had been great excitement in Saratoga. A number of delegates were in favor of renominating Governor Charles S. Whitman on the Republican ticket, but a large and important group of men, in fact, the largest and most important group in the Republican party of New York State, were extremely anxious that Colonel Roosevelt should allow his name to be brought forward as a candidate for governor. Elihu Root, William Howard Taft, and many of the weighty "bosses" of the various counties lent all their efforts toward this achievement. Colonel Roosevelt, on his arrival in Saratoga, took a quiet luncheon with my family, Mrs. Parsons, and myself, after which we adjourned to the large hall in which the convention was to be held. I remember before we left him that Mrs. Parsons suggested the insertion of a sentence in the speech which he was about to make, and his immediate and grateful response to the suggestion. No one had a more open mind to the helpful suggestion of others.

The great hall was already filled to overflowing when we arrived, and it was difficult for us to find our seats, even although they had been carefully reserved for us. The atmosphere of the crowd in the great building was different from that of any concourse of people who had hitherto waited the coming of Theodore Roosevelt. At other times, in other crowds, when their favorite leader was expected, there had always been a quality of hilarity and gay familiarity showing itself in songs and demonstrations in which the oft-repeated "We want Teddy—we want Teddy" almost always was heard, but in this great assemblage there was a hushed silence and solicitude for their beloved friend, a personal outflowing of silent sympathy for the man whose youngest, whose "Benjamin," had so lately paid the final price, and even a few minutes later, when to the strains of the "Star-Spangled-Banner," Colonel Roosevelt was escorted up the aisle by my son, Senator Robinson, and Congressman Cox, from his own Nassau County, the many faces turned eagerly to watch him showed in strained eyes and set though quivering lips their efforts at self-control. As he began his speech, we realized fully that he was holding himself firmly together, but as he poured out his message of Americanism, as he pleaded for the finer and truer patriotism to be brought more closely and definitely into political action, he lost the sense of the great bereavement that had come to him, in his dedication anew to the effort to arouse in his countrymen the selfless desire for service, with which he had always fronted the problems of his own life. Toward the end of the speech, though he never referred to his sorrow, the realization of it again gripped him with its inevitable torture, and again the people who sat in breathless silence—listening to one to whom they had always listened

—followed in their hearts the hard path that he was bravely treading.

The convention adjourned, and he asked the leaders to wait until the following day, at least, for his answer to the Round-Robin request which had been sent to him, but he did not give much hope that he would look favorably upon their desire that he should allow his name to be put in nomination as candidate for governor. I motored him back to Albany and took the train with him for New York. In recalling the hours of intercourse that afternoon and early evening, the great impression made upon my mind by his attitude was one of ineffable gentleness. Never was he more loving in his interest about me and mine; never was he less thoughtful of self. I realized that he needed quiet, and when I found that my seat was in a different car from his, although several people offered to change their seats with me, I felt that after our drive together, it would do him more good to be alone and read than to try to talk to me. I told him I would order our dinner and would come back for him when it was time for the meal, and I left him with his usual book in his hand. When I came back, however, I stood behind him for a moment or two before making myself known to him again, and I could see that he was not reading, that his sombre eyes were fixed on the swiftly passing woodlands and the river, and that the book had not the power of distracting him from the all-embracing grief which enveloped him. When I spoke, however, he turned with a responsive smile, and during our whole meal gave me, as ever, the benefit of his delightful knowledge of all the affairs of the world.

Only once during our talk did he speak of the Round Robin, and especially of my son's desire that he should be the nominee for governor. He used an expression in discussing the matter which gave me at once a sense of almost physical apprehension. Looking at me gravely, he said: "Corinne, I have only one fight left in me, and I think I should reserve my strength in case I am needed in 1920." The contraction of my heart was swift and painful, and I said: "Theodore, you don't feel really ill, do you?" "No," he said; "but I am not what I was and there is only one fight left in me." I suggested that that fight would probably be made easier by this premonitory battle, but he shook his head and I could see that there was but little chance of his undertaking the factional warfare of a state campaign, nor did he seem to feel, as did some others, that to win the election for governor of New York State would be of distinct advantage in connection with the great fight to come in 1920. The following week Theodore Roosevelt definitely refused to let his name be put before the people as a candidate for the governorship of the Empire State.

That evening on arriving late in New York, he would not let me go to the Langdon Hotel with him, but insisted on taking me to my own house. The next morning I went early to the Langdon, hoping for better news, and saw my sister-in-law, whose wonderful self-control was a lesson to all those who have had to meet the ultimate pain of life. I could see that she had but little hope, but for my brother's sake, until the actual confirmation of Quentin's death, she bravely hoped for hope. Later, Colonel Roosevelt made a statement from Oyster Bay in connection with the many telegrams and cables of sympathy which they received. He said: "These messages were not meant for publication but to express sympathy with Quentin's father and mother, and sorrow for a gallant boy who had been doing his duty like hundreds of thousands of young Americans. Many of them indeed, I think, were really an expression of sympathy from the mothers and fathers who have gladly and proudly, and yet with sorrow, seen the sons they love go forth to battle for their country and the right. These telegrams, cables, and letters show the spirit of our whole people."

The noble attitude of my brother and sister-in-law roused deep admiration, and I have always felt that their influence was never more felt than when with aching hearts they continued quietly to go about their daily duties.

On August 3d a letter came to me from Dark Harbor, Maine, where Colonel and Mrs. Roosevelt had gone to visit their daughter Mrs. Derby. "Darling Corinne:—Indeed it would be the greatest pleasure—I mean that exactly,—to have you bring little Douglas to Sagamore in the holidays. [He refers to my grandson, the son of Theodore Douglas Robinson.] All the people here are most considerate and the children a comfort. Little Edie is as pretty as a picture and a little darling; she has been very much of a chimney swallow this morning, clinging to whoever will take her up and cuddle her." In the latter part of the letter he refers to my own great loss nine years before of my youngest son in his twentieth year, and says: "Your burden was even harder to bear than ours, for Stewart's life was even shorter than Quentin's and he had less chance to give shape to what there was in him, but, after all, when the young die at the crest of their life, in their golden morning, the degrees of difference are merely degrees in bitterness; and yet, there is nothing more cowardly than to be beaten down by sorrows which nothing we can do will change. Love to Douglas, Helen and Teddy, and to Fanny if she is with you." The sentence of this brave letter in which my brother speaks of its being "cowardly to be beaten down by sorrows which nothing we do can change" is typical of the attitude which he had preserved through his whole life. Theodore Roosevelt was a great sharer and a great lover, but above all else he was essentially the courageous man who faced squarely whatever came, and by so facing conquered.

A few days later, again a dear letter came from Dark Harbor, and once more he dwells upon the baby girl who comforted him with her sweet, unconscious merriment. He says: "She is such a pretty little baby and with such cunning little ways. I fear I am not an unprejudiced witness. The little, curly-headed rascal is at this moment, crawling actively around my feet in her usual, absurd garb of blue overalls, drawn over her dainty dresses, because otherwise, she would ruin every garment she has on and skin her little bare knees. I heartily congratulate

Teddy on going to camp. Give Corinne and Helen my dearest love and to all the others too." The congratulations sent to my eldest son were indeed deserved, for the serious break to his leg having at last fully recovered, and a new camp near Louisville, Ky., having been started for men above the draft age, my son with real sacrifice resigned from his position in the Senate (having just been nominated for a second term), and started for Camp Taylor, where later he received his commission. My brother was very proud of the fact that, with hardly an exception, each son, nephew, or cousin of the Roosevelt and Robinson family was actively enrolled in the country's service.

On August 18, having returned to Sagamore Hill, a little line comes to me of appreciation of a poem that I had written called "Italy." "I am particularly glad you wrote it," he says, and referring to my son-in-law, he continues: "Joe and Corinne lunched here yesterday; they were dear,—I admire them both so much." He never failed, as I have said before, in giving me the joy of knowing when he admired those most dear to me. The following day, August 19, Mr. Colgate Hoyt, a generous neighbor, wrote to Colonel Roosevelt making the suggestion that a monument should be erected in honor of Quentin in some permanent place in the village of Oyster Bay, as Mr. Hoyt thought it would have an educational influence and value, as Quentin was the first resident of Oyster Bay (and the first officer) to make the supreme sacrifice in giving his life for his country. Mr. Hoyt wished to start this movement, but Colonel Roosevelt sent the following reply, a copy of which Mr. Hoyt gave me:

"My dear Mr. Hoyt:—That is a very nice letter of yours, but I do not think it would be advisable to try to put up a monument for Quentin. Of course, individually, our loss is irreparable but to the country he is simply one among many gallant boys who gave their lives for the great Cause. With very hearty thanks, Faithfully yours."

The above letter and his statement that he and Quentin's mother would prefer that their boy should lie where he fell were but what would have naturally been expected of Colonel and Mrs. Roosevelt.

In September, 1918, Theodore Roosevelt made an address on Lafayette Day, part of which ran as follows:

"Lafayette Day commmemorates the service rendered to America in the Revolution by France. I wish to insist with all possible emphasis that in the present war, France, England, and Italy and the other Allies have rendered us similar services. . . . They have been fighting for us when they were fighting for themselves. [My brother was only repeating in 1918 what he had stanchly declared from the autumn of 1914.] Our army on the other side is now repaying in part our debt. It is now time and it is long behind time for America to bear her full share of the common burden. . . . It is sometimes announced that part of the Peace Agreement must be a League of Nations which will avert all war for the future and put a stop to the need of this nation preparing its own strength for its own defense. In deciding upon proposals of this nature, it behooves our people to remember that competitive rhetoric is a poor substitute for the habit of resolutely looking facts in the face. Patriotism stands in national matters as love of family does in private life. Nationalism corresponds to the love a man bears for his wife and children. Internationalism corresponds to the feeling he has for his neighbors generally. The sound nationalism is the only type of really helpful internationalism, precisely as in private relations, it is the man who is most devoted to his own wife and children who is apt in the long run to be the most satisfactory neighbor. The professional pacifist and the professional internationalist are equally undesirable citizens. The American pacifist has in the actual fact shown himself to be the ally of the German militarist. We Americans should abhor all wrongdoing to other nations. We ought always to act fairly and generously by other nations, but, we must remember that our first duty is to be loyal and patriotic citizens of our *own* nation. Any such League of Nations would have to depend for its success upon the adhesion of nine other nations which are actually or potentially the most powerful military nations; and these nine nations include Germany, Austria, Turkey, and Russia. The first three have recently and repeatedly violated and are now actively and continuously violating not only every treaty but every rule of civilized warfare and of international good faith. During the last year, Russia under the dominance of the Bolshevist has betrayed her Allies, has become the tool of the German autocracy and has shown such utter disregard of her national honor and plighted word and her international duties that she is now in external affairs the passive tool and ally of her brutal conqueror, Germany.

"What earthly use is it to pretend that the safety of the world would be secured by a League in which these four nations would be among the nine leading partners? Long years must pass before we can again trust in promises these four nations make. Therefore, unless our folly is such that it will not depart from us until we are brayed in a mortar, let us remember that any such treaty will be worthless unless our own prepared strength renders it unsafe to break it. . . . Let us support any reasonable plan whether in the form of a League of Nations or in any other shape which bids fair to lessen the probable number of future wars and to limit their scope, but let us laugh at all or any assertions that any such plan will guaranty Peace and Safety to the foolish, weak, or timid characters who have not the will and the power to prepare for their own defense. Support any such plan which is honest and reasonable, but support it as a condition to and never as a substitute for the policy of preparing our own strength for our own defense.

"I believe that this preparation should be, by the introduction in this country of the principle of universal training and universal service, as practised in Switzerland, and modified, of course, along the lines enacted in Australia, and in accordance with our needs. There will be no taint of Prussian militarism in such a system. It will merely mean to fit ourselves for self-defense and a great democracy in which order, law, and liberty are to prevail."

I have quoted this speech because I am under the impression that it was his first actual declaration of any attitude toward a proposed League of Nations. In the early autumn of 1914 Theodore Roosevelt himself had written an article for the New York *Times* syndicate in which he suggested the possibility of a League of Nations, and the fact that he did make that suggestion was frequently used after his death—and, I think, in an unjustifiable manner—by the adherents of the Wilsonian League of Nations, with the desire to make the American public feel that my brother would have been in favor of Mr. Wilson's league. In every pronouncement in connection with a tentative or possible league, my brother invariably laid stress upon an absolutely Americanized type of association. I asked him once about his article written in 1914, and he told me that while still hoping that some good might come from a league or association of nations, his serious study of world situations during the Great War had made him less optimistic as to the possibility of reaching effective results through such a possible league or association.

In another speech at about the same time, he said, in characteristic fashion: "I frequently meet one of those nice gentry in whom softness of heart has spread to the head, who say: 'How can we guaranty that everybody will love one another at the end of the war?' The first step in guarantying it is to knock Germany out!"

On September 12 my husband, Douglas Robinson, the unfailing friend and devoted brother of Theodore Roosevelt, died very suddenly, and my brother and sister-in-law hurried to the old home on the Mohawk Hills which my husband had loved so well. Putting themselves and their own grief for Mr. Robinson and their own late personal sorrow entirely aside, they did all that could be done by those we love to help me in every way. My brother had always cared for Henderson House, its traditions and its customs, and even in the midst of the sorrow which now hung over the old place, he constantly spoke to me of his appreciation of its atmosphere. At the time of my husband's death my eldest son came quickly back for two days from the camp where he was training, to his own home adjoining mine, and his children were with us constantly during those days, as were the children of my nephew and niece, Hall and Margaret Roosevelt, who occupied a little cottage on my place. I remember with what tender thoughtfulness my brother withdrew himself on the Sunday afternoon after the funeral and wrote a long letter to my second son, Monroe, a captain in the 77th Division, then in the Argonne Forest in France. Just as he had found comfort in his own little grandchildren during those hard days at Dark Harbor, Maine, so, while facing the great loss of his lifelong and devoted friend and brother-in-law, he turned to an affectionate intercourse with the little ones of the youngest generation of the family, and on September 19, when he had left me and gone to Oyster Bay, he writes: "I think of you with tenderest love and sympathy all the time. I cannot get over my delight in Helen and Teddy's darling children; and I loved Margaret's brace of little strappers also. Archie and Gracie have hired a little apartment in town." His son Captain Archibald Roosevelt had returned from France sorely wounded in both arm and leg, wounds and disabilities which he bore with undaunted patience and courage.

On October 13, in response to a letter of mine in which I told him that a Monsieur Goblet had wished the honor of dedicating to him a poem, and at the same time had also asked the privilege of translating my verses "To France" into the French language, he writes to me:

"I have written to M. Goblet as you suggested; I feel that you have every right to be really pleased with what he says about your poem—a noble little poem.

"How admirably Monroe has done. It is astonishing how many men I meet who speak of Douglas [my husband] not only with deep affectionate regard but with a keen sense of the loss of an exceptionally vigorous and powerful personality. Tell Helen that I am really counting on that visit from her delightful children. Their attitude touched me very much. I am much concerned at what you tell me about gallant Bye's health. Give her my dearest love."

My sister, Mrs. Cowles, was even more delicate than usual that autumn, and I was with her at the time he wrote me the above letter. His admiration for our older sister was unbounded, and her splendid dauntless attitude toward the physical pain she suffered, and her unbroken patience through suffering, never failed to awake in him a responsive appreciation.

About that time President Wilson entered into a correspondence with Germany of which my brother disapproved. On October 13 he dictated the following statement at his home on Sagamore Hill:

"I regret greatly that President Wilson has entered into these negotiations, and I trust they will be stopped. We have announced that we will not submit to a negotiated Peace, and under such conditions, to begin negotiations is bad faith with ourselves and our Allies."

Again on October 25, in an open letter to his intimate friend Senator Henry Cabot Lodge, "Let us," he says, "amongst other things, dictate Peace by the hammering of guns, and not talk about Peace to the accompaniment of the clicking of typewriters."

Although the extracts which follow were written and published several weeks later than the above quotations, I prefer to give them in this connection, for Colonel Roosevelt's attitude toward "Peace without victory" and a probable League of Nations has been so often misrepresented. The Kansas City *Star*, the newspaper with which Colonel Roosevelt had actual connection during the last year of his life, published an editorial after his death in answer to a remark made by Senator Hitchcock, chairman of the Foreign Relations Committee, in which he expressed the opinion that if Colonel Roosevelt were alive, "he would be found supporting the League of Nations as ardently as President Wilson."

The Star denied this assertion, and said:

"From the beginning of the discussion of the proposed League, *The Star* has been anxious to find practical features which it could support as a real defense toward lasting peace. In the last weeks of 1918, the matter was taken up with Colonel Roosevelt who proved to be of the same mind. He recognized the war weariness of the world,—a weariness in which he shared to the full—and was anxious to further any practical step in international organization. The difficulty was to find the practical basis. After his first editorial approving certain principles of a League, a member of *The Star* staff discussed the matter with him late in December at the Roosevelt Hospital. The suggestion was made that in a contribution he might point out certain things which a loosely organized League might accomplish. He replied that he could see so little that it might accomplish, in comparison with the rosy pictures that had been painted of its possibilities, that he hesitated to write on that line.

"In the course of correspondence, he wrote under date of December 28th, 1918: 'In substance, or as our friends the diplomats say, in number, I am in hearty accord with you. . . . But remember that you are freer to write unsigned editorials than I am when I use my signature. If you propose a little more than can be carried out, no harm comes, but if I do so, it may hamper me for years. However, I will do my best to write you such an article as you suggest and then, probably, one on what I regard as infinitely more important, viz., our business to prepare for our own self-defense.' A few days later, almost on the eve of his death, he wrote the following article printed in *The Star* on January 13th. It was dictated at his home in Oyster Bay on January 3rd, the Friday before his death, and his secretary expected to take the typed copy to him for correction the following Monday, the very Monday of his death. The following then, his final article, represents his matured judgment based on protracted discussion and correspondence. It is of peculiar importance as the last message of a man who, above every other American of his generation, combined high patriotism, practical sense and a positive genius for international relations."

By Theodore Roosevelt

"It is, of course, a serious misfortune that our people are not getting a clear idea of what is happening on the other side. For the moment, the point as to which we are foggy is the League of Nations. We all of us earnestly desire such a league, only we wish to be sure that it will help and not hinder the cause of world peace and justice. There is not a young man in this country who has fought, or an old man who has seen those dear to him fight, who does not wish to minimize the chance of future war. But there is not a man of sense who does not know that in any such movement if too much is attempted the result is either failure or worse than failure.

. . . .

"Would it not be well to begin with the league which we actually have in existence, the league of the Allies who have fought through this great war? Let us at the peace table see that real justice is done as among these Allies, and that while the sternest reparation is demanded from our foes for such horrors as those committed in Belgium, northern France, Armenia, and the sinking of the *Lusitania*, nothing should be done in the spirit of mere vengeance. Then let us agree to extend the privileges of the league as rapidly as their conduct warrants it to other nations, doubtless discriminating between those who would have a guiding part in the league and the weak nations who would be entitled to the privileges of membership, but who would not be entitled to a guiding voice in the councils. Let each nation reserve to itself and for its own decision, and let it clearly set forth questions which are non-justiciable. Let nothing be done that will interfere with our preparing for our own defense by introducing a system of universal obligatory military training modelled on the Swiss plan.

"Finally make it perfectly clear that we do not intend to take a position of an international Meddlesome Matty. The American people do not wish to go into an overseas war unless for a very great cause and where the issue is absolutely plain. Therefore, we do not wish to undertake the responsibility of sending our gallant young men to die in obscure fights in the Balkans or in Central Europe, or in a war we do not approve of. Moreover, the American people do not intend to give up the Monroe Doctrine. Let civilized Europe and Asia enforce some kind of police system in the weak and disorderly countries at their thresholds. But let the United States treat Mexico as our Balkan peninsula and refuse to allow European or Asiatic powers to interfere on this continent in any way that implies permanent or semi-permanent possession. Every one of our Allies will with delight grant this request if President Wilson chooses to make it, and it will be a great misfortune if it is not made.

"I believe that such an effort made moderately and sanely but sincerely and with utter scorn for words that are not made good by deeds, will be productive of real and lasting international good."

No one has the right to declare what Theodore Roosevelt would or would not have done or said in connection with international problems as they arose, after his death, but every one has the right to quote his own words, written under his own signature, and no words could be stronger than those in which he made his plea for America First and for sound nationalism. But I have voluntarily gone far afield from my actual narrative.

Events continued to move with astounding rapidity in that autumn of 1918. My heart, like the heart of many another mother, was wrung by the news of the terrible fighting in the Argonne Forest, and again wrung by alternate hopes and fears as the October days drew to a close. On the 27th day of October my brother celebrated his sixtieth birthday under the quiet portal of his beloved home. As usual, I had sent to him my yearly message, in which I always told him what that day meant to me—the day when into this world, this confused, strange world that we human beings find so difficult to understand, there came his clarifying spirit, his magnetic personality, his great heart, ready always to help the weak and lift the unfortunate who were trying to lift themselves. I used to tell him that as long as he lived, no matter what my own personal sorrows were, life would retain not only happiness but also glamour for me.

In answer to my birthday letter, an answer written on his very birthday in his own handwriting, he sends me the following message. Intimate as it is, I give it in full, for in these few short lines there seems to breathe the whole spirit of my brother—the unswerving affection, the immediate response to my affection, and the wish to encourage me to face sorrows that were hard to bear by reminding me of the rare joys which I had also tasted. The manner in which he joined his own sorrows and joys to mine, the sweet compliment of the words which infer that for him I still had youthfulness, and at the end the type of humor which brought always a savor into his own life and into the lives of those whom he closely touched, all were part of that spirit.

Sagamore Hill, October 27, 1918.

DARLING PUSSIE:—

It was dear of you to remember my birthday. Darling, after all, you and I have known long years of happiness, and you are as young as I am old.

Ever yours,

METHUSALEH'S UNDERSTUDY.

XVIII

"THE QUIET QUITTING"*

For those who must journey
Henceforward alone,
Have need of stout convoy
Now Great-Heart is gone.

—Rudyard Kipling.

ON November 11, 1918, the armistice with Germany was signed by General Foch. The war was over! So many years had passed since that fateful August 1, 1914, that at first the mind of the world was not attuned to peace. It now seemed as incomprehensible that we should be at peace as it had seemed impossible that we should be at war. Just before the armistice was signed the United States had proved by the ballots cast on Election day that the request of President Wilson that a Democratic Congress should be returned was not in accord with the wishes of the American people.

Theodore Roosevelt, in a vivid speech at Carnegie Hall just before Election day, had defined the issues of the future in sharp, terse sentences, and had pleaded for preparedness for peace (for the signs of those days showed that peace was not far off), as he had pleaded so long ago for preparedness for war. He was far from well on the night when he made that speech, which was to prove the last that he would ever make in the hall in which he had so often aroused his fellow citizens to a sense of their civic and national duty. I was ill and could not be present, but Mrs. Roosevelt told me afterward that she had been much concerned for him, for a trouble which he thought was sciatica in his leg was giving him intense pain. No one would have suspected that fact, however, and many in the audience

*Title of a poem written on the death of Theodore Roosevelt by J. Fries, an old veteran of the Civil War.

told me afterward that that speech in Carnegie Hall was one of the most convincing and thrilling appeals to patriotism ever made by Theodore Roosevelt.

A few days later, always true to his interest in the colored people, he made an address under the auspices of the Negro Circle, and again I was to have been present and was prevented by my condition of health. The following week when I was better I telegraphed to Oyster Bay to ask him, if possible, to lunch with me in New York, and to my distress received an answer that he was not well enough to come to New York, but would I come out and spend the night at Oyster Bay instead? When I arrived at Sagamore Hill, I could not but feel worried to find him in bed, and in much pain, which, however, he entirely disregarded, and we had one of the most delightful evenings that I ever remember spending with him. I had brought, thinking that it might interest him, Professor William Lyon Phelps's book on "Modern Poetry," and during the time that I left his room to take dinner with my sister-in-law, he had read so much and with such avidity that I felt on my return to his bedside that he had assimilated the whole volume. In spite of pain and politics, he threw himself into a discussion of modern American poetry, taking up author after author and giving me rapid criticisms or appreciations. He took much interest in both Edgar Lee Masters and Vachel Lindsay, struck with the masterful story-telling quality of the one and the curious rhythmic metre of the other, and the strong Americanism of both.

From poetry we wandered across political fields together, and he discussed the armistice which had just been signed, and which he said he could not but regret from the standpoint of the future. He felt that for all the days to come it would have been better had Germany's army had to return to the Fatherland an insignificant and defeated fraction of its original strength, and had the Allies entered Berlin as victors. This opinion, although very strong, was not in any way advanced as a criticism of the signing of the armistice, which he appeared to feel had been inevitable. We talked until twelve o'clock that night and I have always felt grateful to my sister-in-law for having arranged for me to have that delightful communion with my brother.

There was no serious apprehension about his health when I left the next morning, and the news that he had been taken to the hospital the following week came as a shock and surprise to me. All through those late November and December days, when my brother was an invalid in Roosevelt Hospital (except for a brief thirty-six hours when he was threatened with pneumonia, which trouble he threw off with his usual wonderful vitality), we were not seriously apprehensive of any fatal outcome to his ill health, and, indeed, at times during that detention in the hospital, he gave one the impression of a man fully able to recuperate as he had always done before. Many were the happy hours of quiet interchange of thought and affection passed by me with my brother in the hospital. My sister-in-law had given the order to the nurses that I should always be admitted, and I came and went in the sick-room daily. Sometimes he was well enough to see visitors, and lines of people of the most varied kinds were always waiting in the corridors in the hope of a few words with him. I remember a long talk on American literature to which I listened between Hamlin Garland and himself, and in the middle of December he asked me to telegraph our dear friend Senator Lodge to ask him to come on and discuss certain political matters with him. The senator spent two days with me, and of those two days two whole mornings in the Colonel's room in the hospital. I was with them during the first morning when they discussed the tentative League of Nations, parts of which in problematical form were already known to the public. The different reservations, insisted upon later by Senator Lodge, when the League in its eventual form was presented to the Senate of the United States, were tentatively formulated at the bedside of the Colonel. I do not mean that definite clauses in the League were definitely discussed, but many contingencies of the document, contingencies which later took the form of definite clauses, *were* discussed, and the future attitude toward such contingencies more or less mapped out. He took great pleasure in these talks with Senator Lodge, for, although not always in accord in some of their political views, I know no one in whose stimulating mentality my brother took keener pleasure; and on the fundamental issues of "America First," and of deep-rooted patriotism and practical service to their country, they stood invariably as one man.

One day—in fact, it was the last day that I sat with him in the hospital—he seemed particularly bright and on the near road to recovery. His left arm was still in bandages, but with his strong right hand he gesticulated as of old, and sitting in his armchair, his eyes clear and shining, his face ruddy and animated, he seemed to me to have lost nothing of the vigorous and inspiring personality of earlier days. As usual, he shared my every interest, reiterated his desire to have my little grandson, Douglas, and his sisters pay a visit in the holidays to Sagamore Hill, told me delightedly how he would show Douglas every trophy in the large north room where his trophies were kept, and said that he wanted to know all the children intimately. From family affairs we branched off to public affairs, and speaking of the possibilities of the future, he said he knew much depended upon his health, but that he recognized that even amongst those who had been opposed to him in the past, there was now a strong desire for him to be the Republican candidate for President in 1920. Alluding to his birthday so lately passed, he said: "Well, anyway, no matter what comes, I have kept the promise that I made to myself when I was twenty-one." "What promise, Theodore?" I asked him. "You made many promises to yourself, and I am sure have kept them all." "I promised myself," he said, bringing his right fist down with emphasis on the arm of the chair, "that I would work *up to the hilt* until I was sixty, and I have done it. I have kept my promise, and now, even if I should be an invalid—I should not like to be an invalid—but even if I should be an invalid, or if I should die [this with a snap of his finger and thumb], what difference would it make?" "Theodore," I said, "do you remember what you said to me nearly a year ago when you thought you were dying in this same hospital? You said that you were glad it was not one of your boys that was dying at that time in this place, for *they* could die for their country. Do you feel the same way now?" "Yes," he said, "just the same way. I wish that I might, like Quentin, have died for my country." "I know you wish it," I answered, "but I want to tell you something. Every one of us—even those not as courageous, not as patriotic, as you are—would, I feel sure, if our country were in peril, be willing to bare our breasts to any bullet, could we, by so doing, protect and save our country; but the trouble is that the very people who, in peril, will give themselves, with absolute disregard of the consequences, to their country's service, fail, utterly, in times of peace, to sacrifice anything whatsoever for their country's good. The difference, Theodore, between you and the majority of us is that you not only are willing and anxious to *die* for your country, but that you *live* for your country every day of your life."

Within a few days, in fact on Christmas day, he was moved to Oyster Bay, and at first seemed benefited by the change. On Friday, January 3, I had arranged to go out and spend the day with him, but a message came that he was not quite as comfortable and would I wait until Monday, when he hoped to feel much better and enjoy my visit.

On the Sunday he seemed better again, my sister-in-law told me later, and enjoyed the whole day. He loved, passionately, his home at Sagamore Hill, and the view from it over the Sound on which he had rowed so often from boyhood up. He loved the beauty of the shrubs and trees and undulating wooded hills, and he loved best of all the sense of home there, and the happy family life which, even with a vacant chair, he knew would continue. He expressed his content that evening to Mrs. Roosevelt, in whose companionship he took the same delight as when in their youth he had brought her to be the adored mistress of that home.

Later in the evening he did not seem quite so well and she sent for the doctor, who, after testing him in various ways, pronounced his condition as very satisfactory. Relieved in mind, Mrs. Roosevelt left him in charge of his faithful attendant, James Amos, and shortly after she went out he turned to James and said, "Put out the light." Once again his devoted wife came to his bedside, thinking she heard him stir, but found him sleeping peacefully. At four o'clock James detected a change in the breathing, and realizing that all was not well, called the trained nurse. In a few moments, as Senator Lodge said later in his great oration on his friend before the joint houses of Congress in Washington, "Valiant-for-Truth passed over, and all the trumpets sounded for him on the other side."

That Sunday evening, just before Theodore Roosevelt told his faithful servant to "Put out the light," there was a meeting held in New York under the auspices of the American Defense Society, at which he had hoped to be present. Not able to be there in person, he sent them a letter, and at the moment that he, at his beloved home on the hill, closed his eyes for the last time, his faithful followers listened to his ringing exhortation that there should be "no sagging back in Americanism." The youth, twenty-three years of age, as an assemblyman at Albany had come to his native city to make his maiden address on that theme so near his heart, and the man, whose life-work, replete with patriotism, was drawing to a close, sent the same fervent message in his last hours to his fellow countrymen. All his life long he had been for those fellow countrymen "the patriotic sentinel; pacing the parapet of the Republic, alert to danger and every menace; in love with duty and service, and always unafraid." —From Senator Warren G. Harding's address on "Theodore Roosevelt" before the Senate and House of Ohio, late in January, 1919.

At six o'clock on that very Monday morning when I was hoping to go to him and enjoy his dear companionship, the telephone-bell in my room rang and my sister-in-law's voice, gentle and self-controlled, though vibrant with grief, told me that he was gone, and that she wanted me to come at once to Sagamore. It was not long before my eldest son and I were climbing the familiar hill. As we neared the house, I could not bring myself to believe that the great personality who had always welcomed me there had passed away.

That afternoon Mrs. Roosevelt and I walked far and fast along the shore and through the woodlands he had loved, and on our return in the waning winter twilight we suddenly became conscious that airplanes were flying low around the house. In a tone of deep emotion Mrs. Roosevelt said: "They must be planes from the camp where Quentin trained. They have been sent as a guard of honor for his father."

That night as I stood alone in the room where my brother lay, these lines came to me—I called them "Sagamore," that old Indian word for which my brother cared so much. It means chief or chieftain, and Sagamore Hill, the chieftain's hill.

SAGAMORE

At Sagamore the Chief lies low—
Above the hill in circled row
The whirring airplanes dip and fly,
A guard of honor from the sky;—
Eagles to guard the Eagle.—Woe
Is on the world. The people go
With listless footstep, blind and slow;—
For one is dead—who shall not die—
At Sagamore.

Oh! Land he loved, at last you know
The son who served you well below,
The prophet voice, the visioned eye.
Hold him in ardent memory,
For one is gone—who shall not go—
From Sagamore!